W9-BTI-738

Polling and the Public

Polling and the Public

What Every Citizen Should Know

Third Edition

Herbert Asher
Ohio State University

A Division of Congressional Quarterly Inc.
Washington, D.C.

EMERSON COLLEGE LIBRARY

HM
261
. A74
1995

Copyright © 1995, Congressional Quarterly Inc.
1414 22nd Street, N.W., Washington, D.C. 20037

All rights reserved. No part of this publication may be reproduced or transmitted in any form or by any means, electronic or mechanical, including photocopy, recording, or any information storage and retrieval system, without permission in writing from the publisher.

Printed and bound in the United States of America

Cover design: Ed Atkeson / Berg Design, Albany, New York

Library of Congress Cataloging-in-Publication Data

Asher, Herbert B.
    Polling and the public : what every citizen should know / Herbert Asher -- 3rd ed.
        p.   cm.
    Includes bibliographical references and index.
    ISBN 0-87187-755-4
    1. Public opinion polls.   2. Public opinion--United States.
I. Title.
HM261.A74   1995
303.3'8'0973--dc20   95-10464
                                                                                                            CIP

To the memory of my parents

Contents

Preface

Since the last edition of this book was published, the barrage of public opinion polls on Americans has continued and, in fact, increased. Citizens are given the results of public opinion polls on a wide variety of topics, be it the elections of 1994, the O. J. Simpson trial, the baseball strike, sexual behavior in America, or welfare reform. Because they are closely followed by political leaders as well as by many citizens, polls—and the reporting of poll results—have a growing influence on discourse and decision making in every part of society and at all levels of government.

Despite their prominence, polls are still not well understood. My central objective in first writing this book was to help citizens become wiser consumers of public opinion polls. In twice revising the book, I have maintained that objective. The prevalence of public opinion polls and their frequent misuse make it imperative for citizens to be able to evaluate critically the various assertions made on the basis of the polls. Candidates for public office, incumbents, and many different public and private groups sponsor public opinion surveys to advance their own objectives. As polling data become more central to political discourse, it is more important that citizens understand the factors that can influence poll results.

Chapter 1 explains the types of polls, their importance, and Americans' varying attitudes toward public opinion research. Chapters 2 through 5 address the methodological aspects of polling, such as nonattitude assessment, question wording and order, sampling techniques, and interviewing procedures. These topics are treated in a nontechnical fashion with numerous examples that illustrate major points. Chapters 6 through 8 are more analytical, focusing on how the media cover polls, the role of polls in campaigns and elections, and the interpretation of polls. The last chapter considers the place of polls in a democratic polity.

This book should be readily understandable to a diverse audience—college students taking courses in American politics, public opinion, communications, and journalism, as well as practitioners in the fields of journalism and campaign management. In addition, the general public should find it a helpful guide to evaluating the methods and merits of public opinion polls. As with earlier editions, no statistical expertise is assumed or required.

I appreciate the assistance of Mike Barr in the preparation of this third edition. Also the staff of CQ Press did its usual fine job of editing and getting the book into print in a timely fashion. Finally, I express my deep appreciation to the various polling organizations and newspapers that are so generous in sharing their surveys with the broader public. They provided many of the substantive examples I used here. In particular, the CBS News/*New York Times* polls and the ABC News/*Washington Post* surveys have been invaluable resources in the preparation of this edition, as have many of the newspaper articles about these polls, particularly those by Richard Morin. I also thank the *Times Mirror* and the Eagleton Institute for their generosity in sharing their work with the academic community.

Herb Asher

1 Polling and the Public

Americans today are bombarded with the results of public opinion polls sponsored by news media, candidates for public office, incumbent officeholders, and many different public and private organizations. More than ever before, Americans are learning more about their own attitudes. Indeed, as more nations move toward political systems in which legitimate public opinion polls can be conducted, Americans are also learning more about the attitudes and opinions of citizens of other nations, not only on topics specific to those countries, but also on how they view Americans and the United States. For example, the demise of the Soviet Union and the Soviet empire and the end of totalitarian regimes in other parts of the world have resulted in a flourishing polling industry that regularly assesses citizens' views in these nations about issues of public policy and election preferences. Polls are increasingly used not only to inform Americans about what their compatriots and citizens of other nations believe, but also to convince and even manipulate them in ways advantageous to the polls' sponsors. Therefore the aim of this book is to help citizens become more astute judges of polls so that they will not be misled or deceived by assertions made on the basis of polling data. This will be accomplished by explaining in nontechnical language the various factors that can affect poll results, such as question wording, sampling, and interviewing, and by critiquing various types and uses of polls.

The Importance of Polls

Why should citizens become more astute consumers of polls? One reason is simply to avoid being manipulated by those who use polls inappropriately to promote their own ends. Other reasons are more positive. Some individuals make major economic and career decisions on the basis of public opinion polling. For example, the businessperson who commissions a survey on customer preferences or the television station manager who underwrites a survey on audience demographics will use the information obtained to make important decisions about service or programming. Likewise, potential candidates for public office may commission a poll to assess their electoral prospects before deciding whether to run. In these examples the polling is likely to be conducted by a commercial polling organization. But the more knowledgeable the businessperson and the would-be candidate are about polls, the better able they are to communicate their objectives and requirements to the survey organization and to apply the results of the survey to their own decision making.

Polls are important for the average citizen as well as for the businessperson and potential candidate. Polls have become a major way for Americans to learn what their fellow citizens are thinking. Substantial media coverage of polls allows citizens to compare their own beliefs with their compatriots' and to determine whether their own views are shared by others. As citizens use the polls in this manner, they need to be aware of the factors that affect the poll results so that they do not accept or reject them too quickly or uncritically.

Polling plays an integral role in political events at the national, state, and local levels. In any major event or decision, poll results are sure to be a part of the news media's coverage and the decision makers' deliberations. How should an international crisis, such as the Iraqi invasion of Kuwait, be resolved? What should be the response of the United States to events in Bosnia or Somalia or Rwanda? Should state taxes be raised? What is the best location for a new library in the community? Polls may influence how politicians respond to such issues, and citizens need to understand the essentials of public opinion polling to follow all aspects of the polls.

Finally, public opinion polls are playing an ever larger role in political discourse in the United States because of the improved technology of polling; the introduction of courses in polling methodology in journalism curricula; the widespread assumption (challenged by Benjamin Ginsberg; see chapter 9) that polls are the best way to measure public opinion; and the belief that public opinion polls are instruments of democracy because they allow everyone's views to be represented. All of these factors ensure that future political debate on issues will be characterized by even greater reliance on the polls. To participate in political debate in an informed and analytical fashion, Americans will have to come to grips with the public opinion polls—a useful tool of government and a valuable source of information to citizens and leaders alike.

The Pervasiveness of Polls

That public opinion polling is a growth industry in the United States is undeniable. The polls most familiar to Americans are those conducted for and reported by the major communications media. For example, each of the three major television networks sponsors polls in collaboration with a print medium: CBS News with the *New York Times*, ABC News with the *Washington Post*, and NBC News with the *Wall Street Journal*. Likewise, the major news magazines often commission polls on national issues; thus, *Newsweek* regularly employs Princeton Survey Research Associates, while *Time* uses Yankelovich Partners Inc. and *U.S. News* hires the Tarrance Group and Mellman-Lazarus-Lake.

The pervasiveness of polls is clearly demonstrated by their increased use in major news stories. Recently I examined stories featured on the covers of the three major news magazines, *Time*, *Newsweek*, and *U.S. News and World Report*. The examination showed a sizable increase in the use of public opinion polls as an integral part of cover stories between 1973 and 1993. For example, only about 15 percent of *Time* cover stories in 1973 used polls; in 1993 that number had increased to 46 percent. For *U.S. News* and *Newsweek* stories, the increases were not as large, mainly because both magazines had used polls more heavily in 1973; the comparable figures for *U.S. News* were 31 and 40 percent and for *Newsweek* 38 and 44 percent. Thus, by 1993, more than two in five lead stories in all three news magazines incorporated polling results as part of the coverage. Moreover, the other, non-cover stories in these magazines used polls. The readers of these stories would be more astute judges of the reporting if they were knowledgeable about the strengths and weaknesses of public opinion polls.

The proliferation of polls is also evident in television and newspaper coverage. Typically, these polls survey citizens about their views on political issues, candidates, and incumbents (especially the president); their preferences about possible courses of governmental action; and their general attitudes toward politics and the political process. Major national polls also regularly cover tax reform, social values, hostage crises, abortion, foreign policy, the budget deficit, Supreme Court nominations, and countless other political and nonpolitical topics. In 1994, one of the prime topics of the polls was health care reform, with all sides on the issue trying to use poll results to advance their respective positions.

Sometimes survey questions seem to violate standards of good taste. After President Ronald Reagan's surgery for what turned out to be cancer of the colon, a survey commissioned by *Time* asked respondents how serious they thought the president's health problems were and whether he was likely to serve his full term. An ABC News/*Washington Post* poll asked

Americans whether they thought the president was likely to complete his term. And a *Newsweek* poll inquired whether citizens were concerned that the president might not "be able to meet the demands of a second term." Many citizens undoubtedly had questions in their own minds about the president's health, and therefore the media thought their readers and viewers would be interested in reading about public opinions on the matter—hence the ghoulish speculation.

Indeed, when an issue or event becomes visible and especially controversial, the public is usually surveyed to assess its reaction. For example, the O. J. Simpson case in 1994, which fascinated Americans, was extensively polled. Particularly intriguing to reporters were the sharp racial differences in beliefs about Simpson's guilt or innocence. Likewise, the public's views on acquired immune deficiency syndrome (AIDS) are often publicized. A poll of Americans in the summer of 1985 became a cover story on AIDS in both *Time* and *Newsweek*, and Americans are still being polled about their attitudes and fears about the epidemic and what the government should do to slow its progress. And recently, when a doctor assisted a woman diagnosed with Alzheimer's disease to commit suicide, many polls were conducted on topics such as euthanasia, living wills, and death with dignity. Some issues may seem more frivolous. Whether female sports reporters should conduct postgame locker-room interviews has generated furor and has become an issue for numerous polls. As the final episode of the television show *Cheers* neared in 1993, the Times Mirror Center for the People and the Press queried Americans about such weighty topics as whether Sam should have stayed single, married Diane, or married Rebecca. The survey also asked Americans who their favorite *Cheers* character was and which character they would like to see continue in his or her own series (Mills 1993). All of these examples illustrate that poll results about newsworthy stories often become a part of the news themselves.

In addition to such prominent national polls, so are there visible and reputable state and local polls that focus on specific state and local matters, and on national affairs as well. For example, the *Daily News* (New York) and "Eyewitness News" (produced by the ABC-TV affiliate in New York City) have polled New Yorkers over the years on their views of the New York police, New York mayors, the likelihood of the Yankees and Mets baseball teams making the World Series, and other matters of local concern. Likewise, the *New York Times*, in conjunction with WCBS-TV, has conducted extensive studies of race relations in New York City. Many states have first-rate polling organizations, often affiliated with a university or a major news medium. For example, the Eagleton Institute at Rutgers University, working with the *Newark Star-Ledger*, surveys New Jersey residents about their state government and about New Jersey as a place to live. Finally, publications such as *Public Opinion Quarterly* and *American Enterprise* provide summaries of state and local as well as national poll results.

The polls described thus far are certainly the most prominent and probably the most credible to the American public. Their prominence comes from the often substantial media coverage their results receive; their credibility derives from the public's perception that they are conducted scientifically and that the media and other entities that sponsor the polls are themselves legitimate and objective. The most critical factor in making these polls scientific (and hence valid) is the careful selection of a sample of respondents (most often 1,000 to 1,500 persons). A carefully selected sample enables one to generalize from the specific sample to the larger population from which the sample was drawn. It is impossible to interview directly the entire adult American population of 190 million; a representative sample of 1,500 respondents who have been properly interviewed makes it possible (within certain limits to be discussed later) to make valid statements about the overall population.

Commissioned Polls

Although polls by the major news media seem most prominent, they represent only the tiniest fraction of the public opinion polling done in the United States. Many other organizations conduct polls for purposes other than informing citizens. Many of them are of high quality; others are of lesser repute. Many clients and companies seek answers to questions and therefore commission polls; many academic investigators conduct research that requires the use of surveys. The results of these polls may not attract much public notice, but they still can affect the lives of individual citizens.

An excellent example of a commissioned poll is one paid for by the Internal Revenue Service (IRS) in 1984 to study the problem of tax cheating. Among the items in the survey were these statements with which the espondent was supposed to agree or disagree:

> It's not so wrong to hold back a little bit on taxes since the government spends too much anyway.
>
> The present tax system benefits the rich and is unfair to the ordinary working man or woman.
>
> Since a lot of rich people pay no taxes at all, if someone like me underpays a little, it's no big deal (Sussman 1984c).

The study found that 19 percent of the respondents admitted cheating on their returns and that young, upwardly mobile professionals were the most likely to cheat. The study also investigated ways to reduce cheating and found that Americans strongly rejected the use of paid informants to catch cheaters (Sussman 1985c). Although the honesty of tax cheaters' responses to questions about tax cheating is questionable, the IRS probably gained from this survey some useful insights about the magnitude of the cheating problem and the feasibility of alternative solutions.

This IRS study is typical of thousands commissioned by public and private bodies to address specific concerns. Some of these surveys are based on national samples; others are based on specialized samples that are more appropriate to the research questions being addressed. For example, a promotional brochure of the Gallup Social Science Research Group, a division of the Gallup Organization, listed some of the social research surveys it has conducted. These include:

> American College of Surgeons. A national personal interview survey of the general public and members of Congress to measure opinions related to surgeons and surgical care.

> New Jersey State Lottery Commission. A marketing survey using telephone interviews to . . . aid policymakers in reaching decisions regarding future growth of the New Jersey State Lottery.

> Federal Energy Administration. A series of personal interview surveys on attitudes toward and use of home insulation.

> Catholic Press Association. A television survey of readers of local diocesan newspapers and religious magazines on attitudes toward religious media.

> American Jewish Committee. Semiannual surveys of the national general public on attitudes related to Israel.

> Japan Embassy. An annual national personal interview survey of the general public and mail survey of opinion leaders on attitudes toward Japan.

Commissioned surveys of this type are likely to be high-quality enterprises mainly because the sponsors have a genuine need for accurate information to address some organizational goal or problem. To that end, the sponsors employ a reputable firm, such as the Gallup Organization or Louis Harris and Associates, to design and conduct the survey and perhaps to analyze the data and interpret the results as well. Many other groups, however, conduct surveys for a different reason—not to address a public concern scientifically and objectively, but instead to promote a certain position and to convince the public of the wisdom of that stand. To that end a survey is designed to yield desired results; this is most often accomplished by the use of highly loaded questions, although more subtle methods are also used. Sometimes in such surveys the samples of people interviewed are skewed to ensure a predetermined outcome. In many cases the poll itself is secondary to the real aim of the group — namely, to raise money to support its objectives.

With the advent of computerized mailings, many organizations have entered the business of raising funds and conducting polls through direct mail. Most often the polling becomes a device to generate donations; that is, the sponsoring organization encourages recipients of the mailings to make their views known *and* to contribute to a good cause. Many of these appeals come from political groups, some of them broad in scope, such as the Democratic and Republican parties, and others narrower in focus, such as the Wilderness Society, the Union of Concerned Scientists, the National Right to Work Committee, the Religious Coalition for Abortion Rights, and many, many others.

For example, the Republican National Committee in 1994 mailed a "Republican Agenda Referendum" to thousands of potential contributors on the GOP's mailing lists. The survey included numerous questions as well as a direct appeal for funds (see box on page 8). Until the 1990s, the Democrats had lagged behind the GOP in the use of computerized mailings, but the 1992 "Priority Issues Survey" sponsored by the Democratic Senatorial Campaign Committee demonstrated that they too learned the advantages of attaching a poll to a fund-raising effort (see box on page 9).

Concerned groups and individuals also have used the newspapers to promote their views and conduct polls. On March 7, 1983, the Moral Majority placed a full-page advertisement in the *Washington Post* on the nuclear freeze issue. At the bottom of the advertisement was a three-item questionnaire that readers were encouraged to complete and return to the Reverend Jerry Falwell, who in turn would report the results to U.S. leaders. One of the questions was, "Are you willing to trust the survival of America to a nuclear freeze agreement with the Soviet Union, a nation which rejects on-site inspection of military facilities to insure compliance?" In case the wording of the question was not sufficiently loaded to generate a negative response, the text of the advertisement warned of the Soviet threat.

Indeed, many groups mail extremely biased literature and then ask respondents for their opinions. Consider these examples. The Committee Against Government Waste has asked, "Before you received this letter, were you aware of the gross mismanagement and waste of funds in the U.S. Department of Defense's purchase of parts?" The American Farmland Trust has asked, "Were you aware of the gravity of the problem of our vanishing farmland before receiving this mailing?" In case the literature accompanying the poll does not convince respondents of the correctness of the group's position, a carefully constructed question or statement may achieve the

Republican Agenda Referendum

PART I.

PERSONAL REPLY TO BOB DOLE

Dear Bob,

Thank you for including me in your national REPUBLICAN AGENDA REFERENDUM.

☐ **I agree** that all Republicans must unite immediately to stand up to Bill Clinton and his liberal regime in Washington today - - and to retake control of our nation tomorrow.

Therefore, I am proud to become a Sustaining member of the Republican National Committee — and having completed my referendum, I am rushing my views back to you today along with my most generous donation of:

☐ $15   ☐ $25   ☐ $50   ☐ $75

☐ $100   ☐ $250   ☐ $500   ☐ $1,000

☐ Other $ _____

Please make your checks payable to:
Republican National Committee or the **"RNC"**
Please see reverse side if contributing by credit card.

Contributions to the Republican National Committee are not deductible as charitable contributions for federal income tax purposes.

310 First Street, S.E. • Washington, D.C. 20003

Issued to:

PART II.

Even if you cannot answer all of the questions, it is important that you return this entire document before the Tabulation Deadline Date (listed below) expires. Your individual answers will be kept strictly confidential. Only total results will be reported to the Republican leadership. Thank you!

Please read each question carefully and check the response which best reflects your views.

A) Do you agree with the liberal media's assertion that the Republican Party lost the 1992 Presidential election because it was "too conservative"?

☐ YES   ☐ NO   ☐ UNDECIDED

B) Which of the following policies (**if any**) should the Republican Party abandon or change? *(You may choose none or more than one.)*

☐ Anti-tax-and-spend
☐ Anti-government regulations
☐ Anti-Congressional perks
☐ Anti-pork barrel spending
☐ Anti-homosexuals in military
☐ Anti-military disarmament
☐ Anti-gun control
☐ Anti-socialized medicine
☐ Anti-D.C. statehood
☐ Anti-big government
☐ Pro-tax cuts

☐ Pro-balanced budget amendment
☐ Pro-term limits
☐ Pro-line item veto
☐ Pro-right-to-life
☐ Pro-SDI
☐ Pro-death penalty
☐ Pro-family values
☐ Pro-health care reform
☐ Pro-free trade
☐ Pro-enterprise zones
☐ None
☐ Other _____

Survey continued on back ⬆

S4PJ41
Tabulation Date: 05/09/94

**Democratic Senatorial
Campaign Committee**

Dear Senator Mitchell, You're absolutely right. It is imperative that we keep our Democratic Majority in the Senate. And you can count on me to help build an even stronger Democratic majority in the next election.

I understand that we must begin now to lay the ground-work for an effective campaign to counter the untold millions the Republican Party will pour into campaigns to defeat Democratic candidates.

To make certain that happens, I have completed my 1992 Priority Issues Survey (below) to help Democratic Senators frame the issues and plan their strategy ... and I am making my largest contribution possible to the DSCC for:

❑ **$20**　❑ **$25**　❑ **$35**　❑ **$75**
❑ **$100**　❑ **Other $_____**

Please make your check payable to the DSCC and return it with this entire form in the envelope provided.

Authorized and paid for by the Democratic Senatorial Campaign Committee. Contributions are not deductible on federal tax returns.

430 South Capitol Street, S.E. • Suite L-14 • Washington, D.C. 20003

1992 Priority Issues Survey

Democrats in the 102nd Congress must make vital decisions about what issues to press for and what federal legislation we push for the hardest in 1992.

To make certain the issues we address are of crucial importance to Americans like you, please rank by order of importance **(with "1" being most important)** the priorities you believe should be stressed.

A____ Restructure the tax burden to achieve a more equitable distribution, and direct efforts to support the working people of America.

B____ Pass campaign finance reform legislation that makes public officials more accountable to their constituents.

C____ Support national health care legislation that helps American families deal with the effects of major illness or the long-term care of an elderly relative.

D____ Pass civil rights legislation that restores protection against discrimination guaranteed to women and minorities by the 1964 Civil Rights Act.

E____ Propose comprehensive energy conservation legislation to lessen our dependence on imported oil.

F____ Make education of our children a top initiative and create incentives for states to improve basic reading and math skills.

G____ Support legislation that ensures the decision to terminate a pregnancy remains with the woman, not with the government.

H____ Continue to pass legislation to protect the environment and strongly support efforts to reduce the "green house" effect.

I____ Insist on respect for, and protection of, human rights as a condition for U.S. aid to other countries.

J____ Introduce comprehensive legislation that realistically addresses the problem of treatment and prevention in our fight against the tragedy of drug abuse.

K____ Other: _____
_____
_____

Thank you for your participation.

E/F

same end, as illustrated by the following questionnaire items and their sponsoring organizations:

> Are you in favor of allowing construction union czars the power to shut down an entire construction site because of a dispute with a single contractor, thus forcing even more workers to knuckle under to union agents? *National Right to Work Committee*

> In his speeches and public addresses, the President has always made a point of keeping the American people fully informed of the Soviet threat to world peace. The Democrats, on the other hand, constantly downplay the Soviet threat. Do you think that, during his campaign, the President should continue to bring this issue to the attention of the voters?
>
> —Yes, the President should continue to address the Soviet threat
> —No, I agree with the Democrats who downplay the Soviet threat
> —Not sure *Republican National Committee*

> Were you aware that a good part of why America has been leaning toward nuclear weapons is due to inflated prices of conventional weapons parts? *Committee Against Government Waste*

> The Reagan Administration must replace the James Watt political appointees who have been carrying out destructive land policies and will continue to do so until they're removed.
>
> *The Wilderness Society*

> Teenagers, through the force of law and regardless of circumstance such as rape and incest, should be denied access to abortion services until their parents are notified, or until they have obtained a court order. *Religious Coalition for Abortion Rights*

> Do you endorse the idea that a greater number of smaller farms should be encouraged to relieve the growing burden being placed on large farms to fulfill our agricultural needs? *American Farmland Trust*

> Our nation is still blessed with millions of acres of public lands, including roadless wilderness areas, forests and range lands. Land developers, loggers, and mining and oil companies want to increase their operations on these public lands. Do you think these remaining pristine areas of your public lands should be protected from such exploitation? *Sierra Club*

> Do you feel that all of the TV networks are in serious danger of losing the public's confidence and trust because they hire so many liberal Democratic activists as top corporate executives who formerly worked for Ted Kennedy, Walter Mondale, Gary Hart, George McGovern, Mario Cuomo, Jimmy Carter and the National Democratic Party?
>
> *Fairness in Media*

English is the language of the United States by custom, although not by law. In order to avoid the political upheavals over language that have torn apart Canada, Belgium, Sri Lanka (Ceylon), India, and other nations, would you favor legislation designating English the official language of the United States?   *U.S. English*

As a result of our efforts to save dolphins from getting caught in the nets of tuna fishermen, legislation was introduced in the U.S. that led to "dolphin safe tuna" labels. Do you support the kind of direct action that brought about this labeling to force companies to operate in more responsible ways?   *Greenpeace Update Survey*

Senator Bob Dole has threatened to filibuster health care reform if it requires businesses to pay a portion of health care premiums. Should businesses have an obligation to provide health care coverage to their employees?   *Democratic National Committee*

All of the preceding items were carefully constructed to generate responses sympathetic to the sponsors' objectives. In fact, some readers might raise several reasons these enterprises should not be called "polling." First, in most cases the sample is not scientifically selected; instead, the surveys and fund-raising requests are mailed out to lists of citizens who are thought to be likely supporters. Whether the people who actually respond are at all representative of a larger population is of little concern. Second, the questions are often poorly formulated and fundamentally flawed (deliberately so). Third, if the survey data collected is tabulated at all (and many times it is not) little analysis can be conducted, because the original survey was very short and omitted key questions about the demographic and political characteristics of the respondents. In other words, collecting opinions is not necessarily polling.

Pseudo-polls

Orton (1982) has identified similar examples of what he calls *pseudo-polls*. In such polls the representativeness of the respondents is highly questionable. For example, the print and electronic media often encourage members of their audiences to write or phone to express their views. But even with hundreds or thousands of replies, these "straw polls" are usually not representative, simply because people who voluntarily choose to participate are likely to differ in important ways from the overall population. They may be more interested, informed, and concerned about the topic at hand and thus hold views different from those of the overall population. A prominent example of a pseudo-poll occurred in 1980 when "ABC News" encouraged viewers to call (at a cost of fifty cents) to indicate whether they thought Jimmy Carter or Ronald Reagan had won the presidential debate.

In 1992, shortly after President Bush's State of the Union address, the CBS television program "America on the Line" featured telephone call-in surveys. At the same time, CBS also conducted a scientific poll that included questions that were identical to those on the call-in survey. The results of the two surveys differed. Unfortunately, it was the results of the call-in responses that received the greater attention, despite the fact that the differences between the two sets of results were major. For example, in response to the question of whether they were better or worse off than they were four years ago, 54 percent of the callers in the phone-in poll said they were worse off compared to only 32 percent of the respondents in the scientific survey (Morin 1992a).

Radio talk shows and call-in polls have become prominent in the 1990s. A 1993 *Times Mirror* poll (Kohut 1993) showed that citizens who listened to and called radio talk shows were not representative of the overall citizenry; instead, they tended to be more Republican, more conservative, more male, and slightly more wealthy and educated. Thus it is not surprising that the radio phone-in polls often generate results more conservative and pro-Republican than the outcomes obtained through scientific polling.

Other examples of pseudo-polls are the questionnaires that members of Congress send to households within their congressional districts. Typically, these are addressed to "Postal Customer," with no sure way of knowing just who in the household actually completed the survey. Although thousands of these questionnaires may be returned to a congressional office, it is difficult to ascertain whether the respondents' demographic characteristics and actual opinions on the issues are truly representative of the broader constituency. In some instances the questions themselves are loaded to guarantee responses compatible with a legislator's own predisposition and record. This is not to say that completed questionnaires are ignored or discarded; in most cases the results are tabulated and later reported to the constituency in a newsletter. But, as Sussman (1985h) argues, these questionnaires are mainly "a public relations gimmick, aimed at convincing voters that officeholders care about the folks back home." And Morin (1987) opines, "Too many of these polls reek from a kind of self-serving flatulence that insults the average voter while exposing the unctuous pomposity of the elected official."

Other examples of pseudo-polls are highly publicized surveys on marital relations done by Shere Hite and "Dear Abby" (Squires and Morin 1987; Smith 1988). Hite distributed 100,000 extensive open-ended question-naires to women's groups and to individual women who requested a questionnaire. She received about 4,500 replies, a response rate of only 4.5 percent. In one of her columns, Abby wrote (Smith 1988): "Readers, I need your cooperation for an important survey. Questions: Have you ever cheated on your mate? How long have you been together? You need not sign your name, but please state your age and indicate whether you are male or female." She received more than 200,000 responses.

In both the Hite and Abby surveys, the sampling method and the questions generated unrepresentative and misleading results, despite the large number of respondents to Abby's poll. (Reputable, scientific national polls typically have a sample of about 1,500 respondents.) Hite found that 70 percent of women married five or more years were having extramarital affairs, while 15 percent of Abby's married female respondents claimed to have been unfaithful. As Smith (1988) argues, both surveys could not be correct and, indeed, both were overwhelmingly likely to be wrong because of the pitfalls inherent in the sample selection and the actual questionnaire. Allowing citizens to select themselves into a survey guarantees biased results because of the motivations that lead people to participate in such surveys in the first place.

Since the 1970s, magazines have regularly published the results of sex surveys of their readers. Typically, magazines conduct these surveys by including the questionnaire in the magazine and encouraging readers to complete the survey and mail it back. *Redbook* and *Cosmopolitan* in the 1970s, *Playboy* in the 1980s and *The Advocate* in the 1990s are among the magazines that have sponsored such surveys. In some cases, the response rate was low, but the number of completed questionnaires very large, simply because of the size of a magazine's readership. For example, the *Playboy* response rate was about 2 percent, but this translated into 100,000 replies. In contrast, *The Advocate* response rate was 18 percent with almost 13,000 questionnaires returned (Lever 1994, 18). Despite the large number of replies to a typical magazine survey, one must be very careful generalizing the results to any broader population, whether it be to straight males based on the *Playboy* survey or to gay males based on *The Advocate* poll. That is because self-selection presents a double problem. First, the readers and subscribers to various magazines may not be representative of the broader population of which they are members. Second, those individuals who actually complete the questionnaires may not be reflective of the magazines' readers and subscribers in the first place. Nevertheless, the results of these surveys typically receive a lot of media coverage (and probably enhance magazine sales).

The key point, of course, is that pseudo-polls are highly flawed and may give misleading portraits of public opinion. Because of loaded and unfair question wording, self-selection biases in the respondents, outright efforts to stack the results, or other deficiencies, pseudo-polls are poor ways to ascertain public opinion. However, despite their deficiencies, I prefer to include these unscientific enterprises under the rubric of polling because they are becoming more prevalent in the United States. Citizens are subjected to many different kinds of polls, all of which may later affect them in some way through the decisions that are based on the results. For this reason it is important for citizens to be aware of the gamut of polls and to be able to evaluate them. If citizens are able to recognize unscientific polls and their associated deficiencies (as well as the shortcomings of scientific polls), then they are less likely to be misled by the results of such surveys. This leads us to the central concern of this book—the citizen as a potential consumer of public opinion polls.

The Citizen as a Consumer of Polls

As argued earlier in this chapter, opinion polling is pervasive in the United States. Whatever the quality of these polls, they can affect the attitudes and behavior of citizens. Even media-sponsored polls designed to inform the audience (and perhaps to keep up with the competition and improve ratings) may do more than simply report citizens' attitudes. They may also help *shape* preferences, particularly during a presidential primary season when polling is frequent and the linkages between a candidate's poll standing, media coverage, and primary election fate are pronounced. (The role of polls in elections is considered in chapter 7.)

There are highly specific polls designed to affect behavior; for example, it has become increasingly common to use public opinion surveys in court proceedings dealing with change-of-venue motions (Nietzel and Dillehay 1983) and in cases concerning protection of trademarks and advertising claims (Dutka 1982). Public opinion research has been conducted on almost every conceivable topic, whether it be opinions on pornography (Smith 1987b), the televising of rape trials (Swim and Borgida 1987), acid rain (Pierce et al. 1988), wiretapping (Fletcher 1989), nuclear power (Bisconti 1991), Estonian attitudes toward Yeltsin (Saar and Joe 1992), or the social bases of European feminism (Banaszak and Plutzer 1993).

Americans are major consumers of the results of public opinion research. But are they smart consumers? Americans should be aware of the problems and limitations of polls before they "buy" anything from them. Just as customers in a supermarket often inspect the list of ingredients in a product, so too should consumers of public opinion question what went into a poll before accepting its results. Citizens who are simply passive consumers of poll results need to recognize that often someone is actively promoting the poll results to generate support for his or her objectives. It might be the president citing polls to argue that the American people support his policies. It might be a local builder waving the results of a

BLOOM COUNTY   by Berke Breathed

© 1983, Washington Post Writers Group, reprinted with permission.

neighborhood poll purporting to show local support for a rezoning ordinance to permit commercial construction in an area. It might be a regional transportation commission citing poll results to justify the establishment of bus lanes on freeways. Or it might be a friend or neighbor selectively using poll results to win an argument.

In the course of becoming better consumers of public opinion research, citizens need not become experts at drawing samples, constructing questionnaires, and analyzing data. Instead, they can develop an intuitive awareness of the steps involved in conducting a survey and the possible consequences of these steps so as consumers of polls they are better able to reject bad "merchandise" and to appreciate good buys. Thus, the major aim of this book is to sensitize citizens to the problems and limitations of opinion polling. Readers should note that this book should in no way be construed as a condemnation of public opinion research; most of the highly publicized polls as well as many private polls reflect high standards of polling. Indeed, public opinion polling has improved dramatically over the past fifty years in areas such as sampling design, question wording and format, interviewing techniques, and methods of data analysis (see the fiftieth anniversary issue of *Public Opinion Quarterly* [Winter 1987] for discussions of how polling practices have changed over time). But there is still an art to the conduct and analysis of surveys. An appreciation of that art will leave citizens less susceptible to the intellectual tyranny that can occur when a public opinion poll is deemed by its sponsor to be scientific and its results therefore beyond question or challenge.

Citizens' Views of the Polls

Ordinary citizens' reactions to public opinion polling are generally positive, although there are specific areas of criticism and skepticism. Among political elites the view of polls is often more critical. In 1985 the Gallup and Roper organizations both conducted national surveys that assessed popular awareness of and reactions to the public opinion polls (Clymer 1985, Sussman 1985e). Twenty-five percent of the respondents in the Gallup survey said they regularly followed the results of a public opinion poll in a newspaper or magazine; an additional 16 percent said they did so occasionally. Fifty-nine percent of the respondents said they did not follow a poll regularly in the print medium; of course, they might sporadically read about polls, or they might be aware of the polls through the electronic media.

With respect to the accuracy of the polls, both the Gallup and Roper surveys indicated that Americans held fairly positive views. More than two-thirds of the Gallup sample said the polls were right most of the time, while 56 percent of the respondents to the Roper survey said the polls were almost always or usually accurate. Finally, 76 percent of the persons in the Gallup survey thought that polls were a good thing in our country, while only 12 percent thought they were a bad thing.

Despite these indications of positive attitudes toward the polls, other evidence, often of an anecdotal nature, suggests the public takes a more skeptical view. Most teachers and practitioners of public opinion polling have encountered citizens who have expressed utter distrust of polling. Some citizens complain that they and their friends and relatives have never been interviewed and therefore wonder just how representative samples can be. This kind of skepticism is widespread. Koch (1985) found that people who had never participated in a poll were dubious about the accuracy of the results of surveys.

Others base their doubts on the size of the samples selected. In talking about polling with diverse audiences, I repeatedly hear people ask how a sample of 1,500 respondents can possibly represent 190 million adult Americans. And despite my brilliant answer by analogy—a doctor takes only a sample of a person's blood (fortunately) and a chef need taste only a spoonful of soup (assuming the soup is stirred properly) to test its seasoning—much skepticism about the polls remains. Indeed, one question posed in the 1985 Roper survey showed that only 28 percent of Americans believed that national polls with sample sizes of 1,500 to 2,000 could be accurate, while 56 percent said they could not be (Sussman 1985e).

One substantive area in which the polls have received much criticism is their growing role in elections and election coverage by the media. The argument is often made that polls have contributed to the packaging of candidates; aspiring leaders are accused of first consulting the polls and then staking out their positions, thereby abdicating their leadership responsibilities on issues. Similarly, the use of polls in reporting elections is seen as encouraging a horse-race mentality among the media; instead of focusing on

Reprinted with special permission of North America Syndicate.

DON'T FORGET THAT ELECTION YEAR IS
ALSO LIE-TO-THE-POLLSTERS YEAR.

issues and the candidates' qualifications, the dominant theme becomes who's ahead and who's behind, who's gaining and who's falling back, as measured by the polls. In the context of elections, Americans have become more critical of the polls. A Gallup poll conducted for *Newsweek* in October 1988 found that 52 percent of the respondents believed that news organizations' polls on the presidential contest should not be reported in the final weeks of the campaign. An NBC/*Wall Street Journal* poll in November 1988 showed that 63 percent of Americans believed that voters were influenced too much by the polls.

Exit polls, interviews with citizens right after they have finished voting, enable the television networks to project election outcomes even before the polls have closed. This practice has angered many citizens and political elites. Newspaper columnist Mike Royko has encouraged voters to lie to exit pollsters, while others (e.g. Munro and Gans 1988) have simply encouraged a public boycott of exit polls. Congress has conducted hearings in an effort to get the networks to alter voluntarily the ways they report exit polls and election projections. Other observers have condemned the impact of polls on American politics, none more harshly than Daniel Greenberg, who wrote:

> Given the devastation that opinion surveys have brought to the American political process, we shouldn't be asking how polls can be sharpened but rather why they are endured and how they can be banished.
>
> Polls are the life-support system for the finger-to-the-wind, quick-change politics of our time and, as such, are the indispensable tools for the ideologically hollow men who work politics like a soap-marketing campaign. . . .
>
> The effect of this—on campaigns, as well as on administrations between campaigns—is an obsession with salesmanship rather than with governance. (Greenberg 1980)

The nation's political cartoonists, many of whom are syndicated in newspapers that themselves conduct polls, have had a field day attacking the polls, particularly their frequency, duration, and intrusiveness in the presidential selection process. Smith (1987c, 209) found that polls were treated negatively in 61 percent of the comics and cartoons he analyzed and worried how this would affect citizens' reactions to the polls. And political satirists such as Art Buchwald (1987) and Russell Baker (1988, 1990) also have lampooned the polls.

Various practitioners of polling and survey research have become concerned about what they see as increased disinterest, skepticism, cynicism, or even hostility toward the polls. To combat these views, Black (1991) advocates greater sensitivity to the needs of respondents by (a) making the interview itself a more interesting and rewarding experience for respondents; (b) keeping promises made to respondents in such areas as the length of the interview and the provision of final reports if requested by the respondent; and (c) maintaining high quality throughout the polling enterprise. Lang and Lang worry that some of the more recent entrants into the polling business may have weaker ties to the profession and a lesser commitment to the high standards that should characterize public opinion polling (Morin 1992c). ⁻⁻ careful self-policing by the polling industry to protect the ⅃ ultimately its reputation among the public. Others (e.g. Tanur

1994) recommend better education of citizens as consumers of the polls (which is indeed the main purpose of this book). The point is that there is a growing unease among many practitioners of polling because the lofty status that public opinion assessment has enjoyed may be in some jeopardy.

Although sometimes angry or skeptical about poll results, Americans generally think polls are accurate and fair. Although they often resent the intrusiveness and presumed power of the polls, they eagerly consume the latest public opinion findings about a myriad of topics. This love-hate relationship is probably inevitable in our political system. We all want our voices to be heard, and therefore we attack the polls when we think they are undermining genuine citizen involvement and influence. Yet in a large and heterogeneous nation such as the United States, the polls may be the best mechanism for reflecting the diversity of public opinion. The simple fact that polls generally count all respondents equally bestows upon polls a democratic character that enhances their appeal in a democratic society.

Polling and Democracy

The role of polling in a democratic society has been a subject of controversy. Advocates emphasize that polling is an opportunity for citizens to participate in a democracy and that it permits quick and repeated assessments of the opinions of the public. Polling is particularly valued by those who prefer a democracy in which the people govern directly rather than through intermediaries such as elected representatives. Proponents argue that we should directly poll citizens on their policy preferences and enact these preferences, thereby circumventing the "middleman" — the elected representative. The simplistic version of this proposal clearly ignores many important features of the governing process such as dialogue, exchange, and bargaining. Many within this group are fascinated with the possibility that technological innovations such as interactive cable television might facilitate direct governance by the citizenry. Until its demise in the early 1980s, the QUBE system in Columbus, Ohio, was seen as the wave of the future; Columbus residents on the QUBE system were able to vote from their homes on issues of the day and have their choices tabulated instantly. Indeed, NBC News used the QUBE facilities to conduct an instant survey of viewers' reactions to President Carter's 1979 speech in which he said that reducing America's dependence on foreign oil was the moral equivalent of war. Since then, the communications infrastructure has advanced to such an extent that the virtues and feasibility of direct democracy through technology are being extolled even more.

Some proponents of a more traditional, representative notion of democratic theory also welcome the public opinion polls because they provide systematic information on the preferences of the citizenry. They argue that citizens' opinions should influence the behavior of their elected representatives and that any mechanism, such as polls, that can provide information on citizens' opinions is bound to foster democracy. Obviously, there is mixed empirical evidence on the extent to which popular preferences are actually translated into public policy. We can all cite examples of the government's seeming unresponsiveness to public opinion. For instance, polls have regularly shown that overwhelming majorities of Americans favored some form of gun control, such as handgun registration or waiting periods, yet it took Congress until late 1993 to pass the Brady bill, first introduced in 1987. The Brady bill was the first major federal gun control legislation since 1968. However, a number of empirical studies have found substantial congruence between the attitudes of the public and the actions of government on certain issues (Page and Shapiro 1983, 1992; Erikson 1976). While these studies are careful not to hastily attribute government decisions to popular preferences, they do suggest conditions under which citizen influence is likely to be significant.

Yet another benefit of polls according to poll proponents is the opportunity for citizens to learn about their compatriots and to dispel myths and stereotypes that might otherwise mislead public discourse. For example, poll results reported by Morin challenge the stereotype of evangelical and fundamentalist Christians as monolithic, homogeneous supporters of the religious right (Morin 1993a, 1993e). A *USA Today*/CNN/Gallup Poll conducted in December 1993 showed that classic stereotypes on the gun control issue were misleading. For example, the attitudes of gun owners on various aspects of gun control did not differ substantially from attitudes of non-owners, particularly for less sweeping forms of gun regulation. Other public opinion polls can provide insights, sometimes surprising and unexpected, on the issue of race, ethnicity, and prejudice in the United States. A Louis Harris poll conducted in 1993 showed that the traditional victims of bigotry — blacks, Asians, and Latinos — often express intolerant views of other minority groups. And a study by Sniderman et al. (1993) debunked the simplistic notion that conservatives were prejudiced toward blacks and liberals were not. Although on many items conservatives were less tolerant than liberals toward blacks, the key point for Sniderman and his colleagues was that these differences were often very small.

In contrast to the favorable arguments of proponents, many critics of polling worry about the harmful consequences of polls for a democratic political system. They agree that citizen influence is a key component of a democracy and that public opinion, properly measured, can be useful in governing. But they argue that polls give a misleading impression of how a democracy actually operates. Public opinion is not synonymous with the results of public opinion polls, yet today the two are treated as though they

© ROB ROGERS reprinted by permission of UFS, Inc.

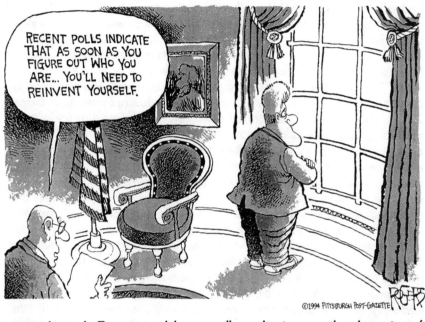

were identical. Focusing solely on poll results ignores the dynamics of opinion formation and change, and often overlooks factors that may shape (and manipulate) public opinion, such as the behavior of leaders and interest groups. Polls may present an overall picture of the distribution of opinion, but the reporting and use of polls often ignore important differences in preferences among subgroups. The result is a misleading picture of similar attitudes across different segments of the American population. Margolis (1984) claims that polls may not be the optimal way to measure public opinion on politically and socially sensitive topics. He argues that in some instances actual behavior provides a more valid expression of public opinion than verbal responses to survey questions do.

A more radical criticism of the polls is that they are simply a sop to the citizenry, that they give people a false sense of being influential when in reality political power is held and exercised by a few elites who may or may not act in the public interest. Social scientist Johan Galtung (1969) made the point most effectively when he argued that surveys are too democratic: they generally count all respondents equally, whereas people are tremendously disparate in the resources and skills they bring to bear on political decisions. To the extent that a survey is seen as a quasi-referendum on issues, it is misleading because the participants in the referendum have different opportunities to shape governmental outcomes.

Another major criticism of the polls concerns their consequences for leadership in the United States. The simplistic version of this argument says that leaders blindly follow the polls rather than work to educate and persuade the public. This argument is exemplified by an editorial in the *Akron Beacon Journal* (May 8, 1994) titled "Foreign poll-icy," which begins with the assertion "The name of Stanley Greenberg may not be familiar to most Americans. It should be. He is Bill Clinton's pollster, and for all intents and purposes, he conducts the country's foreign policy." (Indeed, other observers [e.g. Barnes 1993] have described the critical role Greenberg plays in the Clinton administration just as he did during the presidential campaign itself.) Others argue that leaders have been weakened by the polls because the widespread awareness of public preferences generated by the polls limits the ability of leaders to make unpopular choices. Still others complain that leaders can easily manipulate the polls (perhaps by giving a major televised address that can influence opinions in polls taken right after an address) and therefore generate poll results unfairly supportive of their policies. Some make the fundamental point that polls (and the media) have altered the style and substance of governance, particularly by emphasizing immediate consequences for the next election: the result is a shortsighted approach to problem solving. Compare this with the proponents' defense of the polls' impact on leadership, which argues that officials should have information about citizens' attitudes before they make major decisions, and that the polls, whatever their limitations, are the best way to acquire that information.

What, then, do we conclude about opinion polls in the United States? They are now an integral part of the political and social landscape, and they are likely to become even more prominent in the future. Polls can provide useful information to citizens and leaders; they also can be highly misleading and inaccurate. Polls may enhance the opportunities for citizen influence; they also can serve to manipulate the public. The late George Gallup wrote optimistically about the future of the polls:

> As students, scholars, and the general public gain a better understanding of polls, they will have a greater appreciation of the service polls can perform in a democracy. In my opinion, modern polls are the chief hope of lifting government to a higher level, by showing that the public supports the reforms that will make this possible, by providing a *modus operandi* for testing new ideas. . . . Polls can help make government more efficient and responsive; they can improve the quality of candidates for public office; they can make this a truer democracy. (Gallup 1965-1966, 549)

Nearly three decades have passed since these claims were made, and current discourse about the polls has become much more critical. Nevertheless, as citizens become wiser consumers of polls, Gallup's lofty aspirations for the polls become more likely to be realized.

The chapters that follow consider polls in detail. They raise a number of methodological points, often in the context of important substantive examples. Chapter 2 addresses the problem of nonattitudes; that is, when citizens do not have genuine opinions on a topic and yet they answer the questions. In such cases, the topic is inappropriate for the sample because despite pollsters' best efforts, citizens do often respond to questions on which they have no real opinions, thereby yielding misleading results.

Chapter 3 discusses the wording of questions, and their order and context. Some examples of poorly worded questions likely to produce skewed results have already been cited, but the wording of individual questions is not the only important consideration. A survey, after all, is a series of questions, and the placement and context of those questions can greatly affect the results.

Chapter 4 focuses on various sampling techniques and their advantages and disadvantages. It also deals with sample size and error. Chapter 5 explains in detail how different interviewing procedures can affect results.

Chapter 6 examines how the media report the polls, and chapter 7 analyzes the role of polls in elections. Since Americans learn about polls primarily through the mass media, media coverage of polls greatly influences public opinion. This is particularly interesting in the case of high-visibility national polls, because the medium that reports the polls also is responsible for conducting them. Chapter 7 argues that the polls have come to play an intrusive role in elections and that the use of polls by candidates and the reporting of polls by the media often do a disservice to citizens and to the electoral process. Elections are the most visible opportunity for citizens to influence their government, and to the extent that polls affect that opportunity, citizens should be sensitive to the role of polls in elections.

Chapter 8 explains that the analysis of poll results is more an art than a science, affording many opportunities for manipulative interpretation and dissemination of poll results in order to sway public opinion. Chapter 9 ties together the various themes, offers suggestions about better utilization of polls, and discusses the effects of polls on the American polity.

2 The Problem of Nonattitudes

To produce an informative and accurate public opinion poll, a researcher must successfully perform several tasks. These include constructing a questionnaire with properly worded and ordered questions, selecting a representative sample, correctly interviewing the respondents in that sample, analyzing the data appropriately, and, finally, drawing the correct conclusions. But before any of these tasks can be performed, a researcher must ask a fundamental question: Is the proposed topic of the poll one on which citizens have genuine opinions? If it is, then the topic is suitable for a public opinion survey. But if the topic is so remote from and irrelevant to citizens' concerns that they do not hold real views on it, then any poll on the topic will measure *nonattitudes* rather than attitudes. Any information obtained will be suspect — even if the questions are properly worded, the sample scientifically selected, and the data appropriately analyzed.

The presence of nonattitudes is one of the simplest yet most perplexing problems in public opinion polling. Too often in a survey context, people will respond to questions about which they have no genuine attitudes or opinions.[1] Even worse, the analyst treats the nonattitude responses as if they represent actual public opinions. Under these circumstances a misleading portrait of public opinion can emerge. That is, no distinction is made between people with real views on an issue and those whose responses simply reflect their desire to appear in an interview situation as informed citizens. Unfortunately, it is often difficult to differentiate between genuine attitude holders and persons merely expressing nonattitudes.

It is tempting to assume that citizens are interested in and informed about issues that are widely discussed by public officials and the media. Indeed, researchers do often take for granted that citizens know basic facts about their government and political system. Sometimes these assumptions lead us to include questions in polls on topics that people know very little about even though the topics are prominent. As a result the responses to such questions might reflect nonattitudes rather than genuine opinions. For example, an obvious topic for public opinion polling is the state of the economy. While citizens can certainly express valid opinions about their own and the nation's economic situation, an extended inquiry might be hindered by citizens' ignorance about key facts of economics. Morin (1993c) cites studies demonstrating the public's deficiencies in economic knowledge. Those studies show that only one in five respondents came reasonably close to knowing the national unemployment rate, and only about half of the citizens could identify the correct definition of the federal budget deficit from four choices that were presented to them. Even on more basic factual knowledge about the American political system, there are major gaps in the public's awareness. A study that compared citizens' information levels in the 1940s and 1950s with contemporary information levels found that after controlling for educational levels, Americans today at each level of education are less informed about many aspects of politics than their counterparts in the earlier decades (Delli Carpini and Keeter, 1991). The study speculated that the reason for this phenomenon is a lower level of interest today in politics. Given that respondents with low interest are more likely to express nonattitudes, these results suggest that pollsters must exercise great care to avoid measuring nonattitudes.

The presence of nonattitudes in survey responses has been well documented (Converse 1970; Taylor 1983; Norpoth and Lodge 1985). A particularly intriguing study by Bishop, Oldendick, and Tuchfarber (1980) included a fictitious item in surveys conducted in the greater Cincinnati area. Respondents were presented with the following statement and question about a nonexistent Public Affairs Act: "Some people say that the 1975 Public Affairs Act should be repealed. Do you agree or disagree with this idea?" One-third of the respondents offered an opinion. After an effort to filter out nonattitude responses on this fictitious question, the researchers found that 10 percent of the sample still offered an opinion (the use of screening or filter questions will be discussed later in this chapter). Nonattitudes are definitely a problem for would-be interpreters of public opinion.

The existence of nonattitudes is not surprising; after all, an interview is a social situation in which a respondent interacts in person or by telephone with an interviewer the respondent does not know. Few people in such circumstances want to admit that they are uninformed, particularly on an issue others might expect them to be informed on. Most people answer the questions, and their responses are duly recorded by the interviewer. Before discussing ways to address the problem of nonattitudes, I would like to illustrate how a public opinion survey based on nonattitudes can go astray and mislead the public.

An Example of Nonattitudes

Some years ago I was part of a sample of Ohioans queried about their views on land use problems. The interview was conducted over the phone, and the sample was probably picked from the telephone book. (I surmised this since the interviewer knew my name.) After the interviewer identified herself and the sponsor of the poll, she asked, "Tell me, Mr. Asher, what comes to your mind when you hear the term *land use*?" As a social scientist familiar with public opinion polling, I recognized this as a screening question to determine whether it was worthwhile for the interviewer to proceed with the interview. Surely, if I did not have the vaguest idea what *land use* meant, there would be little point in continuing the interview. In any event I responded, "Hmmm. Land use. How you use the land!" This response must have been sufficiently brilliant for the interviewer to continue with the survey. She then asked me, "Mr. Asher, what do you think is the most important land use problem facing Ohio?" I mentally squirmed and silently gave thanks that the telephone interviewer couldn't see my difficulty in thinking up a land use problem. After a delay of about ten seconds, I responded with something like "planned growth and development." She then asked, "Which level of government — state, county, or local — do you think should have primary responsibility for addressing the problem of planned growth?" I responded, although to this day I cannot recall which level of government I mentioned.

The interview continued, and about three minutes later the interviewer asked me, "Mr. Asher, what do you think is the second most important land use problem facing Ohio?" This time I really had to struggle for an answer. Finally I uttered triumphantly, "Sufficient parks and green space." And, of course, the interviewer then asked me which level of government — state, county, or local — should have primary responsibility for rectifying this problem. I gave an answer (which I cannot recall) and said to myself that if the interviewer asked me about the third most important land use problem facing Ohio, I was going to blast her and the entire research project on the grounds that it was measuring nonattitudes. Fortunately for the interviewer, she never asked that question, and the interview was completed.

Some months later a report based on this survey made statements about which land use problems Ohioans ranked as being of most importance and which levels of government Ohioans wanted to take the lead in addressing these problems. The report made policy recommendations and cited scientific evidence to support its conclusions. As I read the report I

© 1985, Washington Post Writers Group, reprinted with permission.

grew angrier and angrier because the report used survey results derived from what I assume were nonattitudes, opinions from respondents like me who gave answers in response to the questions but had little information about or interest in land use.

As sponsors of public opinion polls should recognize, not every issue of central importance to them will be an appropriate topic of inquiry for the citizenry at large. Different people have different concerns, and those who conduct public opinion polls must incorporate that fact into their plans and proceed accordingly.

The Use of Screening Questions

Researchers can take steps in opinion polls to minimize the problem of nonattitudes. The simplest strategy is to make it socially acceptable for respondents to say they are unfamiliar with the topic of the question. This response would result in that question being skipped. Another strategy is to employ screening or filter questions to separate likely attitude holders from nonattitude respondents. With both strategies the intent is to minimize the number of responses that are superficial reactions to the interview stimulus. For example, the study cited earlier by Bishop and his colleagues (1980) on the fictitious Public Affairs Act employed a variety of screening questions to reduce the frequency of nonattitudes, for example, "Do you have an opinion on this or not?" and "Have you thought much about this issue?" Respondents who could not pass the screening questions were not asked about the Public Affairs Act.

As another example, the 1984 American National Election Study (ANES) conducted by the Center for Political Studies (CPS) at the University of Michigan used a variety of means to lessen the problem of nonattitudes. One item on this survey asked respondents whether they thought the federal government had become too powerful. The exact wording of the question was:

> Some people are afraid the government in Washington is getting too powerful for the good of the country and the individual person. Others feel that the government in Washington is not getting too strong. Do you have an opinion on this or not?

Of the 973 citizens in the sample who were asked whether they had an opinion, 550 (57 percent) said yes and 423 (43 percent) said no. The sizable number with no opinion might surprise the reader, given the recurring theme of Reagan's presidential victories in 1980 and 1984, namely, the need to reduce the scope and power of the federal government. What this example suggests is that topics hotly discussed by political elites may not be of great importance to the average citizen. In this example, asking people whether or not they had an opinion was an effective screening question that eliminated nearly half of the respondents. We can only speculate on how many of the eliminated respondents would have answered the entire survey if the screening question had not been used and if instead people simply had been asked whether they thought the government was becoming too powerful or not. As it was, among the 550 citizens with an opinion on the issue, 311 thought government had grown too powerful, 218 thought it had not, 10 said it depended, and 11 said they did not know (even though they had stated in response to the screening question that they had an opinion on the issue).

Another example of the use of a screening question in the 1984 CPS election study is the following item:

> Some people think the government should provide fewer services, even in areas such as health and education, in order to reduce spending. Suppose these people are at one end of the scale at point number 1. Other people feel it is important for the government to provide many more services even if it means an increase in spending. Suppose these people are at the other end, at point 7. And, of course, some other people have opinions somewhere in between at points 2, 3, 4, 5, or 6. Where would you place yourself on this scale or haven't you thought much about this?

Of the 971 persons who were asked this question, 150 (about 15 percent) said they had not thought much about the matter. This does not mean, however, that the other 85 percent had thought a lot about the issue and had genuine opinions. The following pattern of their responses to this item raises questions about their answers ($N = 821$):

N	Response
48	1. Provide many fewer services; reduce spending a lot.
82	2.
141	3.
293	4.
138	5.
58	6.
48	7. Provide many more services; increase spending a lot.
13	Don't know.

Note that the largest number of responses ($N = 293$) fell in the middle, in category 4. This may reflect large numbers of citizens who are satisfied with the status quo or who genuinely take a neutral position on the issue. Or it may reflect the tendency of some citizens with genuine, nonneutral preferences on the issue to hide their preferences by opting for the safe middle category. Many such responses can be moved out of the middle category by using a branching format question, in which citizens who opt for the middle category are then asked whether they favor one side or the other more (Aldrich et al. 1982).

On the other hand, it is also possible that the large number of people in the middle category may signal problems of nonattitudes in the measurement. Perhaps some proportion of people in the middle category place themselves there because they do not want to admit to the interviewer that they haven't thought much about the issue or are unable to place themselves along the scale. These people might choose the middle category as a safe position that makes them seem informed without having to take sides on the issue. If so, then some of the category 4 responses may be nonattitudes rather than genuinely neutral opinions, and the portrait of American public opinion on this issue may be misleading.

In contrast to the pattern of responses on the spending question, consider citizens' replies to the following item about racial integration, from the same study:

> Some people think achieving racial integration of schools is so important that it justifies busing children to schools out of their own neighborhoods. Others think letting children go to their own schools is so important that they oppose busing. Where would you place yourself on this scale or haven't you thought much about this?

Here only 69 of 968 respondents (7 percent) said they had not thought much about the issue, as opposed to the 15 percent who had not given much thought to the question of government spending. That more people said they had thought about the busing issue seems intuitively correct, since busing is the kind of issue that hits home and captures citizens' attention. Moreover, the distribution of the busing responses reveals relatively few in the middle category; most responses (93%) bunched in the two most antibusing, pro-neighborhood schools categories ($N = 899$):

N	Response
33	1. Bus to achieve integration.
15	2.
25	3.
70	4.
91	5.
186	6.
462	7. Keep children in neighborhood schools.
17	Don't know.

This skewed pattern of responses demonstrates that few Americans are neutral about busing and that the middle category is not the choice for large numbers of citizens with nonattitudes on the issue. It may also be the case that the meaning of a middle position on the busing item is less clear than it is on the question of providing services, so that fewer people would opt for the middle position.

A final example of a screening question occurred in the 1992 American National Election Study in the use of "feeling thermometers." In essence, the use of the feeling thermometer rests on the ability of people to relate points on a thermometer to figurative degrees of warmth and coldness toward objects. Survey respondents were given the following instructions:

> I'd like to get your feelings toward some of our political leaders and other people who are in the news these days. I'll read the name of a person and I'd like you to rate that person using something we call the feeling thermometer. Ratings between 50 degrees and 100 degrees mean that you feel favorable and warm toward that person. Ratings between 0 degrees and 50 degrees mean that you don't feel favorable toward the person and that you don't care too much for that person. You would rate the person at the 50 degree mark if you don't feel particularly warm or cold toward the person. If we come to a person whose name you don't recognize, you don't need to rate that person. Just tell me and we'll move on to the next one.

Ideally, citizens who do not recognize a name or feel that they are unable to evaluate a particular individual would indicate that to the interviewer. However, the instructions may encourage respondents to place individuals at the 50 degree mark, including individuals whose names they do not recognize.

Table 2-1 indicates the proportion of respondents who gave particular ratings to various political figures. (Keep in mind that Bush, Clinton, and Perot were the major presidential candidates in 1992, Buchanan had unsuccessfully sought the GOP nomination that year, and Jackson had been on the national stage many years including earlier runs for the Democratic presidential nomination.)

The percentage of respondents who did not recognize George Bush, Bill Clinton, Ross Perot, or Jesse Jackson or who could not evaluate them is very small, while the comparable percentage for Pat Buchanan is much higher — 19 percent. It appears that the screening questions worked well, since about one-fifth of the respondents did not rate the less prominent Pat

Table 2-1 Thermometer Ratings of Five Political Figures (percentage)

Candidate	Evaluation				
	Rating Other than 50	Rating of 50	Does not recognize	Cannot evaluate	Rating (N)
Bush	85	14	0	1	100 (2,481)
Clinton	84	14	0	2	100 (2,481)
Perot	71	22	3	4	100 (2,478)
Buchanan	54	27	13	6	100 (2,475)
Jackson	78	19	1	2	100 (2,471)

Source: 1992 American National Election Study conducted by the Center for Political Studies, Institute for Social Research, University of Michigan.

Note: Table entries are the percentage of respondents ranking each political figure in each category.

Buchanan. However, it is disquieting that among the citizens who did assign a thermometer score to these political leaders, more citizens give a rating of 50 to Buchanan, Perot, and Jackson than to Bush and Clinton. Of those citizens evaluating Bush on the thermometer, only 14.1 percent $[14/(85 + 14)]$ gave him a score of 50; the comparable percentage for Clinton was 14.3 $[14/(84 + 14)]$. But for Perot, Buchanan, and Jackson, the proportion of citizens using the thermometer who placed them at the midpoint was 23.7 percent $[22/(71 + 22)]$, 33.3 percent $[27/(54 + 27)]$, and 19.6 percent $[19/(78 + 19)]$ respectively.

In one sense it is not surprising that more people placed Buchanan at 50; he was less well known than the other political figures in 1992 and therefore may have been more likely to evoke neutral responses. But there may also have been a problem of measuring nonattitudes here. The greater frequency of ratings of 50 for Buchanan may indicate that the screening questions did not eliminate all those persons who had no genuine attitudes about him.

An indirect test of this notion is presented in Tables 2-2 and 2-3, which show how educational levels and degree of interest in the campaign were related to assigning political figures a thermometer score of 50. One might intuitively expect that citizens with higher levels of education would be able to make more discriminating evaluations and therefore would be

Table 2-2 Frequency of Ratings of 50 for Five Political Figures by Respondents' Education (percentage)

Candidate	Grade school	High school	Some college	College graduate	Post-college
Bush	23	19	10	7	5
Clinton	21	16	18	9	4
Perot	27	24	24	24	21
Buchanan	35	39	33	30	19
Jackson	25	23	19	17	10

Source: 1992 American National Election Study conducted by the Center for Political Studies, Institute for Social Research, University of Michigan.

Note: Table entries are the percentage of respondents assigning a thermometer score who gave the candidate in question a score of 50. For example, the 39 in the "high school/Buchanan" category means that 39 percent of respondents with a high school education gave Buchanan a score of 50; the other 61 percent of high school respondents assigned Buchanan a numerical score other than 50.

less likely to assign thermometer scores of 50. As Table 2-2 indicates, this expectation held across the board.

Table 2-3 relates the frequency of ratings of 50 to the respondents' level of interest in the campaign. As expected, the more interested the respondents, the less likely they were to assign a score of 50 because of their greater awareness of and involvement in the campaign. This pattern held for all five political leaders. But note that less than 30 percent of the low-interest respondents rated Bush and Clinton at 50, while 46 percent rated Buchanan at that midpoint. These numbers may suggest that little information went into the evaluations of Buchanan and raise the question of what the score of 50 represents: is it a genuine neutral point, or simply a convenient and safe home for the expression of nonattitudes that were not filtered out by the screening questions?

Nonattitudes and the Middle Position in Survey Questions

The preceding examples illustrate how difficult it is to assess the magnitude of the nonattitude problem. They also raise another problem in attitude and opinion measurement. What does it mean when a person replies to a survey question "I don't know" or "I can't decide" or "It depends"? Do these responses represent a genuine neutral stance or something else? Should the responses of holders of nonattitudes be included at the neutral or middle point, or should they be at a distinct point off the

Table 2-3 Frequency of Ratings of 50 for Five Political Figures by
Respondents' Interest in the Campaign (percentage)

Candidate	Very much interested	Somewhat interested	Not very interested
Bush	8	15	27
Clinton	8	16	28
Perot	19	26	33
Buchanan	23	40	46
Jackson	17	20	29

Source: 1992 American National Election Study conducted by the Center for Political
Studies, Institute for Social Research, University of Michigan.

Note: Table entries are the percentage of respondents assigning a thermometer score
who gave the candidate in question a score of 50. For example, the 46 in the
"Buchanan/not very interested" category means that 46 percent of the not very
interested respondents who were able to rate Buchanan gave him a 50, while the other
54 percent gave him a score other than 50.

measurement scale in order not to create a misleading image of large
numbers of citizens thoughtfully adopting the middle position?

The response alternatives included in an item affect the extent of
nonattitudes. For example, a CBS News/*New York Times* poll conducted in
November 1985 asked a national sample of Americans, "Who should have
the most say about what cuts should be made to balance the budget—the
President or Congress?" Note that the question did not give respondents the
option of stating that the president and Congress should have an equal say.
About 4 percent of the sample volunteered this response, but one wonders
what percentage of Americans would have opted for this alternative if it had
been explicitly presented. In marked contrast is the following question asked
in a November 1985 ABC News/*Washington Post* poll: "As things presently
stand, who do you think is ahead in military power, the United States or the
Soviet Union, or do you think they are about the same in military strength?"
Twenty-four percent said the United States was ahead, 26 percent said the
Soviets were, 4 percent had no opinion, and 46 percent said that both
nations were about the same in military strength. In fact, in the eight times
between 1979 and 1991 that this question was asked of samples of
Americans by ABC News/*Washington Post,* the percentage of respondents
citing "the same" has ranged from 34 to 55 with an average of 44. One can
only speculate what the responses would have looked like if the middle
choice had not been provided.

Research on the effects of including a middle choice in the response
alternatives shows that including a middle option typically generates about

25 percent more noncommittal responses (Schuman and Presser 1977; Bishop et al. 1980; Presser and Schuman 1980). This suggests that the omission of such a choice will result in many substantive responses that are not very meaningful from citizens who have weak or nonexistent attitudes on a subject. In one study Presser and Schuman (1980) administered two forms of a survey item to random subsamples. The only difference between the two forms was that one offered a middle alternative and the other did not. For example, one item asked about the penalties for using marijuana. It read: "In your opinion, should the penalties for using marijuana be more strict, less strict, or about the same as they are now?" The other version read: "In your opinion, should the penalties for using marijuana be more strict or less strict than they are now?" On average, about 23 percent of the respondents answered "about the same as they are now" when that choice was included in the question, compared with only about 8 percent who volunteered that response when it was not included.

Research by Bishop (1987) further demonstrates how the presence or absence of a middle response alternative can affect survey responses. Based on a series of experiments, Bishop's work confirmed earlier research in finding that citizens are much more likely to choose the middle alternative when it is included in the question than when it is omitted. Moreover, simply mentioning the middle category in the preface of a survey question will encourage respondents to select that option even when it is not listed among the response alternatives. More important, Bishop presents evidence (p. 227) that suggests that "people who select a middle alternative when it is offered would not necessarily answer the question in the same way as other respondents if forced to choose between the polar alternatives" when the middle option is not provided.

The interpretation of a "don't know" response can be especially problematic since "don't know" can mean many different things (Coombs and Coombs 1976-1977; Faulkenberry and Mason 1978). For some people, "don't know" simply reflects the absence of a real attitude on the topic, but for other people it may represent an inability to choose among contending positions. Smith (1984, 229) points out other ways in which "don't know" responses might arise. Respondents may be too insecure to take a stance, or they may decline to state their opinions out of a strong sense of privacy or because they do not want to offend anybody. Some respondents may want to hasten the completion of the interview by saying "don't know," thereby avoiding follow-up questions. Just as respondents' nonattitudes may be disguised as attitudes, so too their middle responses (including "don't know") may mask genuine attitudes. Gilljam and Granberg (1993) found that poll respondents who were induced to respond to a survey item after they had initially given a "don't know" response to that item expressed attitudes

Drawing by C. Barsotti; © 1980 The New Yorker Magazine, Inc.

*"I'm undecided, but that doesn't mean I'm
apathetic or uninformed."*

that were predictive of behavior. They concluded that there indeed were poll respondents who had genuine attitudes, but kept them concealed by opting for the "don't know" response.

Converse (1976-1977) investigated characteristics of respondents as well as properties of survey questions that might affect the frequency of "no opinion" and "don't know" answers. She found, as expected, that the higher the level of education of respondents, the less likely they were to give "no opinion" replies. With respect to question characteristics, she found that the most important feature was the content of the item. As the subject matter of the question became more and more remote from the concerns and interests of citizens, the frequency of "don't know" responses increased.

Other research sheds further light on how survey responses are affected by response alternatives and their ordering. Krosnick and Alwin (1987) found that respondents with less cognitive sophistication—less formal education and limited vocabularies—were more likely to be influenced by the order of responses. Bishop (1990) also found that the effects on responses of using or not using a middle alternative are most pronounced among citizens who are less involved with the particular topic of the survey question. In general, the implications of the Converse, Bishop, and Krosnick and Alwin studies are that the consequences of response alternatives and their ordering are genuine but complex. Therefore one must be sensitive to the potential distortion and even manipulation of responses that might occur because of how the response choices are presented.

Is it a good idea to force responses into polar categories and minimize middle or neutral answers? Or is it better to encourage people to choose the middle position? The answer, of course, is that it depends. If people have genuine attitudes, then the public opinion researcher wants those attitudes clearly expressed. The inclusion of a middle category in such a situation might result in cautious citizens opting for the middle position, particularly on controversial issues where they might not want to reveal their true opinions to the interviewer. Yet the exclusion of a middle category might lead people with weak or nonexistent opinions on an issue to choose one of the genuine response options, thereby creating false impressions of genuine attitudes. A similar dilemma occurs with respect to screening questions. The researcher wants to screen out nonattitudes, but does not want to make it too easy for people to avoid answering questions on which they have real views, or too difficult to answer when they have real, although weak, attitudes.

This is a problem without a simple, neat solution. The public opinion pollster and the consumer of the research must simply be sensitive to whether and in what form screening questions are used on a survey. They must also be aware of the response alternatives provided to the respondents. Finally, the appropriateness of particular substantive questions to particular samples of citizens should always be a central concern of the political analyst and the public opinion consumer. In the political realm one must recognize that issues of great concern to political elites may be of little interest to rank and file citizens.

The "Mushiness Index"

If a survey measures genuine attitudes, the responses should show some degree of stability over time, yet in many instances survey responses fluctuate wildly over a relatively short period. This type of fluctuation raises questions about how real the measured opinions were in the first place. In response to this phenomenon the polling firm of Yankelovich, Skelly, and White developed the "mushiness index." The index was designed to assess the volatility of the public's views on issues, particularly the ones citizens provide answers on even though they have little information and understanding about the issues. The mushiness index has four components in addition to a person's position on a particular issue: how much the issue affects the respondent personally, how well informed the respondent feels he or she is on the issue, how much the respondent discusses the issue with family and friends, and the respondent's own assessment of how likely it is that his or her views on the issue will change (Keene and Sackett 1981). On the basis of these criteria, Yankelovich, Skelly, and White placed issues into three categories ranging from very volatile or "mushy" to firm. They found that, in general, attitudes on domestic policy were less mushy than those on foreign policy.

The usefulness of the mushiness index is illustrated by the following example (Keene and Sackett 1981, 51). A sample of Americans was asked: "Do you favor or oppose restricting imports of foreign goods such as Japanese cars, textiles, and steel, which are less expensive than American products?" Fifty-four percent favored restricting imports, 41 percent opposed restrictions, and only 5 percent were unsure. But when the sample was broken down into three groups according to responses to the four mushiness criteria, the patterns of response were quite different. Among the mushiest group, 39 percent favored restrictions, 37 percent opposed them, and 24 percent were unsure; among the firmest group, 62 percent favored restrictions, 37 percent opposed them, and 1 percent were unsure.

Respondents' knowledge about an issue (one component of the mushiness index) clearly affects their attitudes, as an April 1986 CBS News/New York Times poll made clear. The poll queried Americans about their support for the Nicaraguan contras, rebels fighting against the Sandinista government. Overall, 25 percent of the sample were willing to give aid to the contras, while 62 percent opposed such an action. But when the sample was divided according to whether the respondents knew which side the United States supported in Nicaragua, major differences were observed (Shipler 1986). Among those respondents who knew which side the United States favored, 40 percent supported aid to the contras, and 52 percent opposed it. But for those who were not aware of American policy, only 16 percent favored aid to the contras, while 59 percent opposed such assistance.

The mushiness index is not widely used in surveys, in part because it is too costly and time-consuming to ask all the questions needed to construct the index, particularly when the survey covers multiple substantive issues.

Nevertheless, the concept of mushiness is of interest analytically because it helps explain a number of apparent anomalies in American public opinion. One puzzle is the rapid swings in public opinion often observed after the president of the United States delivers a speech devoted to a single issue, particularly foreign policy. Public opinion is most volatile on issues that seem distant in terms of their likely effects on people and their susceptibility to citizen influence. We often praise a president for his ability to move public opinion, not recognizing that on some issues a somewhat mindless "follow the leader" mentality is at work; a president would be successful in moving public opinion in any direction, assuming he is able to present the issue in ways beneficial both to his own and to citizens' objectives.

The rationale underlying the mushiness index is not new to Yankelovich, Skelly, and White; more than forty-five years ago George Gallup (1947) espoused survey designs that measured multiple aspects of a person's opinion. Indeed, Schuman and Presser (1981) and other investigators have emphasized the need to measure the importance of an issue to a person as well as his or her opinion on that issue in order to better understand the dynamics of attitude change. However, Yankelovich, Skelly, and White had the public relations acumen to coin a catchy phrase for their finding, which built on the results of earlier public opinion studies.

Many survey questions seem to be prime candidates for high mushiness scores, yet unfortunately these scores will not be calculable since the necessary follow-up questions were not asked because of insufficient time and space on the survey. Thus, poll users need to ask themselves whether the topic of the survey is likely to be of concern to the respondents or whether they will see the topic as an abstraction with little immediate and practical relevance. If the former, mushiness and nonattitudes are not likely to be a serious problem. The complicating factor is that the topic of the survey is likely to be of varying importance to different segments of the American population. Unemployed steel and auto workers are more likely to be concerned about foreign imports and thus to have more stable attitudes on that issue than are, say, college students. Likewise, senior citizens are more likely to have well-developed views on Social Security and Medicare than a youthful population group would. Consequently, American public opinion on a particular issue includes the rather divergent views of various subgroups of the population, some of whom have genuine attitudes on the issue while others do not. Moreover, in trying to relate public opinion to the processes and decisions of government, the whole of public opinion may be less important than the opinion of a particular subset of people. It may be that on certain issues, it is the views of a few people with genuine attitudes that will have the greatest impact on government policy and policy makers.

Conclusion

The problem of nonattitudes remains one of the least considered aspects of public opinion polling. Other facets of public opinion research, such as question wording and sampling, receive much more attention, even to the point of being mentioned in television and newspaper reports of results of public opinion polls. But very few people raise the fundamental questions: Was the topic of the survey of interest to the respondents? Did the poll query people on subjects about which they held genuine views?

As discussed earlier, assessing the size of the problem of nonattitudes is a difficult task that is made even more problematic by the tendency of people to respond to questions not in terms of their actual purpose and content, but in terms of the cues provided by the questions and whatever meaning (often idiosyncratic) respondents read into them. For example, a person asked whether she favors selling military equipment to Saudi Arabia might answer the question, not on the basis of any information about Saudi Arabia, but on the basis of a predisposition toward the weapons industry in general (she might be a stockholder in a firm that manufactures weapons). Likewise, citizens asked whether they favor joint American-Russian space ventures might respond on the basis of their underlying view of Russia rather than on the basis of opinions about the best way to explore outer space. The pressure to provide an answer in an interview situation may lead respondents to seek out whatever cues are available in order to answer the question. Because of the absence of attitudes about the topic, citizens may impute a variety of meanings to the question in order to come up with a response. Or because only one question was asked about a multifaceted topic, it may be impossible to disentangle attitudes and nonattitudes.

The problem of nonattitudes should not lead us to disregard polls because on many issues the general public has genuine attitudes and is willing and able to express them. There are other issues on which only a small subset of the public may have real opinions, but even then events may transform such an issue into one that engages the serious attention of the mass public. One should not be surprised when the public seems to be fickle on the issues it cares about and on its positions on these issues. Oreskes (1990) observed that in 1989, 64 percent of Americans said that the drug problem was the most important one facing the nation. Yet a year later only 10 percent cited drugs as the most serious problem. Certainly it was not victory in the drug war that led citizens to downgrade the importance of the drug problem. Instead, it was more a matter of media and presidential emphasis on issues; when the media and the president focused on the drug menace, then many Americans saw the issue as the critical one facing the nation. But as new issues arose and media and political attention shifted,

Americans' views of which issues were critical also changed. Public opinion polls do provide valid assessments of what Americans are thinking; one should simply keep in mind that not all issues are appropriate topics for public opinion surveys.

Nonattitudes are more a problem of the respondent than of the measuring instrument. That is, nonattitudes can arise even when a question is carefully constructed without any loaded words or implied alternatives. The best formulated questions can still result in the measurement of nonattitudes. Nevertheless, deficiencies in the questions themselves can contribute to the problem of nonattitudes, as well as to many other difficulties encountered in public opinion polling. Thus, we now turn to a discussion of how question wording, question order, and question context can affect the results of public opinion polls.

Note

1. I am using the terms *attitude* and *opinion* interchangeably. Many social scientists differentiate between attitudes and opinions by treating the latter as more transitory, as verbal representations of some underlying attitude. That is, they view an opinion as a verbal manifestation of an attitude, words elicited by the public opinion survey. For the purposes of this chapter, this distinction is by no means critical, although the reader should recognize that public opinion data at times may simply be verbal responses (opinions) that we hope accurately reflect some underlying attitudes.

3 Wording and Context of Questions

Of all the pitfalls associated with public opinion polling, question wording is probably the one most familiar to consumers of public opinion research. Common sense tells us that the use of a loaded word or an inflammatory phrase can affect the pattern of responses to a survey question. If one wants a poll to show weak support for federal assistance to financially beleaguered entities (such as the savings and loan industry in the 1990s), all one need do is ask Americans whether they favor a federal "bailout" of these entities. Few people favor a bailout, but many more support federal loans with proper safeguards that the moneys will be repaid. If one wants a poll to indicate scant support for providing foreign aid, one can construct an argumentative and leading question such as: Do you favor giving foreign aid to other nations when there are children in the United States who are suffering from hunger? To demonstrate support for foreign aid, one could "load" the question differently: Do you favor giving foreign aid to other nations in order to help them resist communist subversion and thereby enhance our national security?

Individuals and groups with an ax to grind can easily construct questions that will generate desired responses. The response alternatives they provide to the interviewees can also help them achieve the intended result. As we have seen, if a middle alternative is not listed as one of the choices, then fewer citizens will opt for that choice, and this can alter the interpretation of a poll. For example, if a mayor wants a poll to indicate support for a city's spending policies in the area of garbage collection, he or she might construct this question: Do you think the city is spending too much, too little, or about the right amount on garbage collection? Clearly, the response "about the right amount" is an endorsement of the mayor's current policies. If "about the right amount" were not included as an explicit response alternative, fewer such replies would result because citizens would have to volunteer that response. In turn, a high response to either of the other two alternatives creates an impression of citizen dissatisfaction with the mayor's spending on garbage collection.

Bad question wording may occur when polls are conducted by interested parties whose aim is to generate specific responses. Even so, most professional polls are not blatantly manipulated; instead, questions are typically worded in a nonbiased, fair, and straightforward fashion. But as we shall see, even when the sponsor has no obvious ax to grind, question wording choices can be very consequential to the results obtained. In many instances highly reputable polling organizations have arrived at divergent conclusions simply because they employed different (although well-constructed) questions on a particular topic.

Less obvious than the impact of question wording is the effect on responses of the order and context in which specific questions are placed. A typical public opinion survey includes many questions, and the placement of a particular question can affect the responses to it. Yet most consumers of public opinion research know little about item order and therefore have little sense of how the context has helped to shape the responses.

Consider the following hypothetical example. Imagine a survey assessing popular attitudes toward economic relations with China. The key question measuring support for most favored nation trade status to China is preceded by a battery of items about Chinese human rights violations. Obviously, the prior questions on Chinese human rights violations will predispose respondents to be more hostile toward granting China favorable trade conditions. Or imagine a survey in which the popularity of the president is measured after a series of questions dealing with scandals in his administration and difficulties with the economy and Congress. Certainly, reactions to the president will be more negative when respondents are first reminded of these problems. The point of both examples is that the context in which a particular survey item is embedded can help shape responses to that item.

This chapter presents numerous examples of questions from a variety of real-world settings. It will become clear, if it is not so already, that some "question effects" are obvious and therefore less likely to mislead people, while others are subtle and more problematic and may indeed manipulate and mislead unsuspecting consumers of public opinion research.

Question Wording

Four decades ago Stanley Payne wrote *The Art of Asking Questions*, a fundamental work on interview techniques. In the final chapter he presented a checklist of 100 considerations organized around themes such as the topic being studied, the structure of the question and the response alternatives, the treatment of the respondents, the words themselves, sources of bias, and the readability of the questions. Most of what Payne said then still holds true today and demonstrates that constructing good questions is largely a matter of common sense (Payne 1951).

Some question wording problems are obvious and may even be intentional, particularly in the pseudo-polls (discussed in chapter 1) whose sponsors are seeking specific results. Clearly the use of loaded words will affect the results. For example, referring to labor union officials as union leaders rather than union czars or union bosses will certainly affect opinions about union officials. Likewise, questions can be argumentative, pushing respondents in a particular direction. For example, the American Foundation for AIDS Research asked the following question in 1994:

> The AIDS epidemic is a national emergency. It has already claimed over 180,000 lives in the U.S. alone. Over one and a half million Americans now carry the AIDS virus. Do you think the majority of Americans realize how widespread this tragedy has become, and that the worst is still ahead?

Note that this is a compound question. It asks about two topics — the extent of the epidemic, and its future, yet the respondent is not allowed to distinguish between the two. Sometimes compound questions are more disguised in that the duality of the item is not evident until one interprets responses to the question. Classic examples of such questions are "Do you still beat your spouse?" and "Have you stopped using illegal drugs?" Yes and no answers to both of these questions leave the impression that at some point one beat one's spouse and used illegal drugs. Obviously, the solution here is to use two questions — "Did you ever use illegal drugs in the past?" and "Are you currently using illegal drugs?"

Survey questions are also flawed when they provide false or misleading information in order to influence responses. A 1994 pseudo-poll for the National Republican Senatorial Committee included the following item:

> Do you support President Clinton's tax increase on Americans who earn more than $30,000 a year? (The top tax rate increased from 31% to 36%.)

Among the many things wrong with this question is the possibility that it might leave the citizen who earned more than $30,000 with the incorrect impression that his or her tax rate increased from 31% to 36%.

Wording problems can arise on routine topics included in legitimate surveys. Seemingly straightforward questions that employ relatively simple language can seem ambiguous to respondents. Even basic questions about the number of persons in a household or the number of children in a family can present difficulties. For example, in surveys in which the wife and husband were both interviewed independently, their responses did not agree perfectly about such factual items as the number of children they had (Asher 1974b). Perhaps errors were made in transcribing their responses. Or perhaps the question was ambiguous. One spouse might have responded in terms of children living at home, the other in terms of the total number. Or one spouse might have included children from a previous marriage, while the other might not have. Measurement of a respondent's age has also proven to be surprisingly problematic. Peterson (1984) showed that four different ways of measuring age in a survey yielded substantially different refusal rates (that is, the percentage of respondents refusing to answer the question), although the age data obtained were very similar across the four formats.

Fowler (1992) argues that survey questions, even apparently straightforward ones, must be adequately pretested before they are included in an actual poll. He discussed seven questions used in national health surveys that were subjected to extensive pretesting and were found to have a number of ambiguous terms. For example, the very simple question "Do you exercise or play sports regularly?" was found to be ambiguous because different respondents had different views on what constituted exercise. The question was then modified to read "Do you do any sports or hobbies involving physical activities, or any exercise, including walking, on a regular basis?"

Imagine the ambiguity that can arise from the simple question "Have you taken a vacation in the last few years?" Does "last few years" mean one or two years, or could it mean three, four, or five years to some respondents? And what constitutes a vacation? Does one have to go somewhere in order to have a vacation or does staying at home by the swimming pool count?

If question wording can affect measurement of objective matters such as a person's age and the number of children in a family, then how much might wording affect more subjective phenomena? The answer, of course, is that wording can make a great difference. For example, Sussman (1985i) reported on three different versions of a question used in ABC News/*Washington Post* surveys to measure the public's attitudes toward President Reagan's Strategic Defense Initiative (SDI), commonly known as "Star Wars." In 1983 the survey asked Americans if they had "heard or read of a proposal by Reagan that the United States develop defensive military weapons using lasers and particle beams to shoot down enemy missiles." It then queried, "Well, do you favor or oppose developing such defensive weapons, or what?" In this survey 65 percent of respondents knew of SDI. Fifty-four percent were in favor, 37 percent opposed, and 9 percent undecided.

A July 1985 poll began by telling respondents that SDI weapons "could destroy nuclear missiles fired at the United States by the Soviet Union or other countries." It then stated:

> Supporters say such weapons could guarantee protection of the United States from nuclear attack and are worth whatever they cost. Opponents say such weapons will not work, will increase the arms race, and that the research will cost many billions of dollars. How about you: Would you say you approve of plans to develop such space-based weapons?

Here the results were 41 percent in favor, 53 percent opposed, and 6 percent undecided, a pattern far different from the 1983 results.

Because the July 1985 version of the survey included two positive and three negative arguments, a third version of the question was tried in October that omitted the clause "such weapons will not work." The results of this version were 48 percent in favor, 46 percent opposed, and 6 percent undecided. In each case, different question wording yielded different results although some of the differences in results may have reflected genuine changes in attitudes over the time period in which the questions were asked.

The impact of question wording on responses can be seen in innumerable examples. In 1982 the Advisory Commission on Intergovernmental Relations sponsored three surveys asking Americans which services they would cut if funds were short (Herbers 1982). Respondents were asked, "Suppose the budgets of your state and local governments have to be curtailed, which of these parts would you limit most severely?" About 8 percent of the respondents cited "aid to the needy" when that response was listed as one of the service areas that could be cut. But when the term "public welfare programs" was used in place of "aid to the needy" and the other choices remained the same, many more respondents (39 percent) opted to cut welfare. Obviously, aid to the needy is much more popular than public welfare, and the program label used in the survey strongly influenced the results. It has been a common phenomenon for the American public to complain about welfare in general, but to be highly supportive of specific programs that could justifiably be included under the rubric of welfare.

Poll results about presidential preference in 1980 provide another example of the importance of question wording (Townley 1980). In May 1980 an NBC News poll asked a sample of citizens an open-ended question about whom they would like to see elected in 1980; the question did not mention any specific candidates. The leading choice was "not sure" with 25 percent, followed by Carter and Reagan, each with 24 percent, and John Anderson far back at 5 percent. A week later a Harris poll asked likely voters, "If you had to choose right now, would you vote for Reagan, Carter or Anderson?" This time the results were 39 percent for Reagan, 34 percent for Carter, 24 percent for Anderson, and only 5 percent undecided. It is highly unlikely that any political event in the week between the two polls caused these highly divergent results. Instead, the explanation must lie with question wording and the fact that one question specifically mentioned candidates while the other did not.

One general rule in constructing survey questions is to avoid double negatives. Yet such a mistake was made in a 1992 Roper poll conducted for the American Jewish Committee on the Holocaust. The results of this poll and the subsequent media coverage generated a lot of controversy and consternation (Moore and Newport 1994; Morin 1994e, 1994f; Kifner 1994; Ladd 1994). The Roper question asked:

> Does it seem possible or does it seem impossible to you that the Nazi extermination of the Jews never happened?

Fully 22 percent of the respondents said that it seemed possible that the Holocaust never occurred and another 12 percent did not know. When these results became known, there was shock and concern about American ignorance of the Holocaust and fears about the success of anti-Semitic revisionist historians.

It turned out that these results were largely due to a convoluted question. The Roper Organization itself was so dismayed that such a poorly worded question had seen the light of day that it redid the survey for the American Jewish Congress. This time the question was worded:

> Does it seem possible to you that the Nazi extermination of the Jews never happened, or do you feel certain that it happened?

With this wording, only 1 percent of the respondents said it seemed possible that the Holocaust had never occurred. The Gallup Organization also tested the impact of alternative question wording and got results similar to those of Roper (Ladd 1994). The pain and confusion caused by the first Roper question shows how careful one must be in wording questions.

Often in providing respondents with some background to a question, a pollster may go too far. In a June 17, 1985, editorial entitled "A Grain of Salt, Please," the *Washington Post* complained about the increasingly common practice of informing respondents about a topic in order to ascertain their opinion on it. Obviously, the content of the information provided to the respondents will have a lot to do with their subsequent expression of their views on the issue. The *Post* editorial cited an example from a Harris poll that demonstrated how ludicrous matters can become. The following agree/disagree statement was presented to a sample of Americans in January 1985: "When [Bernard] Goetz said in his confession

FRANK AND ERNEST ©by Bob Thaves

IT SEEMS TO ME THAT "HOW MANY IN YOUR HOUSEHOLD?" WOULD BE A SIMPLE QUESTION TO ANSWER, DR. JEKYLL.

© Reprinted by permission of NEA, Inc.

that he used dum-dum bullets, that he was sorry he didn't gouge out the eyes of the four [young men] he shot, and that if he could have reloaded his gun fast enough, he would have taken out after them, he looks more like a *Death Wish* gunman out stalking to kill criminals, not an innocent victim just trying to defend himself [from a mugging]." As the *Post* opined, "The wonder is not that a majority agreed with the statement, but that 38 percent of the respondents had the gumption to disagree."

My favorite example of an argumentative question purporting to inform respondents comes from the 1982 Democratic primary race for governor in Ohio. Three major candidates were running: the former lieutenant governor, Richard Celeste; the incumbent attorney general, William Brown; and the former mayor of Cincinnati, Jerry Springer. The pollster for the attorney general (Pat Caddell's Cambridge Survey Research) included the following question in a statewide survey:

> As you may know, in 1974, Jerry Springer, who had gotten married six months earlier, was arrested on a morals charge with three women in a hotel room. He also used a bad check to pay for the women's services, and subsequently resigned as mayor of his city. Does this make you much more likely, somewhat more likely, somewhat less likely, or much less likely to support Jerry Springer for governor this year?

In addition to being factually incorrect on a number of points, this question was a blatant effort by the pollster first to feed consumers information that would generate negative responses about a candidate, and then to use the replies in a highly selective way for political purposes. In the context of our discussion of nonattitudes in chapter 2, this was an attempt to create attitudes on the basis of the interview situation—something that can be done in a variety of ways. One technique is to present hypothetical situations to citizens and then ask them to react to these situations. More often than not, the information obtained is of dubious utility because the hypothetical situations have forced the respondents into a world that has little real meaning for them.

Many other examples of the impact of question wording can be cited. Smith (1987a) showed that Americans are much more likely to support spending for the "poor" than spending for "welfare." Similarly, Rasinski (1989) found that support for spending in policy areas other than welfare was affected by how the issue was labeled; for example, respondents were more supportive of "solving the problems of big cities" than they were of "assistance to big cities." Smith and Squire (1990) found that the use of prestige names (e.g. President Reagan) in survey questions not only influenced the direction of responses, but also the frequency of "don't know" answers. Based on the evidence, the authors speculated that the inclusion of a prestige name provides a cue or stimulus that encourages less educated persons to respond to the survey question; this cue is not necessary for more educated respondents, who may be more familiar with the topic of the question.

Sometimes the response alternatives that a question provides can also affect survey results. For example, Kagay and Elder (1992) examined attitudes toward Clinton and Bush as measured in two July 1992 polls, one conducted by Gallup and the other by CBS News/*New York Times*. The Gallup poll first asked voters if their opinions of a candidate were favorable or unfavorable; respondents could volunteer that they did not know enough to offer an opinion. In contrast, the CBS News/*New York Times* poll initially presented respondents four choices: favorable, not favorable, undecided, or haven't heard enough about a candidate to have an opinion. Needless to say, the CBS News/*New York Times* found fewer Americans offering an opinion than did the Gallup poll since the former survey provided two opportunities for citizens to refuse to rate the candidates while the Gallup poll provided no such opportunity. Thus, the CBS News/*New York Times* poll showed 36 percent of Americans favorable to Clinton, 24 percent unfavorable, 31 percent undecided, and 9 percent stating that they hadn't heard enough. The Gallup poll, in contrast, found 63 percent favorable toward Clinton, 25 percent unfavorable, and only 12 percent volunteering "don't know."

Morin (1993f) has shown that slight modifications in the choices presented in the standard presidential approval question can alter the results. The standard question reads: "Do you approve or disapprove of the job that Bill Clinton is doing as president?" Respondents are next asked whether they strongly or somewhat approve or disapprove. Another way of asking the question is to combine opinion and intensity in one item that reads: "Do you strongly approve, somewhat approve, somewhat disapprove or strongly disapprove of the job Bill Clinton is doing as president?" In Morin's study these different wordings affected the results. The half of the sample that received the first wording gave Clinton a 53 percent approval rating and a 38 percent disapproval. But the other half of the sample, responding to the second version of the question, gave Clinton a 62 percent approval rating (the two approval responses combined) and a 32 percent disapproval rating (the two disapproval responses combined). A *Time*/CNN poll in August 1994 asked Americans, "Who is more responsible for today's gridlock in government?" Unfortunately, there were only two choices offered to respondents — Clinton or Republicans in Congress. "Democrats in Congress" was not an option, yet this was certainly a logical possibility. The results showed 48 percent of the respondents blaming the Republicans, 32 percent blaming Clinton, and 12 percent volunteering that both were equally at fault. While Democrats in Congress might be tempted to trumpet these results, it is clear that they are partially an artifact of the choices provided to the respondents.

Krosnick and Berent (1993) have shown that the treatment of response alternatives to a question with respect to branching and labeling can be very consequential for such matters as the apparent stability of attitudes. Branching refers to follow-up questions asked after some initial query is presented to respondents. For example, political scientists typically measure party identification by a series of questions. The first question simply ascertains whether a person is a Democrat, a Republican, or an Independent. If respondents initially say Democrat or Republican, then they are next asked whether they are strong or not very strong Democrats or Republicans. If respondents first say that they are Independents, then they are asked whether they lean to the Democrats or the Republicans. Note that at each stage of the questioning, the response alternatives are labeled, that is, each response option is specified in words. An example of a non-labeled set of options can be found when respondents are asked to place themselves on a scale that ranges from one to seven where only the endpoints are labeled with words; this type of scale has often been used to measure citizens' policy attitudes and positions. Social scientists have shown that political party loyalties seem to be more stable than citizens' policy attitudes. But Krosnick and Berent argue that this finding may simply be the result of measuring party identification by a labeled branching technique and assessing policy attitudes by a non-labeled procedure.

A final aspect of question wording is using multiple questions to measure some topic and combining the responses to these questions into an index or scale. Often no single questionnaire item can adequately measure the multifaceted construct that a public opinion analyst is studying. Hence, the researcher may ask a series of questions and combine the results into an index. For example, *political efficacy* is a concept that has been of great interest to political scientists (Asher 1974a). It refers to a citizen's feelings of

Reprinted with special permission of King Features Syndicate, Inc.

effectiveness in dealing with government. Early measures (since modified) of political efficacy generally relied upon four statements:

1. I don't think public officials care much what people like me think.
2. Voting is the only way that people like me can have any say about how the government runs things.
3. Sometimes politics and government seem so complicated that a person like me can't really understand what's going on.
4. People like me don't have any say about what the government does.

These items are usually included in surveys in an agree/disagree format, with a disagree response representing the efficacious position on all four items. A researcher could construct an efficacy index by simply counting the number of items to which the respondent gave an efficacious answer. This number could range from zero to four; three or four efficacious responses might be classified as high in efficacy, two efficacious answers as medium, and one or zero as low.

The use of an index is justified on both substantive and methodological grounds (Asher 1974c). Substantively, the index does a better job of representing the complexity of the concept being studied than any single item could. Methodologically, the use of a multiple-item index can lessen the harmful effects of the random measurement error that is present in survey data. Whenever one measures opinions, the very process of measurement may yield results that are not perfectly accurate. If the measurement error is random, the obtained results are just as likely to be above or below the true value. Thus combining a number of items in an index will tend to cancel out some of the random measurement error. However, consumers of public opinion polls are often not provided sufficient information about the components of an index, including the actual wording of the questions. Moreover, consumers are not informed of the ways in which separate items relate to each other and how they are combined into an index; they often must accept on faith that the index has been constructed properly from individual items that themselves were appropriately worded. Chapter 8 presents some substantive examples of situations in which multiple items on a topic were available for analysis.

Question Order and Context

Question order can dramatically affect responses to survey items by altering the framework and context within which the question is answered. An excellent example of the effect of question order occurred in 1980 when the Harris organization employed a "double vote" question to measure citizens' candidate preferences in the presidential primaries. The Harris organization asked respondents at the beginning of the interview whether they intended to vote for President Jimmy Carter or Senator Edward M. Kennedy in the hotly contested Democratic nomination battle. Next followed questions about domestic and foreign policy, including items about inflation and the economy, American hostages in Iran, and the Soviet invasion of Afghanistan. Toward the end of the interview, the respondents were again asked how they intended to vote. Surprisingly, over the course of the interview, support for President Carter declined sharply. The only explanation for this drop was that as respondents thought about Carter's record, their views of him became more negative.

A similar phenomenon occurred in an ABC News/*Washington Post* study of the placement of a presidential popularity question in a survey (Sussman 1984a). In November 1983 a sample of Americans was asked about presidential popularity twice, once at the beginning of the interview and again at the end, with a variety of issue questions in between. Unlike the preceding example of Kennedy versus Carter, there was very little difference in the overall distribution of the responses at the two time points. Initially, 59 percent approved of the president's performance, 37 percent disapproved, and 4 percent had no opinion. Later, 59 percent approved, 39 percent disapproved, and 2 percent had no opinion. However, more than 15 percent of the sample changed their opinion about the president over the course of the twenty-minute interview, with 8 percent moving from approval to disapproval and 7 percent moving the opposite way. An experimental study by Sigelman (1981) yielded similar results. The distribution of responses to the presidential popularity item was barely affected by the placement of the question within the overall survey. However, Sigelman's study showed that the willingness of people to provide an evaluation of the president, whether positive or negative, was affected by the placement of the popularity item; asking the question at the beginning of the survey resulted in a smaller proportion of respondents offering an evaluation of presidential popularity, an effect particularly pronounced among persons with low levels of education.

In early 1984 the major national polls were yielding highly divergent results in a presidential trial heat between Ronald Reagan and Walter Mondale (Sussman 1984b). A CBS News/*New York Times* poll showed Reagan ahead of Mondale, 48 percent to 32 percent; two other polls showed the race to be much closer, Gallup calling it even and the ABC News/*Washington Post* poll showing Reagan ahead by three points. The discrepancy among the three polls was largely attributed to the placement of the trial heat questions. The latter two polls asked the vote intention question at the end of the interview, while the CBS News/*New York Times* survey asked it at the beginning. Experts argued that asking the question at the beginning benefited the president since he was so much better known than Mondale, while asking it after a battery of questions on troublesome issues lessened the president's advantage.

Many researchers have studied the effects of question order and context. Schuman and Presser (1981) demonstrated that effects of question order were prominent, particularly on general, somewhat amorphous questions that had little direct relevance to respondents. They warned that in examining the distribution of responses to identical questions asked at multiple points in time, one must take into account whether the context in which the questions were asked was also identical. The significance of this point was supported by the work of Bishop, Oldendick, and Tuchfarber (1982), who argued that the decline in Americans' level of political interest uncovered in a 1978 survey was partly attributable to changes in the context and order in which the question about political interest was asked; the real decline in political interest was not nearly as worrisome as originally thought.

A 1984 study by Bishop, Oldendick, and Tuchfarber found that respondents' reports of how much they follow government and politics depended on the context in which the question was asked. For example, if respondents were asked how much they follow government and public affairs after they were asked some difficult questions about their knowledge of their representative's record, they were likely to lower their estimate of their attentiveness to politics. But if respondents were first asked about their attentiveness to politics, they tended to assert a higher level of interest.

The works of Eubank and Gow (1983) and Gow and Eubank (1984) further illustrate the effects of question order and context. They examined the 1978, 1980, and 1982 American National Election Studies, which are national sample surveys of Americans that political scientists have used extensively to study the effects of incumbency on citizens' vote choices in U.S. House elections. Political scientists have found that incumbency is a very strong factor in voting, but Eubank and Gow argue that this finding is somewhat artificial because of the placement of questions in the American National Election Studies. They pointed out that before respondents were questioned about their vote for Congress, they were asked a series of questions about their incumbent U.S. representative. This sequence of questions made it more likely that respondents would claim to have voted for the incumbent when in fact they had not, a tendency especially pronounced among less knowledgeable citizens, who are generally more susceptible to the effects of question order.

The ability of one question to affect responses to another has been demonstrated by Hyman and Sheatsley (1950), Schuman and Presser (1981), and Schuman, Kalton, and Ludwig (1983). Their studies have examined responses to the following two items:

> Do you think the United States should let Communist newspaper reporters from other countries come in here and send back to their papers the news as they see it?

> Do you think a Communist country like Russia should let American newspaper reporters come in and send back to America the news as they see it?

When these two questions were asked in the order just given, support for letting communist reporters come to the United States was much lower than when the questions were asked in the reverse order. The explanation for this pattern seems clear: it was difficult for the respondent to deny communist reporters the opportunity to come to the United States if they had already said that American reporters should be allowed to go to the Soviet Union. This effect of context is strong when the questions are contiguous in a survey, but the effect remains strong even when the items are separated by many other questions.

Another example of context effects is provided by Schuman, Presser, and Ludwig (1981). They studied the consequences of different orderings of a general and a specific question on abortion. The items read:

> Do you think it should be possible for a pregnant woman to obtain a legal abortion if she is married and does not want any more children? [general]

> Do you think it should be possible for a pregnant woman to obtain a legal abortion if there is a strong chance of serious defect in the baby? [specific]

The authors found that responses to the general item were very much influenced by whether the item came first or second, while responses to the specific question were not affected by item order. More specifically, support for abortion in general was much higher when the general item came first. Their explanation for this finding, although speculative, suggests the kinds of cognitive calculations that may shape a response:

One plausible explanation for the effect turns on the fact that there are a number of different reasons for supporting legalized abortion. A possible defect in an unborn child is a specific reason that appeals to a large part of the population. When the more general item is asked first, some respondents may say yes but mainly with such a specific reason in mind. When the item on abortion because of a defective child is asked first, however, this indicates to respondents that the general item which follows does not refer to that specific case. Thus respondents who are reluctant to favor abortion except within narrow limits should find it easier to oppose the general rationale after having favored (and "subtracted") the more specific rationale about the defective child. (Schuman, Presser, and Ludwig 1981, 220)

In contrast to the example concerning communist reporters, in which a particular question order promoted consistency, here a particular ordering generated divergence, since some respondents favored abortion in the specific case but opposed it more generally.

A final example of the effects of question order comes from an analysis by Abramson and colleagues (1987). The authors were puzzled that between 1980 and 1984, the percentage of citizens disagreeing with the statement, "If a person doesn't care how an election comes out then that person shouldn't vote in it," dropped from 58.7 percent to 42.8 percent. This statement was one of four items that had traditionally been used to measure feelings of citizen duty. In surveys before 1984, this item had been preceded by two related statements with which Americans typically expressed high levels of disagreement. But in 1984, this item, while worded identically to earlier versions, was not preceded by the other two questions. Abramson and his colleagues provide convincing evidence that the apparent decline in citizens' feelings of duty between 1980 and 1984 was not real, but was instead a consequence of the different questions that preceded this item in the survey. The general lesson here is that before one concludes on the basis of survey data that attitude change has occurred over time, one must be able to rule out other explanations for change, such as differences in question wording and question order.

Although the ordering of specific survey items among other questions is considered context, "context" also refers to the substantive framework within which questions are placed. Pollsters can choose the framework within which they ask questions, and this choice can be very consequential. A survey about the U.S. military buildup posed in the context of the successful bombing of Iraq would probably elicit more supportive attitudes toward defense spending than would a similar survey framed in the context of the huge national debt. In their work on white Americans' attitudes toward affirmative action, Kinder and Sanders (1986) found clear differences in the factors that affect opinion depending upon whether the questions were presented in the context of reverse discrimination (affirmative action discriminates against whites) or in the context of undeserved advantage (affirmative action gives blacks advantages they haven't earned). For example, whites' opinions were more racially motivated when affirmative action was placed in the context of undeserved advantage.

Finally, context can refer to the broader environment in which an interview is occurring. Personal circumstances, recent societal events, and the content of media coverage can alter the meaning of a survey question for respondents. An identically worded question can mean dramatically different things to respondents depending upon the frame of reference they bring to the interview situation. And one part of that frame of reference will be the social and political context at the time of the interview.

Conclusion

Citizens are in a better position to evaluate the effects of question wording than they are to assess the consequences of question order for a number of reasons. First, much of what is involved in question wording is common sense; people can often recognize that a question is worded in a misleading and loaded fashion. More important, when public opinion results are reported, the media often provide the wording of the survey questions. This allows citizens to form their own judgments about the quality of the question wording. But the newspaper and television reports give consumers no information about the overall structure and content of the survey, although the major news organizations are very willing to mail the complete report of a poll to interested citizens who request it. Because information is limited, citizens normally do not have any basis to form independent judgments about whether their responses to a particular item have been affected by its placement within the questionnaire. Moreover, the effects of question order and context are likely to be subtle, thereby making it difficult for citizens to assess these effects even when the text of the complete survey instrument is provided.

Fortunately, polling organizations are becoming more sensitive to the consequences of question order, and survey research textbooks are at last addressing the problem in more detail. Today reputable pollsters give more attention to effects of context and are more likely to inform the consumers of their polls about the potential consequences of question order. Nevertheless, it remains quite easy for the unscrupulous pollster, intent upon generating a preferred response to a particular question, to mislead and manipulate the public by embedding that question in the survey in order to yield the desired answer.

4 Sampling Techniques

Among the many aspects of public opinion polling, sampling arouses the greatest skepticism among Americans. One source of this skepticism is the actual composition of the sample, as reflected in the plaintive question, "How come no one has asked me about my opinion on that issue?"

An experience I had in October 1984 exemplifies Americans' suspicion of polls. I was to speak about the 1984 presidential election before a group of about seventy labor union leaders. As he introduced me, the president of the Ohio AFL-CIO, who was obviously disturbed by national polls showing Democratic nominee Walter Mondale badly trailing President Ronald Reagan, conducted his own two-part poll. He first asked the audience how many were for Mondale and how many supported Reagan. Everyone was for Mondale. He next asked how many people in the audience had been interviewed by national pollsters concerning their presidential preference. None had. He then concluded by expressing disdain for the entire enterprise of polling. After that inauspicious introduction, he turned the platform over to me so that I might give my poll-based analysis of the 1984 campaign.

Sampling is the selection of a subset of respondents from a broader population. In a good sampling process this subset will be representative of the broader population. This chapter covers several aspects of sampling so that consumers of public opinion research can better understand how and why samples are selected. It includes a nontechnical review of various sampling designs followed by a brief discussion of some factors that affect sample size. It also discusses sampling error and confidence levels in relation to the interpretation of poll results. The chapter concludes with a discussion of *total* sample size versus *actual* sample size. Too often reports of poll results pay little attention to the actual number of cases on which a conclusion is based—a number that can be substantially smaller than the total sample size.

Sampling Designs

The aim of a good sampling design is to select a sample that is appropriate for the research topic and within the investigator's budget. Because it is impossible to interview an entire population — whether that of the United States, of New York, of all doctors, or of all senior citizens — a sample of that population is selected. The key requirement of the sample is that it must enable the researcher to generalize from the sample results to the broader population from which the sample was drawn. Typically, the sample is of interest because of what it reveals about the overall population and not because of the actual sample characteristics themselves. Hence, researchers need to be able to select samples that accurately reflect the broader population from which they are drawn. This can be done in a variety of ways, depending on the nature of the respondents, the objectives of the research, and the resources available to the investigator.

All of the designs to be discussed here are examples of *probability sampling*, the dominant and preferred mode of sampling public opinion. Probability samples have a number of advantages. Foremost is that they tend to be more representative than other kinds of samples because in large part they avoid the selection biases inherent in nonprobability samples in which the investigator has discretion over who should be included in the sample. That is, probability sampling entails procedures for selecting the sample that eliminate subjective biases about sample composition.

Another advantage of probability samples is that they allow researchers to use statistical theory to ascertain the properties of the survey sample. One such property is called the *sampling error* (discussed later in this chapter), which enables the investigator to estimate, with a certain level of confidence, how discrepant the sample results are from the true population values. The defining characteristic of a probability sample is that it permits the researcher to determine the probability of any single person being selected in the sample.

On the other hand, nonprobability sampling does not enable one to determine the sampling error. For example, the television reporter who stands at a street corner and interviews people passing by in order to assess public opinion on an issue has actually selected a nonprobability sample. The reporter has no way of telling how representative these interviewees are or how accurate the sample results are. Radio call-in surveys are also based on nonprobability samples since the callers may or may not be representative of the larger community. Likewise, the questionnaires mailed by U.S. congressional representatives to all the households in their districts exemplify a nonprobability sampling procedure. Thousands of questionnaires may be returned, but there is no assurance that they constitute an accurate sample of the district. In these examples, selection biases affect who is included in the sample.

Simple Random and Systematic Sampling

One method of probability sampling is simple random sampling. In simple random sampling, every element in the population has an equal chance of being selected in the sample. Moreover, every configuration of elements has the same chance of composing the sample. The chief requirement for simple random sampling is a list or an enumeration of the persons in the overall population. With such a list, the actual process of sampling is straightforward. The researcher assigns a unique number to each person, and then selects a sample of these numbers. A primitive way of selecting the sample would be to put all the numbers in a hat, mix them up, and then draw the sample. A more likely method today would be to use a table of random numbers or computer-generated random numbers to select the sample. Simple random sampling is appropriate when a reasonably complete and current listing of the population is available.

For a number of reasons, simple random sampling of individuals is not a feasible way to select a national sample of Americans. First, there is no complete and up-to-date list of all Americans (not even the census list). Then, even if there were a good list, random sampling would not be useful, particularly if a researcher were planning to interview respondents personally rather than on the telephone. That is, a randomly selected national sample would require sending interviewers all over the country, which would make the cost of the poll prohibitive. However, cluster sampling techniques (discussed later) have been developed to select samples from large geographical areas when personal interviewing is to be used.

Systematic sampling is a variant of random sampling. In systematic sampling, one picks every Nth name from the list after picking the first name at random. For example, to select a sample of 500 students from a student directory of 25,000 names (a 2 percent or one-fiftieth sample), one might first pick at random a number between one and fifty. Suppose that number were twelve. Then the sample would consist of the twelfth name in the directory, the sixty-second name, and every fiftieth name thereafter.

Systematic sampling is easily done; the only caution to be noted is that the listing of the names should have no cycle or periodicity to it lest the skip interval coincide with the periodicity. Normally, names listed in alphabetical order present no problems of periodicity, as opposed to, say, a list in which male and female names alternate. In the latter case, if the skip interval were an even number, the sample would be composed entirely of either males or females, thus introducing a bias to the study. A less obvious example of a periodicity problem might be a list of homes in a major housing development. In picking a sample of homes in order to interview the owners, one would want to ensure that there is no special pattern in the listing of homes. That is, if every tenth house on the list were on a corner lot, one might inadvertently select a sample that includes only corner homes. This could introduce a serious bias to the study since corner-lot houses tend to be larger and more expensive and thus owned by wealthier people than houses on the rest of the block. In systematic sampling, every element in the population has an equal chance of being in the sample, as is the case in random sampling. But unlike random sampling, every configuration of elements does *not* have the same chance of composing the sample.

Stratified Sampling

The key characteristic of stratified sampling is that the population is divided into subsets, or strata, according to some characteristics of interest to the investigator. After stratifying the population, researchers may sample randomly or systematically within the strata. For example, to interview a sample of members of the U.S. House of Representatives, one might first stratify the members according to political party affiliation (Democratic versus Republican) and seniority (for simplicity, high versus low), two characteristics of relevance to the research, rather than pick a random sample. This stratification creates four categories: high seniority Democrats, low seniority Democrats, high seniority Republicans, and low seniority Republicans. One would then sample within each of the strata.

To stratify the population requires knowledge of the characteristics of the individuals in the population. However, stratification guarantees that a sample will include a sufficient number of cases with characteristics of interest to the researcher, since the researcher can determine the size of the sample within each stratum. The major advantages of stratified sampling are a reduction in sampling error and a guarantee of representativeness with respect to the variables used in stratifying. The reduction in sampling error occurs if the strata differ from each other, but internally are relatively homogeneous. For example, if one wanted to compare the attitudes of northern and southern Democrats in Congress, it would be more efficient to set up these strata and sample within them than to pick a sample from among all Democrats.

Cluster and Multistage Sampling

Cluster sampling entails multiple interviews within the same geographical area, typically a neighborhood. The advantage of cluster sampling is economic. It is expensive to support an interviewer in the field and to send that interviewer to a particular site to conduct an interview. The overall cost of a field survey is lower if the interviewer conducts multiple interviews at one site.

Cluster sampling is often part of a multistage sampling scheme employed by organizations that wish to interview personally a national sample of Americans. The Survey Research Center (SRC) of the University of Michigan is one such organization; it utilizes multistage sampling in which geographical areas, not individuals, are sampled at all stages except the last. Typically, the SRC's sample design selects a sample of counties; then within the sample of counties a sample of cities, townships, and unincorporated areas; then from the sample of cities, townships, and unincorporated areas a sample of city blocks and land tracts; and then a sample of residential dwellings that are located on the sampled blocks and land tracts. For example, Cook County, Illinois, might be included in the sample of counties. Then the city of Chicago might be selected within Cook County. Then a number of blocks would be selected from within Chicago, and then some dwelling units would be chosen from the selected blocks.

Note that up to this stage in the example, geographical units and not individuals have been sampled. Sampling geographical units is relatively straightforward. It is easy to pick a sample of counties and a sample of localities within the counties, since lists of counties and municipalities are readily available. Likewise, it is fairly easy to pick samples of blocks and dwelling units since local governments keep such information for the purpose of tax assessment. At each step in the typical multistage design, the probability of a geographical unit being included in the sample is proportional to its population. Thus, Cook County and Los Angeles County are almost certain to be included in a sample of counties, while sparsely populated rural counties will have very little chance of being included. A sample concentrated in the major metropolitan areas of the country helps control the cost of supporting and transporting interviewing staff.

In cluster sampling, once interviewers arrive at selected dwelling units, they consult instructions provided to them to determine whom to interview; it is not left to the interviewers' discretion to decide whom to interview. These instructions are usually couched in terms of the age and gender composition of the dwelling unit; an interviewer might be instructed to survey the oldest male or the second oldest female in a household, for example. Note that this information about the characteristics of individuals within the household does not have to be known to researchers earlier in the sampling process; indeed, this kind of sampling scheme requires no prior knowledge about individuals — information that can be difficult to acquire — but only knowledge about geographical entities, which is easily obtained.

Sampling Techniques for Telephone Interviewing

The preceding sampling designs are the classic ones covered in most textbooks on survey research. However, the preceding designs do not include the dominant technique used by major polling organizations: conducting telephone interviews. Telephone surveys are the type most frequently used to measure public opinion for several reasons. The first reason is speed: often pollsters want to assess as quickly as possible the public's reaction to a major event, such as the Iraqi invasion of Kuwait in 1990 or the outbreak of war in 1991 when U.S. and allied troops were sent to oust Iraq from Kuwait. In such cases, personal interviews and mailed questionnaires take too much time. Another reason is that telephone interviews are substantially cheaper to conduct than personal interviews, yet they still enable the interviewer to collect detailed and pertinent information from respondents. Although respondents tend to become fatigued much more quickly in a telephone interview than in a personal interview, there usually is enough time to conduct a reasonably extensive interview. Third, in many instances a telephone interview has the virtue of being less threatening and intrusive to private citizens; they do not have to let a stranger into their home in order to participate in the interview.

At one time telephone-based samples were considered suspect because of the obvious class bias in the use of telephones; poor families were less likely to have phones. Today almost all Americans have home phones, which makes telephone samples more appropriate even though some class bias still exists. According to Lavrakas (1987, 14-15), most estimates indicate that at least 95 percent of households in the United States have telephones, although across the fifty states there are variations in telephone ownership. Those without telephones are more likely than telephone owners to be uneducated, poor, in a minority group, of low occupational status, and living in a single adult household.

In earlier years telephone directories served as the basis for picking samples. Although directories are still used today, particularly for local samples, a number of problems are associated with their use. One is that telephone directories are always out of date because of the high level of mobility of the U.S. population; the older the book, the worse the problem. Moreover, picking a national sample from telephone directories is a logistical nightmare — one would have to consult almost 5,000 of them. But the most serious problem with the use of telephone directories is the popularity of unlisted telephone numbers. It is estimated that in 1993, 30.4 percent of American households had unlisted phone numbers compared to only 21.8 percent in 1984 (Survey Sampling, Inc. 1994). In some metropolitan areas, particularly in California, the percentage of households with unlisted phone numbers exceeded 60 percent, topped by Sacramento at 64.7 percent.

Both Lavrakas (1987) and Piekarski (1989) refute the common assumption that upper-income white households are more likely to have unlisted telephone numbers. Instead, they find that unlisted households are more likely to be younger, unmarried, lower income, minority, less educated, and more mobile. Lavrakas cites a general rule that the proportion of households with unlisted phone numbers drops the farther one samples from the central city (1987, 33). He cites the Chicago area as an example, noting that within the city, about 50 percent of the households have unlisted numbers. In contrast, inner-ring suburbs have an unlisted-number rate of about 20 percent to 30 percent, outer-ring suburbs a rate of 10 percent to 20 percent, and rural areas a rate of about 5 percent.

One way around the problems inherent in the use of telephone directories is a technique called *random-digit dialing*, in which random numbers are generated to produce the telephone numbers to be called. With random-digit dialing, it is critical to know the area codes and exchanges (the first three digits in the seven-digit telephone number) in an area. Once this information has been collected, a computer random-number generator or a table of random numbers can be used to provide the last four digits of telephone numbers to be dialed. This procedure does result in unlisted numbers being reached, as evidenced by the surprised reactions of respondents who ask, "How did you get my number? It's unlisted!" When a residential household is reached through random-digit dialing, the interviewer does not automatically interview whoever answered the phone. Instead, interviewers typically first collect information about the number of adults in the household and the number of males and females. Then the interviewers must follow a set of instructions that tells them, for example, to interview the oldest male in the first household or the youngest female in the second household or the second oldest male in the third household. The combination of random-digit dialing and the instructions about respondent selection generates a sample highly representative of American households.

Sample Size

Sample size is a major puzzle for Americans who wonder how a national sample of 1,500 respondents can accurately represent the views of 190 million adult Americans. Contributing to the confusion is the fact that an equally accurate statewide survey might require a sample of 750 to 1,000 respondents, even though any state's population is only a small proportion of the national total. The few cases required for a good sample and the weak relationship between the size of the sample and the size of the population from which it is drawn make many citizens who are aware of these apparent anomalies skeptical of the validity of the entire polling enterprise.

Statistical and probability theory explain why such small sample sizes suffice to generate valid results, but these theories are not very enlightening to people who lack an extensive mathematical background. More helpful perhaps is an analogy: To perform a blood test a medical technician draws only a drop or two of blood from the patient. This very small sample of the total amount of blood in the patient's body is sufficient to produce accurate results because any particular drop has properties identical to those of the remaining blood. The technician does not need to choose the specific blood cells to be tested. Indeed, one would not want the technician to draw too large a sample of one's blood, lest the blood test be more harmful than the potential ailment being investigated.

Another analogy of sample size is a chef testing whether more spices need to be added to a large kettle of soup. The chef might sample the soup's flavor by tasting one spoonful, certainly a very small sample. Now, all spoonfuls of soup may not be comparable unless the chef first carefully stirs the mixture. But if the soup is stirred properly, a spoonful would be sufficient to determine whether more spices should be added.

Because the major cost in public opinion polling is interviewing the selected sample, it is critical that the researcher select a sample that suits both the purposes and the budget of the project. There is no particular virtue in large samples. If poorly selected, large samples provide no guarantees of accurate results. The classic example is the infamous *Literary Digest* poll of 1936, which confidently predicted a sweeping victory for Republican presidential candidate Alf Landon based on a sample of over 2 million; Franklin D. Roosevelt carried forty-six of the forty-eight states in the November election. The *Literary Digest* poll failed because of unrepresentativeness of the respondents who were selected from telephone directories and automobile registrations, a procedure that skewed the sample to the upper end of the socioeconomic continuum. This method of sample selection had worked well for the *Literary Digest* in previous elections, but it failed in the depression year of 1936. Squire (1988) argues that the sample was only one of the problems affecting the *Literary Digest* poll in 1936. The additional problems with low response rates and a nonresponse bias were such that those who did respond to the poll were more likely to be for Landon than for Roosevelt.

About Sampling Error

One determinant of sample size is the amount of sampling error that can be tolerated in a poll. *Sampling error* is simply the difference between the estimates obtained from the sample and the true population value—for example, the percentage of people in the sample who approve of Clinton's performance versus approval of Clinton in the overall population. Investigators often select national samples of sufficient size to generate a sampling error of about 4 percent; this means that if the sample indicates, for example, that 52 percent of the respondents approve of the president's performance, the actual value is likely to be in the range of 48 percent to 56 percent (52 plus or minus 4 percent). How likely it is that the actual value will fall within that range is measured by the *confidence level*. In this example a 95 percent confidence level would mean that in 95 out of 100 samples that might be selected, the sample would generate an estimate of approval within the range of 48 percent to 56 percent. One way to reduce a sampling error is to increase the sample size, but larger samples entail higher costs. A 4 percent sampling error is normally considered acceptable.

A number of caveats about sampling error should be kept in mind. First, in some instances a 4 percent error will be too large, given the predictions the investigator wants to make. For example, if the sample shows 51 percent of voters planning to vote Republican with a 4 percent sampling error, then the election outcome cannot be firmly predicted, since the Republican vote could be as low as 47 percent or as high as 55 percent. But if the poll indicates that 70 percent plan to vote Republican, then a sampling error of 4 percent or even higher will scarcely affect the conclusions.

Second, although the sampling error of the overall sample may be only 4 percent, the sampling error associated with estimates based on subsets of the sample can be substantially higher, particularly for small groups within the sample. In subgroup analysis the original sample is subdivided into a number of mutually exclusive subsets. For example, if one were interested in comparing the political attitudes of Protestants, Catholics, and Jews based on a national sample of about 1,500 respondents, one would subdivide the sample into these three religious groups. The sampling error associated with estimates for the Jewish subgroup would be much higher, since there would be only 40 to 60 Jewish respondents, given the percentage of Jews in the overall population. (The sample would contain 350-400 Catholics and about 1,000 Protestants.) If one wished to compare across religious *and* gender groups simultaneously, then the same sample would be divided into six categories: male Protestants, male Catholics, male Jews, female Protestants, female Catholics, and female Jews. The sampling error associated with these classifications would be even larger. In general, as the original sample is subdivided into increasingly smaller subsets, the sampling error becomes larger and larger.

A controversy about the level of support enjoyed by President Reagan among black Americans illustrates, among other things, the need to be sensitive to the large sampling error associated with small subsets of respondents. A CBS News/New York Times poll in December 1985 became a major news story (Clymer 1986a) when it "showed" that 56 percent of black respondents approved of President Reagan's performance and only 24 percent disapproved, a level of support dramatically higher than the president had ever had. Yet an ABC News/Washington Post poll in January 1986 found that only 23 percent of blacks approved of the job the president was doing, and 63 percent disapproved. Which poll was more accurate? The Reagan administration preferred the positive poll, while critics of the administration believed the negative results.

In retrospect, it seems clear that the positive results in the December 1985 CBS News/New York Times poll were misleading and incorrect. The poll interviewed a national sample of 1,358 Americans, of whom 150 were black. Thus, the sampling error for the estimates about blacks was high (9 percent). In contrast, the ABC News/Washington Post survey was based on a specially designed national sample of 1,022 black Americans. With a sampling error of 3.5 percent, it was much more reliable than the CBS News/New York Times poll. Other polls conducted at about the same time confirmed the ABC News/Washington Post results; a Gallup survey showed Reagan with a 23 percent approval rating among blacks, while a Los Angeles Times poll showed 37 percent support.

The next CBS News/New York Times poll took place in January 1986. This one was in line with other polls, showing the president with 37 percent support among blacks and thereby contradicting the December 1985 CBS News/New York Times survey. Adam Clymer, director of polling operations at the New York Times, attributed the discrepancy between the two polls to a bad sample and sampling error:

> It now appears that our December poll had a very unrepresentative black sample, especially of black men, and the findings plainly exceeded normal sampling error. This month's sample appears, on matters from education to household size, much more representative of the black population as a whole. (Apple 1986, A-14)

Although at that time the controversy about black support for the president was resolved, Sussman (1986a) noted that a puzzle still remained, namely that the January 1986 CBS News/New York Times poll showed the president to have 37 percent approval, a rate considerably higher than the 23 percent reported in the same month by the ABC News/Washington Post poll. He cited three possible reasons for the difference. The first was sampling error: the ABC News/Washington Post poll had an error of 3.5 percent as mentioned earlier, whereas the CBS News/New York Times poll had an error of 7 percent since there were 189 black respondents in the total sample of

1,581. Another source of divergence was the race of the interviewers. The CBS News/*New York Times* poll employed white and black interviewers, while the ABC News/*Washington Post* poll used black interviewers only, some of whom may have "sounded black" over the telephone. This may have led black respondents to the ABC News/*Washington Post* poll to be more negative toward the president because that seemed to be the "appropriate" black response. Finally, Sussman noted that the ABC News/*Washington Post* poll began with an explicit statement that it was a survey of blacks. This may have led the respondents to take more of a black perspective and therefore to be more critical of the president.

Informing the Consumer About Sampling

Different survey organizations provide their audiences with different amounts of information about their sample surveys. Most tell the date of the interviews, the method of data collection, the size of the actual sample, and the sampling error of the overall sample. For example, on April 7, 1986, *Newsweek* provided the following information to its readers concerning a poll, which it had commissioned the Gallup Organization to conduct, on American reactions to the bombing of Libya: "The Gallup Organization interviewed a representative national sample of 606 adults by telephone March 26 and March 27. The margin of error is plus or minus five percentage points. Some 'Don't know' responses were omitted."

News releases from the media vary in the amount of information they provide. For example, the releases on CBS News/*New York Times* polls (in contrast to *New York Times* articles) typically include a simple and not very informative statement like this one: "The poll was conducted among a nationwide random sample of 1,084 adults interviewed by telephone June 5-8, 1990. The error due to sampling could be plus or minus three percentage points for results based on the entire sample."

The Newark, New Jersey, *Star-Ledger*/Eagleton Institute at Rutgers University poll provides more information, including a definition of sampling error. Its background memo released March 10, 1991, warned that "sampling error does not take into account the possible sources of error inherent in any study of public opinion." The memo did not specify, however, the sources of these other nonsampling errors. ABC News provides much more information about its methodology and is more explicit about the sources of error than is CBS News. For example, in its February-March 1986 release, in addition to the standard information, ABC News explained how the telephone sample was selected; informed readers that the survey responses were "weighted by age, sex, education and race using the latest U.S. Census figures"; warned that in addition to sampling error "inaccuracy may occur from the wording of certain questions or the order in which they are asked"; and presented "full results of poll questions in the order they were asked." With respect to poll information provided in newspaper articles, the *New York Times* and the *Washington Post* maintain an enviable standard of reporting (see the conclusion of chapter 6).

Obviously, the more information that is provided about the methodology of a poll, the better consumers can judge the soundness of the poll results. For example, consider two polls conducted in Chicago in the same week in 1986. The polls obtained sharply dissimilar results concerning mayoral election trial heats between incumbent mayor Harold Washington and former mayor Jane Byrne. An ABC News/Station WLS survey showed Washington ahead of Byrne by a 23 point margin (58 percent to her 35 percent), while a Northwestern University poll had Byrne ahead of Washington, 43 percent to 34 percent.

Paul Lavrakas analyzed the differences between the two polls and pointed out three factors that might have affected the results. The first concerned callbacks, that is, efforts made to interview respondents who initially could not be reached for some reason. Because the Northwestern University survey was conducted over three evenings, in contrast to two for the ABC News poll, and thus had more time for callbacks, the Northwestern survey may have done a better job of tracking down hard-to-reach respondents. A second difference was that the Northwestern survey weighted its results to reflect the demographics of Chicago's adult population. The ABC News poll did not weight its data and, according to Lavrakas, overrepresented blacks in its sample because it sought to have the distribution of blacks and whites in the sample reflect the 1980 census estimates of Chicago's *overall* racial composition as opposed to its *adult* racial composition. Finally, the trial heat question used by ABC News followed a question that asked respondents to choose among three candidates — Byrne, Washington, and Richard Daley, son of another former mayor. Because of hostility between supporters of Byrne and Daley, this question may have affected the responses to the Byrne-Washington query so that Daley supporters opted disproportionately for Washington. Although Lavrakas refused to conclude that the Northwestern University poll results were likely to be more sound, his analysis does indicate how information about poll methodology can help consumers of public opinion polls sort out conflicting claims and results (Lavrakas 1986).

Total vs. Actual Sample Size

When a sample of citizens is interviewed, not every question has a response from every respondent. Some respondents may refuse to answer, others may give answers that are screened out because they reflect nonattitudes, and still others may have no opinion on the matter. In some instances there may be a substantial difference between the total sample size and the actual number of people responding to or being included in the reporting of the results of a particular question.

Consider the following hypothetical situation in which 1,500 Americans are asked about their vote preferences one month before an election. Perhaps only 80 percent of the sample are registered to vote, and only 60 percent of those registered will actually vote on election day. If the investigator wants to report the vote preferences of likely voters only and is able to identify that group (a difficult task), then the effective sample has shrunk from 1,500 to 720 (0.80 x 0.60 x 1,500) with an attendant increase in sampling error. Of these 720, 3 percent might refuse to reveal their preference, and another 22 percent might be unsure, thereby reducing the 720 to 540 likely voters with definite vote preferences, or just 36 percent of the original sample of 1,500. This is the actual sample, out of the total sample. Of the 540 likely voters, 300 may intend to vote Democratic and 240 Republican, a 56 percent to 44 percent split. It would be important for the pollster to report this split and describe the subset of the sample from which it is calculated.

A real-life example of the importance of reporting actual sample size is provided by a July 1985 ABC News/*Washington Post* poll on President Reagan's Strategic Defense Initiative ("Star Wars") (Lardner 1985). The three questions and responses were:

Q. Have you read or heard about plans by the Reagan administration to develop weapons in outer space that could destroy nuclear missiles fired at the United States by the Soviet Union or other countries? Reagan calls the research on these weapons SDI, for Strategic Defense Initiative, and some people refer to it as "Star Wars."

Yes, have read or heard	84%
No, have not read or heard	16%
Don't know or no opinion	1%

Q. Supporters say such weapons could guarantee protection of the United States from nuclear attack and are worth whatever they cost. Opponents say such weapons will not work, will increase the arms race, and the research will cost many billions of dollars. How about you: would you say you approve or disapprove of plans to develop such space-based weapons?

Approve	41%
Disapprove	53%
Don't know or no opinion	5%

Q. (For those who approved) Currently the United States and the Soviet Union have an anti-ballistic missile treaty that prohibits both nations from developing certain weapons. Suppose the U.S. had to violate or abandon that treaty in order to develop the space-based weapons. Would you still favor development of those space-based weapons or not?

Yes, would still favor	63%
No, would not still favor	32%
Don't know or no opinion	5%

Fortunately, Lardner was very careful in his reporting of the responses to the last question, for without the appropriate qualifications, one might interpret the result as showing strong support for development of the weapons even if the United States had to scrap the treaty. Note that the 63 percent favoring SDI represents only 26 percent (0.41 x 0.63) of the original sample of 1,506 and only 22 percent (0.41 x 0.63 x 0.84) of those respondents who had read or heard about the plans initially. It would obviously be misleading and unscrupulous to release only the results of the last item without the necessary qualifiers. Unfortunately, advocates of causes have at times been highly selective in their use of poll information with the conscious aim of swaying the public to their position.

One increasingly frequent problem for pollsters is *nonresponses;* people who have been selected for the sample either refuse to participate in the interview or else cannot be contacted (Stinchcombe, Jones, and Sheatsley 1981; Steeh 1981). With respect to the treatment of nonresponses, poll consumers are very much at the mercy of polling organizations. One approach by pollsters is to weight the sample according to known population characteristics obtained from census data. This procedure assumes a similar distribution of answers among respondents and nonrespondents with similar demographic characteristics, an assumption that is sometimes faulty.

Nonresponse rates are becoming more worrisome today, as the percentage of Americans unavailable or unwilling to participate in public opinion polls rises. Reputable survey organizations take extraordinary steps to increase the response rate by requiring multiple callbacks, careful training of interviewers, and flexibility in the scheduling of interviews. But ultimately some Americans simply refuse to participate in surveys. And as the percentage of refusals increases, it will be necessary to conduct additional research to try to determine whether survey respondents are indeed representative of nonrespondents.

The problem of refusal is less serious for major polling organizations conducting national public opinion polls than it is for market research polls asking Americans about their buying habits and product preferences. But the response rates to both public opinion and market research surveys have likely suffered because of increasing resentment on the part of Americans toward telephone solicitations (telemarketing), which more and more frequently intrude upon citizens' private lives, using computer-based telephone dialing as the agent of annoyance.

Changes in telephone technology may affect responses in other ways. The rapid growth in telephone answering machine ownership by Americans has led pollsters to wonder whether ownership of the machines would have a harmful impact on response rates since one reason to have an answering machine is to screen incoming calls. But various pieces of research (Oldendick and Link 1994; Xu, Bates, and Schweitzer 1993; Piazza 1993; Tuckel and Feinberg 1991) suggest that thus far answering machines do not have a negative impact on the response rate and the representativeness of telephone samples. Indeed, households with answering machines may ultimately be more likely to participate in a poll, but it takes more callbacks to complete an interview. Because about two-fifths of American households have answering machines, a proportion that continues to grow, careful attention will need to be given to the potential effects of answering machines.

Conclusion

For many Americans, sampling is the most problematic feature of public opinion polling. Many citizens doubt whether the "small" samples reported in the media can adequately represent the population of whatever entity is being studied. They may question the wording of a poll, but it is difficult for them to offer informed criticism of sampling procedures unless the polling organization provides sufficient information about such matters as the size of the sample, sampling error and confidence levels, the dates of the interviews, and the method of interviewing. Even though sampling is considered to be a statistical and scientific procedure, sampling problems can arise that may undermine the results and interpretations of public opinion polls. Normally, however, citizens must trust the polling organization to select a good sample.

 # 5 Interviewing Procedures

Unless one has participated in a public opinion survey, it is difficult to appreciate the critical role that the interviewer plays in measuring public opinion. In general, polling organizations provide the general public with little or no information about the interviewing process. Consequently, one cannot make an independent judgment about the quality of the interviews and must assume that they have been conducted competently. This is undoubtedly a safe assumption about the major, prestigious, and highly visible polls.

Nevertheless, as someone who has agreed to be a respondent in public opinion, market research, and academic research surveys, I have been surprised by the obvious disparities in the training and competence of the interviewers. Often, when I am a respondent, I will ask the interviewer what a certain question means or complain about the range of alternatives available to me. Some interviewers are well trained to handle such reactions, but others are not. One interviewer agreed with my frustration about a particular item and informed me that there had been many complaints about the survey. Another interviewer, when I strenuously objected to the alternatives, pleaded with me to pick one of the given choices since he did not know how to handle volunteered responses. In yet another situation the interviewer told me that she would place my aberrant response in the category in which she thought it would best fit.

The purpose of this chapter is to alert the consumer of polls to the potential effects of the interviewing process on poll results. The first section explains the methods used to collect data and discusses the advantages and disadvantages of three approaches: mailed questionnaires, telephone interviews, and personal interviews. The second section examines the interview situation itself and factors such as sex, socioeconomic status, race, and ethnicity of the interviewer, that can affect responses.

Methods of Collecting Polling Information

Mailed Questionnaires

Mailed questionnaires are a common method of assessing opinions, one that is frequently used by organizations with access to good mailing lists. As discussed in chapter 1, interest groups often use mailed surveys in conjunction with their fund-raising efforts. Mailed questionnaires have a number of advantages, but the main one is their low cost. Because mailed surveys are self-administered by the respondent, they require no interviewers to train and support, and thus dramatically reduce costs. Moreover, interviewer bias does not affect results. The privacy in which a mailed survey can be completed may reassure respondents about the anonymity and confidentiality of their responses and may encourage them to respond more frankly, particularly on sensitive topics. For example, a study by Aquilino (1994) showed that self-administered questionnaires used in the context of a personal interview generated a higher level of admitted illicit drug and alcohol use than a telephone or personal interview without a self-administered questionnaire did.

These advantages of mailed questionnaires are typically outweighed by their limitations. Foremost among these is the fact that response rates tend to be lower for mailed surveys than for telephone and personal interviews. However, this disadvantage may be lessening, in part because of the higher refusal rates in personal and telephone interviews (see chapter 4) and because of improved techniques for generating satisfactory response rates to mailed questionnaires (Goyder 1985).

Researchers continue to investigate ways to improve response rates for mail surveys. A study by Fox and colleagues (1988) found that university sponsorship (as opposed to private business sponsorship) of a mail survey increased the response rate. Other important factors in improving response rates included notifying respondents about the survey beforehand by letter, sending the survey by first-class postage, using postcard follow-up, and providing stamped return postage. Another significant factor was the color of the paper on which the questionnaire was printed. The work of James and Bolstein (1990) demonstrated that providing respondents with a monetary incentive to return the survey, along with follow-up mailings urging them to complete the questionnaire, increased response rates. Similar results are found in the works of Yammarino, Skinner, and Childers (1991) and Church (1993), which review a large number of studies of the factors that affect response rates.

Low response rates are not the only limitation of mailed surveys. A related problem is the difficulty of ascertaining the extent to which respondents are representative of the actual population, a particularly acute problem when the response rate is low. If the respondents are representative of the broader population even when the response rates are low, then there is less need to incur the costs required to increase the response rate. A study by Bernick and Pratto (1994) addressed the two issues of response rates and the representativeness of respondents with a four-step process to survey registered voters' attitudes toward local government. They first sent the sample a letter along with the questionnaire and a postage-return envelope. One week later they sent a postcard. Two weeks later they sent another mailing similar to the first mailing. Finally, three weeks later, using certified postage, they sent a special mailing to those people in the sample who had not yet replied. This last mailing did stimulate responses, particularly among less educated respondents. Moreover, early and late responders did differ somewhat in their attitudes, leading the authors to conclude that in this case it was worthwhile to expend the extra resources to enhance response rates. That is, simply weighting or adjusting the respondents obtained from the first three mailings according to the known population distribution of educational levels would not have fully resolved the problem of the response bias in the sample.

Another limitation of mailed surveys is that much information cannot be collected in self-administered surveys. For example, one cannot be sure who actually completes a questionnaire—a serious limitation when surveying elite populations, such as members of Congress or state legislators who, because they are bombarded with mailed questionnaires, may have a staff person fill out the survey form. Also not available is information about respondents' reactions to a survey and about the environment in which a survey is completed. Because no interviewer is present to assist respondents who have difficulty with a questionnaire, instructions must be explicit and questions must be as unambiguous as possible. There is no opportunity for clarification.

Mailed questionnaires must not be too burdensome for respondents or the response rate will plummet. Whenever I receive a questionnaire in the mail, I first check the number of open-ended questions that would require me to write mini-essays. If there are many, I'm likely to toss the questionnaire into the circular file unless it addresses a topic of particular interest to me. Mailed questionnaires encourage response when they are largely limited to highly structured, fixed alternative questions. However, even the structured items are often annoying to citizens, particularly to political elites who complain that the political world is too complicated and their own opinions too complex to be captured in a fixed alternative item.

The burdens imposed by a mailed questionnaire are not uniform across the population. Poorly educated respondents will have more difficulty with a mailed survey, and illiterate persons may simply have to ignore it. In addition, there is no way of knowing the order in which any particular respondent answered the questions. Certainly, some people will read the entire survey before responding, while others will start at the beginning and proceed sequentially. This means that the questionnaire may elicit different responses from individuals depending on the order in which they approached the questions. Finally, mailed questionnaires are inappropriate if an investigator needs a quick response to a topic such as a presidential debate or foreign policy crisis. Experienced researchers allow several weeks for questionnaires to be returned.

Telephone Interviews

Unlike mailed questionnaires, telephone interviews can complete a survey quickly (often in only two to four days and sometimes in a single evening), thereby providing an almost instantaneous reaction to a political event. Another advantage is that by using random-digit dialing techniques (see chapter 4), researchers can easily pick a representative sample. Although more expensive than mailed questionnaires, telephone interviews are less costly than personal interviews, and they generate a good response rate, although typically not as high as that for personal interviews. In some situations telephone interviewing may succeed where other methods can fail, perhaps because of the sensitivity of a topic or because respondents will not allow a stranger in their home to conduct a personal interview.

Telephone interviews also have shortcomings. Despite widespread possession of telephones, telephone interviews are still somewhat biased against respondents of low socioeconomic status who cannot afford phones. Also, respondents become fatigued more quickly in a telephone interview than in a personal interview, which limits the scope of a telephone survey (although recent experiences indicate that telephone surveys can be lengthier than was originally thought). Training interviewers in order to avoid unwanted effects from the interviewing process adds to the cost of the project. Finally, use of the telephone eliminates the possibility of using visual aids during the interview unless materials are sent to respondents in a preliminary mailing.

In the past decade a number of developments have made telephone interviews faster, more efficient, and more accurate. The foremost of these is *computer-assisted telephone interviewing* (CATI). With CATI, the interviewing is done at video display terminals by interviewers who feed the responses directly into a computer and thereby eliminate a separate keypunching step. The overall flow and logic of the interview are controlled by a computer program. Among other things, the program ensures that questions are asked in the correct sequence and that responses are consistent with the question(s) being asked (Frey 1983, 144-145). Running totals are easily generated with CATI, so that survey results are available almost instantaneously. As CATI systems become more sophisticated, investigators who use them can save money, particularly as the sample size grows larger.

Personal Interviews

Personal interviews generally provide the richest and most complete information in public opinion polling. Respondents are willing to participate in lengthy personal interviews, particularly if the interviewer is skillful in developing rapport with them. The response rate tends to be high, and representative samples can readily be selected and interviewed. The presence of the interviewer allows for an assessment of respondents' problems with and reactions to the survey. The interviewer can directly record not only the verbal responses of the interviewee but also nonverbal behavior such as fidgeting, nervousness, and other signs of unease or lack of interest in the interview situation. Moreover, the opportunity to ask follow-up questions (and to know when to probe) is greater in a personal interview than in a telephone survey.

The obvious drawbacks of personal interviews are their cost and the danger of introducing substantial interviewer effects and biases. Costs are high because of the need to train interviewers and to support them in the field, often with housing, meals, and transportation allowances as well as their regular salary. Because the interview is a social situation, poorly trained interviewers may alter the interpersonal dynamics of the interview and thereby influence respondents' answers in undesirable and often unpredictable ways. Such interviewer effects and biases are the topic of the next section.

Interviewer Effects in Public Opinion Polling

Interviewer effects can occur in both telephone and personal interviews, although they are likely to be more pronounced in personal interviews because of the face-to-face interaction between the interviewer and the respondent. For most respondents, the personal interview is a new experience with all the attendant uncertainties and ambiguities of unfamiliar activity. Unsure of how to behave, respondents may look to the interview situation for appropriate cues. The two most important sources of cues are the survey instrument itself and the person who administers the questionnaire, the interviewer. The cues provided by the survey instrument are

© 1994, Raleigh News & Observer.

direct (even if the questions are flawed), but the cues provided by the interviewer can be far more subtle. Moreover, if interviewers are inconsistent in the cues they give to different respondents, the reliability of the survey results may be undermined. At minimum, interviewers must not change the question wording, question order, or voice intonations from respondent to respondent. And because most polls use more than one interviewer, the interviewing process must be standardized as well as possible, which requires careful training of interviewers.

This emphasis on consistency and uniformity in the interviewing process reflects a concern with the *reliability* of the measuring instrument (the questionnaire). One type of reliability measure is based on equivalence, the extent to which different investigators applying the same measurement instrument to the same individuals obtain consistent results. Ideally the identity of the interviewer should not affect the responses that the questionnaire generates in the interview.

The reliability of an instrument can be distinguished from its *validity*, the extent to which the instrument measures what it is supposed to measure. For example, consider one of the political efficacy items discussed in chapter 3: "Voting is the only way that people like me can have any say about how the government runs things." A "disagree" response to this item is considered an efficacious reply; it presumably means that the respondent believes that he or she can be influential in ways other than voting. But what if someone rejects this statement out of a belief that there is no way that people can have influence? In this case, then a "disagree" response signals a lack of efficacy, and the item itself is not a valid indicator of the underlying concept of political efficacy. Because of the problem with validity, this item has been eliminated from the American National Election Studies.

An interviewer's general demeanor, competence, and performance have much to do with the success of the interview. Clearly, interviewers must be able to establish rapport with respondents, making them feel at ease and receptive to the survey. If rapport is not established, respondents may refuse to cooperate or fail to provide complete and accurate information to interviewers. Ideally, interviewers are well informed about the purposes of the research and the intention of specific questions so that they know whether a respondent has fully answered a question and how to ask follow-up questions for clarification.

Interviewers should not inject themselves into the interviewing process by making editorial comments about respondents' replies. Although they should follow instructions carefully and ask all appropriate questions, they should also be able to handle unexpected events such as a respondent's volunteering additional information. Interviewers must also record and transcribe responses as accurately as possible, even when the answers do not fall neatly into one of the predetermined response categories.

The difficulty of an interviewer's job depends on the nature of the questionnaire as well as on the characteristics of the respondents. For example, highly structured survey items require less guidance and judgment from an interviewer, while relatively unstructured instruments require more. For interviews of political elites that use open-ended questions, an interviewer must not only be a good listener and prober who takes few or no notes during an interview; he or she must be able to write up the results of the interview after the question-and-answer session has ended. Sometimes such interviews are taped, which eliminates the need to take extensive notes, but taped interviews must be transcribed to be usable.

In addition to demeanor and skills, the personal characteristics of an interviewer can affect responses to a poll. For example, many interviewers are middle-aged women because this group is least threatening to male and female respondents, particularly in a personal interview in a home. Also, female interviewers often are able to establish rapport more successfully than men.

Morin (1990) cites research that shows that men and women answer poll questions differently depending on the gender of the interviewer. In a poll on abortion conducted by the Eagleton Institute, women were much more likely to give pro-choice responses to female interviewers than to males, while the response pattern for men was weaker. For example, when given the statement, "The decision to have an abortion is a private matter that should be left to the woman to decide without government intervention," 84 percent of the female respondents interviewed by women agreed, compared to only 64 percent of those women who were interviewed by men. Seventy-seven percent of the male respondents interviewed by women agreed with the statement, compared with 70 percent of those who were interviewed by men.

A growing body of research indicates that women are more likely to give traditional, nonfeminist responses to male interviewers and more feminist responses to female interviewers. Likewise, men are somewhat more likely to give feminist responses to female interviewers than to males. Kane and Macaulay (1993) found that both men and women were more likely to express more egalitarian gender-related attitudes and more criticism of gender-related inequalities to female interviewers than to male interviewers. Huddy and Bracciodieta (1992) obtained similar results in their research except that they also found gender-of-interviewer effects on topics such as party identification and authoritarian attitudes which are not directly related to gender. For example, both men and women gave more feminist, Democratic, and anti-authoritarian responses when interviewed by a female than a male. Therefore, on gender-related survey topics such as abortion and perhaps even on gender-neutral topics, researchers must be sensitive to the potential for interviewer-gender effects.

Like personal characteristics, the social distance between interviewers and respondents can influence an interview. If an interviewer is of obviously higher social status than a respondent, the respondent may tend to defer or acquiesce to the interviewer by providing answers intended to win approval. Even an interviewer's manner of speech can affect a respondent's replies, since a person's speech may reflect his or her geographical origin, social class, age group, or level of education.

An interviewer's race and ethnicity are additional factors that can affect responses to a poll (Campbell 1981; Cotter, Cohen, and Coulter 1982; Hatchett and Schuman 1975-1976; Schuman and Converse 1971; Weeks and Moore 1981). When black respondents are queried about the American political system, they are more likely to give supportive, positive answers to white interviewers than to black interviewers. Likewise, white respondents are less likely to reveal attitudes of racial hostility when interviewed by blacks than when interviewed by whites. A January 1987 *New York Times*/WCBS-TV News poll of New Yorkers' reactions to a racially motivated attack on some young black men in the Howard Beach section of New York City found that the race of the interviewer had a substantial effect on responses, even in telephone interviews, since, as pointed out earlier, interviewers may "sound" black or white. An earlier study by the same organizations had shown that telephone respondents can correctly identify the race of the interviewer about three-fourths of the time. In the Howard Beach poll, which asked whether the lawyer for one of the black victims had acted responsibly, nearly half the black respondents interviewed by whites thought he had not, and only about one-fourth thought the lawyer had acted responsibly. But among blacks interviewed by fellow blacks, the results were reversed (Meislin 1987).

Similar patterns of race-of-interviewer effects occurred in a 1989 ABC News/*Washington Post* poll (Morin 1989c). On a number of race-related questions, white responses shifted about 5 percent to 10 percent depending on the race of the interviewer. For some questions the effect was greater. For example, 62 percent of whites interviewed by whites said that most of the problems now faced by blacks were "brought on by blacks themselves"; only 46 percent of white respondents interviewed by blacks gave that same response. A study by Anderson and colleagues (1988b) found that "blacks interviewed by whites were much more likely to express warmth and closeness toward whites than were blacks interviewed by blacks" (p. 289). Finally, a study (Finkel, Guterbock, and Borg 1991) of race-of-interviewer effects in a preelection poll in the 1989 Virginia gubernatorial contest between black Democrat Douglas Wilder and white Republican Marshall Coleman showed that white respondents interviewed by black interviewers were more likely to state a preference for Wilder (52.2 percent) than those queried by white interviewers (43.8 percent). This pattern was particularly pronounced among white Democrats and among whites who were less sure of their vote intention.

A study by Reese and colleagues (1986) on the effects of interviewer ethnicity — white versus Hispanic — found that ethnicity did affect the responses to certain questions, especially items that related to the culture of the interviewer. That is, when Anglos were asked questions by Hispanics about aspects of Mexican-American life, they responded more sympathetically than when they were asked the same questions by fellow Anglos. Why? The general explanation is that respondents try not to give answers that might offend an interviewer, particularly on matters that relate to the interviewer's race and ethnicity.

Anderson and colleagues (1988a) showed that the interviewer's race can affect behavior as well as attitudes and responses. They examined the 1964, 1976, 1980, and 1984 National Election Studies of the Survey Research Center. These involved pre- and postelection interviews with respondents as well as officially validated measures of whether respondents had actually voted. The investigators found that of black respondents living in northern central cities, 63.3 percent of the respondents interviewed by blacks actually voted, while only 51.7 percent of the respondents interviewed by whites actually voted. For the South, the comparable percentages were 58.1 and 45.2, respectively. The authors concluded that the preelection interviews conducted by black interviewers in the central cities of the North and South induced actual voting. No such race-of-interviewer effects could be isolated for white respondents, since they were almost all surveyed by white interviewers.

Conclusion

The method of interviewing and the actual conduct of the interview measurably affect the responses to a public opinion poll. In most instances consumers of polls are in a weak position to evaluate these effects, mainly because pollsters provide little information about interviewing procedures. Nevertheless, consumers might raise a number of questions about the interviewing process, particularly if they have been selected to be respondents in a poll. For example, consumers who refuse to complete a mailed questionnaire might ask themselves why. Is it because of the subject matter, because the questions are too simplistic, or because the questionnaire is too time consuming? Consumers who choose to participate in the survey might examine their reactions to question wording and question order, to the overall experience itself, or to other specific elements of the questionnaire.

One question that poll consumers will never be able to answer is whether the same results would have been obtained had a different interviewing method been used. Some research suggests that the choice of interviewing method can affect the responses because of the different interpersonal dynamics that characterize different interviewing modes. For example, in two studies on substance use, personal interviews showed higher levels of alcohol and drug use by respondents than telephone interviews did (Aquilino and Losciuto 1990; Johnson 1989).

Respondents to personal or telephone polls also should make some mental notes about the skill of the interviewers. How effective was the interviewer in establishing a good climate for the interview? How well did the interviewer handle the respondent's questions and problems? Did the interviewer do or say anything that seemed to lead the person to respond in certain ways? Did the interviewer have any characteristics or traits that either facilitated or hindered the interview? The answers to these and other questions should alert poll respondents to biases that can influence the interviewing process and the answers it generates.

6 The Media and the Polls

The media's role in public opinion polling is essentially twofold: to inform the public of poll results and to sponsor polls. The print and electronic media, especially newspapers and television, are the major sources of what Americans learn about polls because most citizens do not have direct access to reports prepared by polling organizations. And because media are the sources citizens rely on, they need to recognize that many organizations that sponsor surveys try to manipulate the media to cover poll results in ways that promote their objectives. Likewise, candidates often attempt to get advantageous media coverage of private campaign polls by selectively leaking results.

Some of the most publicized and widely disseminated public opinion polls are directly sponsored by the national television networks and their local affiliates, the major news magazines, and newspapers throughout the country. Thus, the media generate public opinion data, which in turn become the subject matter for news stories presented by these same media. For some observers, this situation raises questions about a conflict of interest. That is, the definition of what is newsworthy may be unduly influenced by media-sponsored polls on particular topics. In addition, the fact that the media make substantial investments in developing their capability for public opinion polling may result in a tendency to use that capability even when it is not appropriate to the topic at hand.

Because of the media's pivotal role in developing citizens' awareness of polling, this chapter evaluates the media's reporting of public opinion polls, both those sponsored by the media and those sponsored by other organizations. The discussion focuses on two distinct aspects of poll coverage: the treatment of the polls' technical features (for example, sampling error and question wording); and the presentation of substantive results and interpretations based upon the poll data. The chapter concludes by considering the numerous problems inherent in media-sponsored polls.

Standards for Reporting Results

As mentioned above, media reporting of polls may not always be reliable. For that reason, various organizations have adopted standards to govern the disclosure of poll results to citizens. For example, the National Council on Public Polls (NCPP), an entity composed of polling organizations, has adopted the following Principles of Disclosure (Frey 1983, 189-190):

> All reports of survey findings of member organizations, prepared specifically for public release, will include reference to the following:
>
> —sponsorship of the survey;
> —dates of interviewing;
> —method of obtaining the interview;
> —population that was sampled;
> —size of the sample;
> —size and description of the subsample, if the survey report relies primarily on less than the total sample;
> —complete wording of questions upon which the release is based;
> —the percentages upon which conclusions are based.

The recommendations go on to state:

> When survey results are released to any medium by a survey organization, the above items will be included in the release. . . .
> Survey organizations reporting results will endeavor to have print and broadcast media include the above items in their news stories and make a report containing these items available to the public upon request.

The American Association for Public Opinion Research (AAPOR) has adopted a similar set of standards, with the additional recommendation that sampling error and confidence levels also be reported.

But how much protection do these standards provide for consumers of public opinion research, assuming that polling organizations adhere to them? The answer is that they provide less protection than is apparent at first glance, although they have contributed to improved media coverage of the polls. One reason the standards are not as effective as they appear is that they apply primarily to survey organizations and pollsters who release results rather than to the media that are covering the results; the impact of the standards is thus limited. However, in some cases, when the survey organization and the disseminator of the results are part of the same news organization, coverage of in-house polls is usually more in line with the NCPP and AAPOR standards.

Here is an example of how the standards may be applied when the

Drawing by Dana Fradon; © 1980 The New Yorker Magazine, Inc.

survey organization and the disseminator of the results are the same. One can learn about the results of a CBS News/*New York Times* poll from four distinct sources: (1) the story that appears in the *New York Times*; (2) the report presented on the "CBS Evening News"; (3) the news release issued by the *New York Times*; and (4) the release prepared by CBS News. The first two sources are readily available to citizens; the latter two are not. Normally, the news releases prepared by CBS News and by the *New York Times* and the news story in the *Times* comply closely with the NCPP and AAPOR standards; the story presented on the "CBS Evening News" may be less complete because air time is limited.

On the other hand, if the organization reporting the poll is different from the group that sponsored it, the poll release and the actual news story may show major discrepancies in meeting the NCPP and AAPOR recommendations. For example, most newspapers do not conduct their own polls.

Instead, they rely on syndicated polls from organizations such as Gallup and Harris, or on news releases in the public domain that are issued by polling organizations. In these situations the NCPP recommends that the sponsoring organization attempt to ensure that the medium that reports its results conforms to the NCPP standards. But there really is no way to enforce this requirement with news organizations once the poll release has become a public document. Moreover, the interests of the sponsoring organization may not be well served by full disclosure of the technical features of the poll, particularly when the sponsoring organization has manipulated the poll to generate a desired set of results. Complying with the standards is voluntary. Because organizations may choose not to observe them or may not be able to observe them, the effectiveness of the standards is diminished.

Another reason the NCPP and AAPOR standards are less effective than they might be is that they do not specify reporting of all the technical aspects of a poll that can markedly affect the results. For example, the NCPP standards recommend reporting the "complete wording of questions on which the release is based." Complete wording is not necessarily identical to the complete questionnaire. That is, without an entire survey instrument it is difficult to ascertain whether question order and placement have influenced the results reported in a release. For the major news organizations this is less of a concern since their releases typically include entire questionnaires showing the order in which items were asked. Moreover, the television networks and major newspapers are willing to distribute complete poll releases to interested citizens.

A more serious problem arises, however, when a news organization prepares a news analysis based on a subset of items from a questionnaire and does not inform readers or viewers about question wording and question order. When this occurs the news analysis may or may not accurately represent the content of the entire survey. Obviously, the items chosen for analysis and the perspective given to those selected items can dramatically affect the resulting coverage.

The NCPP and AAPOR standards ignore other technical specifications. For example, they do not require reporting of adjustments made to the sample, such as weighting (used to achieve demographic representativeness [see chapter 8]) or filtering (used to identify likely voters within the sample). A poll release will often state that weighting and filtering have been done, but in most cases it will not tell how. As a result, the poll consumer, ill-equipped to assess the soundness of the poll, is at the mercy of the decisions made by the news organizations.

As will be discussed in chapter 7, pollsters use different methods to identify likely voters, methods that can affect sample-based predictions in important ways (sizable changes in results, for instance). A *Denver Post* poll

on the 1986 U.S. Senate race in Colorado between Democratic representative Tim Wirth and Republican representative Ken Kramer illustrates the
consequences of screening for likely voters. Among the entire sample,
Kramer led Wirth, 44 percent to 41 percent, but among "most likely"
voters, Kramer was ahead, 52 percent to 39 percent (Rothenberg 1986c,
14). Nonetheless, Wirth won the election, which makes one wonder what
criteria the *Post* used to determine who was most likely to vote. The
outcome supports the politicians' cliché that the only poll that really counts
is the one held on election day.

Finally, the NCPP and AAPOR recommendations do not include the
response rate and procedures, such as callbacks, that are used to increase
the response rate. Poor response rates may require adjusting the interviewed sample to make it representative of the broader population. If
respondents who are called back multiple times in order to complete an
interview differ in systematic ways from respondents who are interviewed on
the first attempt, then the decision on whether to use multiple callbacks can
affect the substantive findings of the poll. Unfortunately, in most situations
poll consumers receive little if any information about response rates and
related matters.

Observing the Standards

How closely do the media actually conform to the NCPP and AAPOR
standards in their reporting of polls? Miller and Hurd (1982) conducted a
study of how well three newspapers — the *Chicago Tribune*, the *Los Angeles
Times*, and the *Atlanta Constitution* — followed the AAPOR guidelines. In a
sample of 116 polls reported between 1972 and 1979, compliance was
highest for sample size (reported 85 percent of the time) and sponsorship
(reported 82 percent of the time), and lowest for sampling error (reported
only 16 percent of the time). Miller and Hurd found no marked trend
indicating improved poll reporting over time, but they did find that
compliance with the AAPOR standards on sampling error was better for
election polls than for nonelection surveys. In general, compliance was better
when newspapers reported on their own in-house polls than on polls
provided by external sources. When newspapers did not publish information
called for by the AAPOR standards, in some instances the external polls did
not provide the information but in other cases the newspapers simply edited
out that information (Miller and Hurd 1982, 246).

Another study (Salwen 1985b) examined the reporting of public
opinion polls by the *Detroit News* and the *Detroit Free Press* in presidential
election years from 1968 to 1984. Salwen did find improvement over time in
the reporting of some of the information required by AAPOR, although the

exact question wording and the timing of the poll were reported less frequently (about 28 percent and 61 percent of the time, respectively) and reporting on those aspects showed no improvement during the sixteen-year period. Reporting of sampling error did improve over time, but in 1984 only 50 percent of the news stories about polls mentioned sampling error. Like Miller and Hurd, Salwen found that newspapers did a much better job of presenting the methodology of their in-house polls than of polls from external sources.

Miller and Hurd and Salwen did see positive signs that newspaper reporting of polls had improved over the years. They attributed the improvement to an increased collaboration between journalists and social scientists, the availability of readable books and texts on polling, and the increased frequency of in-house polls (newspapers do a better job of reporting their own polls because of local interest in them and because reporters have greater access to information about their technical aspects).

The positive findings of these studies must be tempered by the fact that they both dealt with major daily newspapers of reasonably high quality. One might expect such papers to have expertise and competence in reporting polls. Moreover, many of the polls the researchers analyzed were election surveys, which are more likely to report information such as sample size and sampling error than are nonelection surveys. However, another study by Salwen (1985a) found that with respect to question wording and method of interviewing, reports of nonelection polls were more descriptive than those of election polls, a finding speculatively attributed to the fact that question wording and interviewing method are more self-evident in election polls and therefore need not be reported. In smaller daily and weekly newspapers without the resources to conduct in-house polls and employ their own survey research experts, poll coverage is probably much poorer.

If newspaper reporting falls short of the NCPP and AAPOR standards, what must television's coverage be like? Newspapers have a number of obvious advantages in reporting polls. One is that they provide the reader with hard copy that can be reread and referred to, in contrast to the television message that (unless taped) "disappears" as soon as it is presented. Another is that newspapers can more easily present a lot of information. Consider the difference in learning about question wording from a newspaper story versus a television report. Television is less likely to present the complete question wording, in part because it typically faces more severe time and space constraints than does a daily newspaper.

Paletz and colleagues (1980) have conducted one of the few empirical studies of the treatment of polls by network television. They examined every poll reported on the CBS and NBC evening news shows and in the *New York Times* in 1973, 1975, and 1977, years deliberately chosen to avoid presidential elections. Their conclusion was that the television networks generally did a poorer job of reporting details about polls than did the *Times*, although the latter's performance was not stellar. (Keep in mind that during the 1970s the networks and the *New York Times* had not yet begun extensive in-house polling; in-house polls are better reported than external surveys.) Among the findings was that the sponsor of a poll was almost never mentioned on the networks and mentioned only about 25 percent of the time in the *Times*. Sample size was presented in two-thirds of the *Times* stories, but in only 26 percent of the television reports. The time of interviewing was given in 43 percent of the *Times* accounts and in 30 percent of the television reports. And in only 30 percent of the *Times* stories and 5 percent of the television reports was the complete wording of particular questions provided. Beyond these details, the report provided virtually no other technical information about the polls (Paletz et al. 1980, 504-505).

An analysis of Australian television coverage of election polls (Smith and Verrall 1985) generally concurred with Paletz and his colleagues that television coverage was superficial and lacking in methodological details. Smith and Verrall argue that the heterogeneity of the television audience requires that coverage be kept brief and simple. One way to foster brevity and simplicity is to omit methodological information.

As the available evidence suggests, the media could do a much better job adhering to the NCPP and AAPOR standards in reporting poll results, especially for surveys that are not conducted in-house. This would enable citizens to become more technically proficient in assessing and evaluating poll results. Methodological sophistication in poll reporting is increasing as survey research skills are acquired by journalists, political practitioners, and even the media audience. Moreover, as more media organizations conduct their own in-house polls and ignore polls from other sources, the overall quality of poll reporting will probably improve. Nevertheless, "the way methodological information about polling is reported in the media tends more to reassure than alert the audience about the possible defects of poll data" (Paletz et al. 1980, 506).

Two examples of excellent reporting of the mechanics of a poll are provided by the *Columbus Dispatch*. The newspaper conducted its own in-house mail surveys and commissioned the Gallup Organization to conduct statewide telephone polls on the 1994 elections in Ohio. With respect to its own poll, the *Dispatch* indicated:

> The *Dispatch* poll was based on returns from 1,456 registered Ohioans who intend to vote Nov. 8. The *Dispatch* bought a computerized list of all registered Ohio voters. A *Dispatch* computer

randomly chose those to receive ballots, modeled as closely as possible after the state's official ballot layout. Voters receiving the ballots were asked to describe themselves by party affiliation, age, sex, race, education, income, religion, union membership and how they voted for president in 1992 and governor in 1990. Ballots of different colors were sent to various regions of the state so *The Dispatch* could ensure that each area was represented in proportion to its actual voting strength. The areas, patterned on groupings of the state's media markets, are: northeast (20 counties); central (20 counties); southwest (8 counties); northwest (12 counties); west (14 counties); and southeast (14 counties). The standard margin of sampling error in a scientific poll of the size conducted by *The Dispatch* is plus or minus 2.5 percentage points in 95 out of 100 cases. This means that if a scientific poll is conducted 100 times, in 95 cases the result will not vary by more than 2.5 percentage points from the result that would be obtained if all registered voters in Ohio were polled and responded. Error margins are greater for poll subsamples. Like all polls, *The Dispatch* Poll is subject to possible error other than sampling error. Other sources of error can be unintentional bias in the wording of questions, data entry error or nonresponse bias. Nonresponse bias means that those who responded to the poll may not necessarily reflect the views of those who did not participate. The response rate was 19 percent. The results were adjusted slightly to compensate for demographic differences between poll respondents and the Ohio electorate as a whole. Although precautions are taken to ensure that the sample reflects the demographic characteristics of the Ohio electorate, precise estimates for total possible error cannot be calculated. The poll was designed, conducted and financed by *The Dispatch*. (*Columbus Dispatch* 1994a, 5)

With respect to the Gallup Poll, the *Dispatch* reported the following information provided by the Gallup Organization:

The results of the Gallup survey are based on telephone interviews with a randomly selected statewide sample of 803 registered voters, conducted Tuesday through Thursday. Data were weighted to ensure appropriate representation by age, sex, education, race and geographical location. Household telephone numbers were generated by a computer to ensure that all areas of the state were represented in proportion to the actual population in that area. This method ensures that both listed and unlisted telephone numbers are included in the sample. Respondents were asked whether they were registered to vote in their precinct or election district. For all respondents—registered or not—information was obtained on their gender, age, education and race, so that the overall sample of registered and unregistered adults could be weighted to conform to the census statistics. Registered voters also were asked their likelihood of voting and how interested they were in the election. These two questions were used to compute a "likely voter" category, which includes 483 respondents. For results based on the statewide sample of 803 registered voters, one can say with 95 percent confidence that the error attributed to sampling and other random effects could be plus or minus 4 percentage points. For results based on the "likely voter" category, the margin of error is plus or minus 5 percentage points. In addition to sampling error, question wording and practical difficulties in conducting surveys can introduce error or bias into the findings of public opinion polls. (*Columbus Dispatch* 1994b, 2)

Note that in addition to the standard information about sampling error and confidence levels, both of these descriptions discussed weighting or adjusting the data and mentioned the different sampling error for subgroups. They also mentioned other sources of error, although they did not develop these points. It is to the credit of the *Dispatch* that it commissioned an outside poll for results that could be compared to the results of its in-house surveys.

Substantive Interpretation of Polls

As we have seen, without access to the complete results of polls, citizens cannot easily evaluate how well the media report on the technical aspects of polling. It is even more problematic for them to evaluate how well the media describe and interpret the substance of public opinion polls. Because interpretation of poll data can be highly judgmental and value laden, it may be difficult to demonstrate that one particular interpretation is superior to another except in cases where obvious misreadings of the data have occurred or where blatant biases have been built into the analysis. Even simple description can pose a problem if time and space constraints force the media to cover only a subset of the items on a topic.

In this section, a number of examples illustrate how the media use and interpret polls and how much leeway the media have in deciding what parts of a poll to emphasize. The first example deals with Americans' reactions to the bombing of Libya as measured in a CBS News/*New York Times* poll conducted in April 1986. At the time of the poll the government of Libya was seen as sponsoring terrorism and as hostile to the American military presence in the Mediterranean Sea. After a number of incidents, the United States launched a retaliatory air attack against Libya. The reports of the poll in a CBS News release, in the *New York Times*, and on the "CBS Evening News" were consistent, the lead being that Americans overwhelmingly approved the bombing by a margin of 77 percent to 14 percent, even though a plurality of 43 percent thought it would lead to more terrorism while only 30 percent thought it would reduce terrorism. The *Times* story was, of course, far more detailed about the poll's results than was the "CBS Evening News" presentation, but the overall consistency of both reports suggested a common interpretation.

In addition to asking citizens whether they thought the Libyan bombing would reduce or increase terrorism, respondents were asked a related item about the efficacy of American military action in general: "If the United States made it a policy to take military action against a government it believes has trained or financed terrorists, do you think that would reduce terrorism in the long run, or would it only make things worse?" Fully 57 percent said it would reduce terrorism, and only 27 percent thought it would make the risk worse. In their treatment of this item, the *Times* story and the CBS press release differed. The *Times* reported this question at the very end of an article that ran forty-four column inches, while in a twelve-paragraph CBS press release the item was detailed in the fourth paragraph. Neither the *Times* nor CBS News made much of the discrepancy between citizens' doubts that the Libyan bombing would reduce terrorism and their belief that a policy of taking military action against terrorist governments would reduce terrorism. But imagine the divergent portrayals of public opinion that could be painted if one or the other item had been reported, but not both. One headline could read, "Americans question effectiveness of Libyan bombing," while another might proclaim, "Americans support military response to terrorism."

A good example of the choices that face the analyst is Adam Clymer's *New York Times* story on attitudes toward abortion, based on a survey of Americans conducted in late 1985. In Clymer's view, the wording of questions about abortion has a tremendous impact on citizens' responses, a "clear indication of uncertainty and conflict" in the public's attitudes on the topic (1986b). Three items in the survey illustrate the complexity of popular attitudes:

What do you think about abortion? Should it be legal as it is now, legal only in such cases as saving the life of the mother, rape or incest, or should it not be permitted at all?

Legal as is now	40%
Legal only to save mother, rape or incest	40
Not permitted	16
Don't know, not ascertained	4

Which of these statements comes closest to your opinion? Abortion is the same thing as murdering a child, or abortion is not murder because a fetus isn't really a person.

Murder	55%
Not murder	35
Don't know, not ascertained	10

Do you agree or disagree with the following statement? Abortion sometimes is the best course in a bad situation.

Agree	66%
Disagree	26
Don't know, not ascertained	8

Markedly different stories could be written based on this survey, depending upon which items were emphasized and how particular items were interpreted. By focusing only on the first item, one could write a pro-choice story that argued that 40 percent of Americans favor the current abortion law, another 40 percent favor legalized abortion in more limited circumstances, and only 16 percent oppose abortion outright. One could also write an antiabortion story based on the first item, by stressing that 56 percent of the sample (40 percent plus 16 percent) favor limiting somewhat the current availability of abortion. A writer could use the second item to document an antiabortion story that emphasized that a majority of Americans think abortion is murder. But a story based only on the third item would suggest that a strong majority of Americans think abortion is sometimes the best course of action. Clymer's article reflects the complex and even contradictory nature of popular attitudes on abortion; imagine the advocacy piece he could have written if he had adopted a blatant pro-choice or antiabortion perspective.

News articles that include polling data in the *New York Times*, *Washington Post*, and other major newspapers usually integrate the polling information into the body of the article, often presenting detailed breakdowns of the data and a reasonable amount of information about the poll and its characteristics. Newspapers not only use polls to supplement a news story, but also print articles in which polls are the subject.

In contrast, news magazines such as *Time* and *Newsweek* often commission polls to use as sidebars to news stories. Sometimes the poll results are placed in a separate box, with little reference made to them in the accompanying story. For example, a four-page story about the beating of a black man by Los Angeles police officers appeared in the March 25, 1991, issue of *Time*, which also commissioned a poll on the subject. No

From what you have read or seen, do you think the Los Angeles police clubbing of a black man was racially motivated?

YES 43%	NO 20%

Should criminal charges be brought against these officers, or should this matter be left to the police for disciplinary procedures?

Criminal charges 67%	Police discipline 17%

How often do you think incidents occur in your community where police use violence against private citizens?

Very often	9%
Fairly often	13%
On occasion	48%
Never	23%

From a telephone poll of 500 American adults taken for TIME/CNN on March 13 by Yankelovich Clancy Shulman. Sampling error is plus or minus 4.5%. "Not sures" omitted.

Source: Copyright © 1991 The Time Inc. Magazine Company. Reprinted by permission.

mention of the poll was made in the story; the poll was presented simply as an inset in the article (see box above).

Note the scant analysis of the poll. There is no breakdown by subgroups, even though a black-white comparison would have been of obvious interest (although the sample size would probably have not allowed for a reliable comparison). Also, no statement is made about any filtering or screening of those people who had not heard or read about the incident.

After some major political event or development, news organizations regularly sponsor polls to assess popular reactions. For example, after a House-Senate conference committee agreed upon a compromise tax reform proposal in August 1986, most of the major news organizations either conducted or commissioned a poll measuring citizens' attitudes toward tax reform. A *Newsweek* poll included the following items (September 1, 1986):

Do you approve or disapprove of the new tax bill approved by a House-Senate conference committee?

Approve very strongly	16%
Approve not so strongly	24
Disapprove very strongly	17
Disapprove not so strongly	17
Undecided	26

Do you think the new tax bill would make for a fairer distribution of the tax load among all taxpayers?

Fairer	33%
Not much different	30
Not as fair	24
No opinion	13

Do you think the new tax bill will benefit the nation's economy generally, hurt the nation's economy or not have much effect?

Benefit	27%
Hurt	20
Not much effect	41

These items are typical of the tax reform questions asked by other organizations. They scarcely recognize the problem of nonattitudes and how uninformed people are on this topic. Instead, respondents' answers are treated as if they reflected genuine attitudes. The epitome of silliness on this issue was reached when the following question was asked in an August 1986 Harris survey reported in the *National Journal* (September 13, 1986):

Do you favor or oppose Congress passing a tax reform bill that will cut individual taxes by $105 billion over five years, will increase business taxes by the same amount, will reduce the tax rates that most people pay, will cut the maximum tax rate for both individuals and corporations and will increase the minimum tax that wealthy individuals and corporations pay?

Favor	77%
Oppose	17

This is such a complex and multifaceted question that it is not clear what citizens were responding to when they answered "favor" or "oppose." The Harris poll also queried citizens on specific provisions of the tax reform proposal, such as the minimum tax that wealthy individuals and corporations would have to pay, the investment tax credit for corporations, and the special deduction for two wage earners in the same family. It would have been helpful to know first whether citizens actually understood what these provisions were. Undoubtedly, the amount of information citizens had on some of these topics was limited, so that many of the responses reflected nonattitudes rather than genuine views.

The following three examples suggest that media reports of polls conducted by other organizations are particularly susceptible to misinterpretation. Krosnick (1989) investigated the *New York Times* coverage of a poll commissioned by Aetna Life and Casualty on the public's attitudes toward the civil justice system and tort reform; the poll was conducted by Louis Harris and Associates. Aetna had a vested interest in tort reform. When the poll was completed, Aetna issued a press release that began, "An overwhelming majority of Americans support a number of specific reforms to improve the nation's civil justice system." Throughout the press release and the Harris report of the survey results were assertions that Americans supported and favored many changes. However, the survey questions themselves did not ask respondents whether they supported or favored these changes; instead, they asked whether respondents found these changes to be acceptable. Clearly, to find something acceptable is not the same thing as supporting or favoring it. Nevertheless, the news story on the poll that appeared in the *New York Times* failed to recognize this distinction and made strong claims that the poll results demonstrated "broad public support for *changes* in the civil justice system" and "reflected the public's *demand* for reform" (Krosnick 1989, 108). As Krosnick concluded, the *Times* coverage of the poll results most likely overstated public support for the changes that Aetna desired.

Another *New York Times* article shows how a reporter can become so creative in describing poll results that he or she fails to convey to the reader what the results really mean. The Graduate School of the City University of New York in 1990 commissioned a major national survey about religion in the United States. One item in the survey asked Americans what their religion was; 7.5 percent responded that they had no religion. At the state level, Oregon led the nation with 17 percent of its population reporting "no religion." The *New York Times* story about this poll began with the simple declarative sentence, "The state with the highest proportion of [atheists] is Oregon" (Goldman 1991). This is certainly a catchy lead that would draw the reader into the story, but it also distorts the meaning of the poll results: having no religion does not necessarily mean that one denies the existence of a higher being.

A more serious example of media misreporting and misinterpreting of polls occurred in the late 1970s as the U.S. Senate considered ratification of the Panama Canal treaties that would lead to Panamanian control of the canal. Smith and Hogan (1987) found that as the debate progressed in the Senate, many media organizations were reporting that public opinion was shifting toward support of the treaties — a finding that, if true, would obviously make it easier for senators sympathetic to the treaties to vote for ratification. But when Smith and Hogan examined the myriad poll results from this period, they found a pattern of stable opinion (which was hostile to the treaties), not one of change. They attributed the misleading interpretations to the variety of questions asked by different polling outfits, flaws in these questions, misinterpretation of key findings, and other factors. For our purposes, the key point of the research was their evaluation of how different media actually reported the polls. They wrote (p. 27):

> In general, CBS and the *New York Times* provided accurate and perceptive accounts of public opinion on the treaties. But the *Time*, *Newsweek*, and NBC stories ... display serious flaws. During the crucial period of Senate deliberation (January through April 1978) all claimed a massive shift in approval based on comparison of responses to different questions asked, in most cases, by different pollsters. Furthermore, the coverage is littered by errors of fact and inference and shows little understanding of the complex issues involved. . . .
>
>   Equally disturbing are certain common omissions. After January 1978, most findings of continued public opposition were simply ignored. . . . Also omitted were the methodological details that would have allowed an educated reader or viewer to discover the misinterpretations embedded in the media coverage. Only two articles, both in the *New York Times*, provided the complete text of a question; only one, also in the *Times*, included all of the information required by the American Association for Public Opinion Research (AAPOR) Standards of Disclosure for poll reports. In *Time* and *Newsweek* almost no information was given.

Certainly it is possible that the way the media portray public opinion on an issue as controversial as the Canal treaties may affect the public policy decisions that are ultimately made.

The previous examples have suggested some of the problems that can be encountered in interpreting poll results. Often, however, the media do not actually interpret poll results, but instead present simple, straightforward descriptive statements about them. Sometimes poll data are integrated into a news story that may or may not present and use the data appropriately. In some cases there is in-depth substantive analysis of the poll and its implications. An excellent example of this is a February 25, 1986, *New York Times* article by William Robbins on the farm crisis. The article effectively incorporated polling data from a February survey conducted by CBS News/*New York Times*. Robbins reported Americans' replies to questions such as "How many farmers are facing serious economic problems today?" and "What do you think will happen to food prices if more small farmers lose their farms?" He also pointed out where agricultural economists disagreed with popular opinion. In addition, Robbins highlighted counterintuitive features of the poll, such as the fact that urban dwellers were less likely to assign blame to the farmers for their predicament than were rural residents. Throughout the news story Robbins included information about federal farm policies and linked it to citizens' attitudes where appropriate.

With respect to the statistical presentation of polling data, the most common form is simple percentage distributions for individual questions. Reports often include a breakdown by demographic subgroups such as men and women or blacks and whites, but seldom offer a cross-tabulation that shows the relationship between two survey items. Measures of association, correlation analysis, and multivariate statistical analyses are virtually nonexistent, probably out of fear of intimidating and alienating the audience. The positive side of this is that the statistical procedures such as percentages used in poll reporting are likely to be understood by most of the adult population. It is fair to say that the media's substantive interpretation of poll results is reasonably accurate as far as it goes, in part because poll coverage is not very ambitious given the media's perception of what their audiences want and are able to comprehend.

Media, Polls, and the News Reporting Emphasis

A frequent criticism of the media is that they promote the polls to such a position of prominence that the polls themselves become regular topics for news stories. Indeed, some observers complain that the media in their role as sponsors of polls have gone into the business of *creating* the news rather than simply *reporting* it. More and more media have developed their own polling capabilities, and, as mentioned earlier, in order to justify this sizable expenditure they may increasingly report poll-based stories that are not newsworthy in the traditional sense. Consider this hypothetical example. A news organization conducts a poll on American attitudes toward mass transportation. Even though this topic is not on the national agenda and not a focal point for public debate, the news organization publishes a story reporting the results of this survey. Such a story comes very close to being news that is created by the media rather than news that is coverage of real events. The media also come close to generating news in their constant reporting of presidential popularity polls; the latest blip in the trend line of presidential popularity becomes a topic for a news story.

Another concern is that as more news organizations develop their own polling capabilities, they will increasingly fail to cover polls conducted by their rivals. Obviously, most of the media pollsters query citizens on matters such as presidential election trial heats, but usually their news reports do not mention the competition's results, particularly when those results disagree with their own. One can envisage situations in which the media might explicitly choose to play an agenda-setting role by conducting a poll on an issue not yet in the limelight and then trumpeting the results of that poll until some public official seizes the issue as his or her own.

The media's treatment of election polls has received especially harsh criticism. The most common complaint is that the media treat elections as sporting events — the comparison is usually to horse races (see chapter 7) — and use the polls to help handicap the outcome. Campaign coverage by the media frequently emphasizes candidates' relative electoral standing, often as measured by the polls (Broh 1980; Asher 1992), rather than their stances on the issues. As Robinson and Sheehan (1983, 252) argue:

> The main problem with polling . . . is that it is objective and so "newsworthy" (at least for the moment) that it drives out all other forms of news. Polls have a higher priority in the newscast than most other forms of campaign reporting. And, of course, polls tend to be among the least substantive kinds of political journalism.

In 1988 and 1992 the many criticisms of the presidential election polls focused on their numbers, their intrusiveness, and their inconsistency. For example, Elving (1989) noted that in August 1988, fourteen major polls on the Dukakis-Bush presidential contest had results that varied by nineteen percentage points, a situation that generated confusion and annoyance with the polls. In defending their enterprise, many pollsters deflected criticism by shifting the blame to the media. Elving cites some pollsters' criticisms of how the media handled the polls in 1988:

> "Did I see [1988] polls that annoyed me? No, but I did see reporting on them that did," says Linda DiVall of American Viewpoint Inc. "I wish the press had less desire to be conclusive and say the race is over when it's 10 points and it's May."
>
> Ed Goeas, president of Tarrance & Associates, says newspaper polls can be manipulated by the campaigns. "When newspaper polls are in the field the campaign can learn of it and do things to pump their guy up."
>
> But, Goeas contends, the real problems come when the data are in hand: "Newspapers are hurting the credibility of the industry because they are not prepared to analyze the data correctly.". . .

"They're getting better, but I am always amazed at how many reporters are covering polls . . . without training or background," says Bud Lewis, the veteran pollster for the *Los Angeles Times*. "It's like sex—everybody thinks they're good at it automatically."

The 1992 elections offer another example. In the pre-convention period, different polls had either Bush or Perot ahead (though not by large margins). The media coverage of these polls was often very dramatic and definitive, with little recognition in many cases of how unstable early presidential preferences can be (Morin 1992d). Likewise, Harwood (1992) complained about media coverage of post-convention polls that showed dramatic swings in support for Clinton and Bush. He argued that the media did a poor job of accounting for these swings, often simply attributing them to the convention "bumps" that each candidate received, when in fact much of the fluctuation might be due to limitations inherent in the polls themselves.

The criticisms do not stop at problems with inconsistency. A number of observers have pointed out problems inherent in media-sponsored public opinion polling, problems that reflect structural flaws of the polling and news reporting enterprises. Ladd (1980, 576) questions whether polling and journalism can ever fit together well, given that *newsworthiness* for the media is characterized by speed and timeliness, whereas good polling, despite the current technology for quick assessments of public attitudes, requires "extensive, time-consuming explanation and exposition." This potential conflict is exacerbated by the space and time constraints faced by news organizations. Consequently, the media are often unable to present a poll-based story that includes complete details about the poll itself as well as adequate substantive background and context. Ladd also argues that good reporting is often characterized by a sharp focus and relatively unambiguous conclusions; good survey research, however, often reveals uncertainty, ambiguity, and low levels of public information and interest on matters of public policy. Often the portrait of public attitudes revealed by polls is a complex, contradictory one that may not make a "good" news story.

The media's treatment of polls is shaped by properties of the news reporting enterprise itself as well as by the capabilities of journalists to analyze and report about the polls. Because of changes in the curriculum of academic journalism programs, one can expect reporters to become increasingly skillful in reporting on the polls. But even so, there are characteristics of the journalism profession that will continue to affect how polls are presented and discussed. Crespi (1980, 473) argues that journalistic requirements affect polling in both positive and negative ways:

Positive	Negative
Journalistic requirements place a high value on factual documentation of poll results, in the form of actual percentages rather than fuzzy generalizations.	There is a preoccupation with reporting numbers, the "objective" poll results, with a corresponding lack of interest in their underlying meaning or patterning.
Subjective editorializing is devalued insofar as poll reports are concerned, reducing the likelihood that the personal views of pollsters will introduce bias.	Superficiality and lack of analysis too often characterize coverage of even the most complicated issues.
Attention is focused on opinion regarding specific events and issues, thereby making poll results relevant to the real-life experiences and problems of the public, and to the political process.	Topics that can be expected to create front-page headlines dominate, leading to a spasmodic coverage of the agenda of public concerns.
Sensitivity to changes in public opinion, resulting from the effects of events, is enhanced.	There is limited continuing coverage of long-term trends, and background news is often neglected.

Conclusion

Although one need not agree entirely with Crespi, it is clear that the relationship between polling and the media can be difficult and complex. If poll sponsors recognize both the uses and limitations of polls, the relationship also can be very beneficial and informative to citizens. After all, the ability to ascertain public opinion in a timely and accurate fashion on matters of civic importance is an amazing accomplishment. But the media need to take whatever steps are necessary to ensure that they provide their audiences with sufficient information to make informed judgments. Reporting sample size and sampling error is the beginning of good poll coverage by the media, not the end. Standard practice should include presenting question wording and question order, factors that can have a much greater effect on the responses than can sampling error.

Beyond this, the journalism profession must be more sensitive to and reflective about the possible linkages between polls and news coverage. The media can easily play an agenda-setting role by bringing certain issues to the public's attention through news reporting; sponsoring and conducting polls on these issues; and reporting the results of their polls which further reinforce the visibility of the issue to the electorate. Citizens can become highly concerned about an issue even though its prominence is largely due to media coverage and media-sponsored polls. For example, Morin (1994a) argues that public concern about drugs in the late 1980s and fears about crime may be largely media driven, both by media coverage of the issues themselves and by media coverage of polls on these issues. He points out that in January, 1989, only 19 percent of poll respondents cited drugs as the most important problem facing the nation. By October of the same year, the percentage had increased to 53. But less than a year later, only 16 percent of Americans named drugs as the country's major problem. He attributes much of the rise and fall in the public's concerns about drugs to the media's heavy attention to the drug problem followed by media inattention to drugs.

Journalists also need to be more perceptive about the frailties and limitations of polls, and how the reporting of polls can influence people in unintended ways. Attention to these and other aspects of polls will improve journalistic treatment of the polls. Gawiser and Witt, in a pamphlet sponsored by the National Council on Public Polls, compiled a list of twenty questions that journalists should ask about poll results. Their elaborations of and answers to the following questions are required reading for journalists.

1. Who did the poll?
2. Who paid for the poll and why was it done?
3. How many people were interviewed for the survey?
4. How were those people chosen?
5. What area: nation, state, or region—or what group: teachers, lawyers, Democratic voters, etc.—were these people chosen from?
6. Are the results based on the answers of all the people interviewed?
7. Who should have been interviewed and was not?
8. When was the poll done?
9. How were the interviews conducted?
10. Is this a dial-in poll, a mail-in poll, or a subscriber coupon poll?
11. What is the sampling error for the poll results?
12. What other kinds of mistakes can skew poll results?
13. What questions were asked?
14. In what order were the questions asked?
15. What other polls have been done on this topic? Do they say the same thing? If they are different, why are they different?
16. So, the poll says the race is all over. What now?
17. Was the poll part of a fund-raising effort?

18. So I've asked all the questions. The answers sound good. The poll is correct, right?
19. With all these potential problems, should we ever report poll results?
20. Is this poll worth reporting?

The *New York Times* and the *Washington Post* usually do a good job of informing their readers about the technical features of their surveys. An April 17, 1986, *Times* article included on page nine the following description of a poll:

> The latest *New York Times*/CBS News Poll is based on telephone interviews conducted on April 15 with 704 adults across the United States, excluding Alaska and Hawaii.
>
> The sample of telephone exchanges called was selected by a computer from a complete list of exchanges in the country. The exchanges were chosen so as to insure that each region of the country was represented in proportion to its population. For each exchange, the telephone numbers were formed by random digits, thus permitting access to both listed and unlisted numbers.
>
> The results have been weighted to take account of household size and number of residential telephones and to adjust for variations in the sample relating to region, race, sex, age and education.
>
> In theory, in 19 cases out of 20 the results based on such samples will differ by no more than 4 percentage points in either direction from what would have been obtained by interviewing all adult Americans. The error for smaller subgroups is larger. For example, the potential error for men is plus or minus 6 percentage points, and for women it is plus or minus 5 percentage points.
>
> In addition to sampling error, the practical difficulties of conducting any survey of public opinion may introduce other sources of error into the poll.

Note that in addition to the standard information, the *Times* briefly described random-digit dialing, explicitly stated that the data had been weighted, and discussed sampling error for subgroups. The last sentence of the statement mentioned other sources of error, but unfortunately did not provide examples of them or elaborate on their potential consequences. Despite this major omission, the *New York Times*'s description of its polls remains one of the best available in spite of the prevalence of polls today. Even more important than describing the technical details of polls, the media should conscientiously ensure that the substance of their stories accurately reflects the polling data.

# 7 Polls and Elections

The type of polling most likely to be familiar to Americans is election surveys. Like surveys on presidential performance, election surveys receive substantial and continuing coverage in the media. They also generate the most controversy, particularly when preelection polls incorrectly predict the election day outcome. Although the most prominent election polls focus on the presidential contest, the use of polls has expanded to include congressional contests as well as many state and local races. Indeed, American-style campaigns replete with polling, media ads, and spin doctors have spread throughout the world.

Sponsors of Election Polls

Election polls are sponsored by a variety of organizations and individuals such as the media, candidates for office, and political parties. Sponsors use polls as research tools, collecting information in order to devise and implement winning campaign strategies. Typically, candidate-sponsored polls survey citizens on their sociodemographic characteristics, their perceptions of candidates, and their views on issues. Because these polls assess the relative strengths and weaknesses of the candidates with respect to their personal attributes as well as their issue stances, they enable candidates to determine how well they are running overall, how their campaigns are going within electorally important subgroups, and how campaign events and media advertising affect their standing among the voters.

A second major set of sponsors of election polls is the mass media. Polls are a central focus of their election coverage. Indeed, the media have been criticized (Asher 1992, 273-278) for treating elections as if they were horse races, emphasizing not what the candidates say on the issues, but their relative standing in the polls: Who's ahead? Who's behind? Who's gaining?

Who's falling back in the pack? Of course, media polls often go beyond recording levels of support for the candidates by addressing topics such as patterns of support for the candidates among groups of voters defined by their demographic characteristics and issue stances.

The distinction between candidate- and media-sponsored polls is often blurred. This is particularly so when candidates try to manipulate the media so that the results of both kinds of polls show the candidates in the best possible light, or at least minimize the damage caused by an adverse poll result. It is not uncommon for candidates to selectively leak their own polls in hopes of getting a helpful story in the media. Candidates may also criticize the accuracy of media-sponsored polls to minimize their negative effects.

This chapter describes the types and uses of polls common to election campaigns. It examines candidates' and parties' attempts to use polls for purposes other than research and to manipulate media coverage of polls. It also covers the role of polling during the presidential primary season and general election and how and why polls can go wrong in making election predictions. The chapter concludes with a speculative analysis of how polls can affect the way citizens vote.

Types of Election Polls

The differences among the many kinds of election polls occur less in their methodology than in the purposes they serve. For instance, some of the candidate- and party-sponsored polls, such as tracking surveys, can be private tools of a campaign; media-generated surveys, such as exit polls, often become topics of public controversy. It is important for consumers of public opinion polls to be aware of the different kinds of surveys and what they can tell about elections.

Benchmark Survey

A benchmark survey is usually conducted after a candidate has decided to seek office. This kind of survey collects standard information about the public image of candidates, their positions on issues, and the demographics of the electorate in order to provide a baseline for evaluating the progress of a campaign. Three important pieces of information often gathered in a benchmark survey are the candidates' name-recognition levels, their electoral strength vis-à-vis their opponents', and citizens' assessments of an incumbent officeholder's performance.

One problem with a benchmark survey is its timing. The earlier it is done, the less likely the respondents are to know anything about the challenger and the more likely it is that the political and economic situation might change dramatically by the time the election nears. Nevertheless, useful information can be collected about voters' perceptions of the strengths and weaknesses of the incumbent, their perceptions of the ideal candidate, and their views on major policy issues. The results of a benchmark survey normally are not publicized or leaked unless they show the candidate doing surprisingly well.

Trial Heat Survey

Technically, a trial heat survey is not a survey but a question or series of questions within a survey. Trial heat questions pair competing candidates and ask citizens for whom they would vote in that contest.

The typical wording of a trial heat question reads: "If the election were held today, would you vote for X or Y?" Sometimes questions are asked about hypothetical matches, particularly in the earlier stages of the presidential selection process. For example, in the first part of 1992, many polls paired various potential Democratic nominees against President Bush. It is the results of these trial heat questions that facilitate the "horse race" emphasis in media coverage of election campaigns. Such questions are fun and they often become the grist for interesting political speculation and gossip.

A number of caveats apply to the results of trial heat questions. The most important one is that much can change between the time a question is asked and the actual voting on election day. This is best illustrated by the dramatic fluctuations in support for the presidential candidates in 1992. For example, a Gallup/*Newsweek* poll in August of that year gave Clinton a 27 percent lead over Bush; by early October (right after Perot's reentry in the race), Clinton's lead had dropped to eight percentage points in the Gallup/*Newsweek* poll. The same dramatic changes can occur over a much shorter time period. For example, a *New York Times*/WCBS TV poll done less than two weeks before the 1993 New Jersey gubernatorial contest showed incumbent Democratic Governor Jim Florio with a 49 to 34 percent lead among registered voters over his Republican opponent Christine Todd Whitman (and an even larger lead among likely voters). But on election day, Whitman was the victor. In California's election for governor in 1994, Democratic challenger Kathleen Brown was more than 20 points ahead of incumbent Republican Pete Wilson in trial heat polls conducted months before the election. But on election day, Wilson defeated Brown by a 15 percent margin.

Trial heat questions far in advance of an election measure name recognition more than anything else, particularly in less salient election contests. Thus, one must be careful not to view trial heat placements as

cathy®   **by Cathy Guisewite**

Cathy, copyright 1988 Cathy Guisewite. Reprinted with permission of
Universal Press Syndicate. All rights reserved.

immutable nor should one be surprised when the standing of the candidates
changes dramatically over the course of the campaign. Also, because the
results of a trial heat question depend on how the question is constructed,
one must be careful in assessing the results. For example, when the political
party affiliation of the candidate is given, the outcome is bound to be
affected. With well-known candidates, it makes little difference whether
party affiliation is mentioned, but in less prestigious races between less well
known candidates, it can make a substantial difference if the question is
phrased "Mary Doe versus Joe Blitz" or "Mary Doe, the Democrat, versus
Joe Blitz, the Republican."

Tracking Polls

Tracking polls provide the most up-to-date information on which to
base changes in campaign strategy and media advertising. Because they are
a tremendous resource for candidates, campaign managers often conduct
these polls on a daily basis near election day in order to monitor closely any
late shifts in support. Tracking polls are expensive, so they rely upon *rolling
samples*. For example, samples of 100 different people may be collected on
four consecutive days. Although an N of 100 is small and has a large
sampling error, an N of 400 is much more reliable. But much can happen
between the first and fourth day of interviewing, perhaps making the oldest
interviews less interesting to the campaign. Hence, on the fifth day another
100 people would be interviewed and added to the sample and the first 100
responses discarded. And on the sixth day, another 100 people would be
interviewed, while the 100 interviews done on the second day would be
eliminated. This procedure guarantees an overall sample of 400 that

includes 100 new interviews each day, thereby allowing a close and timely monitoring of voters' reactions to the campaign. One danger of tracking polls is that any single day's interviews could be highly aberrant; the candidate and campaign must be careful not to overreact to what might be only a statistical blip.

One of the best examples of the value of tracking polls occurred in 1982 in the race for U.S. Senator from Missouri, in which incumbent Republican U.S. senator John Danforth was challenged by Democratic state senator Harriet Woods (Newman 1983). Danforth was the strong favorite to win, but the Woods campaign caught fire toward the end, creating an extremely close contest. The Danforth campaign had ample resources to conduct tracking polls that provided valuable information about Woods's surge and enabled the campaign to respond effectively with new television ads. Danforth ultimately won the election by 27,500 votes out of 1.5 million cast. Broder (1982, 1) pointed out that in 1982 the Republican Senatorial Campaign Committee spent more than a half million dollars on tracking polls in U.S. Senate races that were expected to be close or in which polls indicated a narrowing race.

Cross-Sectional vs. Panel Surveys

When the major polling organizations conduct multiple polls over time on an election contest, they generally use a *cross-sectional design* in which different samples of citizens are selected for each round of interviewing. For example, in the 1988 presidential contest CBS News/*New York Times* polled a telephone sample of 1,282 registered adult Americans between August 19 and 21 about their presidential choice. Among the probable electorate Bush-Quayle led Dukakis-Bentsen, 46 percent to 40 percent, with 12 percent expressing no opinion and 2 percent voluntarily indicating that they would not vote. A few weeks later, from September 8 to 11, CBS News/*New York Times* conducted another poll, this time of 1,043 registered adults; Bush-Quayle led Dukakis-Bentsen among the probable electorate, 47 percent to 39 percent, with 13 percent undecided and 1 percent saying they would not vote.

Each of these surveys provides a picture of where the electorate stood at a single point in time, and each is based on a different sample. In comparing the results of the two surveys, we can say that the Bush lead went from 6 percent to 8 percent (subject to sampling error) and that the *net gain* for Bush was 2 percent. But we cannot tell what pattern of movement produced this net gain. Perhaps 1 percent moved from Dukakis to Bush, or 10 percent moved from Bush to Dukakis and 11 percent from Dukakis to Bush, or 30 percent moved from Bush to Dukakis and 31 percent from

Dukakis to Bush. All of these hypothetical scenarios yield a net gain of 2 percent. But the total percentage of citizens who changed their preferences varies dramatically — 1 percent in the first instance, 21 percent (10 plus 11 percent) in the second, and 61 percent (30 plus 31 percent) in the third.

Unfortunately, cross-sectional surveys tell us only the net amount of change that has occurred; they cannot tell us about the gross amount of change or about the pattern of individual changes that produced the net result. If one is interested simply in net changes in the relative standing of the candidates, then cross-sectional surveys are fine. But if the total volatility of voters' attitudes and preferences is the key concern, then a *panel design* is needed.

The key characteristic of a panel design is that the same individuals are interviewed two or more times. This makes panel surveys more costly and difficult since the same respondents must be located repeatedly, no easy task in light of the mobility and mortality of respondents. For example, panel surveys of college students conducted over a period of months or years can be burdensome because of the high mobility of that group. Another problem is that respondents may not be willing to participate in multiple interviews; moreover, respondents who do agree to be reinterviewed may differ in distinct ways from those who do not. A final problem with panel surveys is that the experience of being interviewed at one point in time may affect the respondent's answers at the next interview. Despite these difficulties, panel surveys provide better information about the dynamics of the campaign and of voter decision making than do cross-sectional surveys.

Focus Groups

Focus groups can be an important campaign tool even though the voter may never hear of them. Technically, focus groups are not polls but in-depth interviews with a small number of people (usually ten to twenty) who often are selected to represent broad demographic groups. A focus group might watch a candidate debate and offer reactions, thereby helping the candidate to prepare better for the next debate. Or a group might be asked to react to a political commercial so that campaign managers can gain some insight into the commercial's effectiveness before spending money to air it. Focus group discussions are also useful in raising and developing questions that may later be incorporated in a public opinion poll.

Probably the most famous example of the effectiveness of focus groups occurred in the 1988 election, when the Bush campaign team called on a group to identify the "hot button" issues that they later used with devastating effect against Dukakis in the general election. The Bush campaign team invited two dozen New Jersey residents to a local hotel to talk about the candidates. Many of the participants were blue-collar and Catholic Democrats who had supported Reagan, but were intending to vote for Dukakis even though they knew little about him. Because these Reagan Democrats were seen as critical to a Bush victory, the focus group leader pushed until issues were identified that moved participants away from support for Dukakis. These issues turned out to be Dukakis's opposition to the death penalty, his opposition to a bill requiring Massachusetts schoolchildren to recite the Pledge of Allegiance, and his support of a weekend furlough program for prisoners (among them the infamous Willie Horton). The reactions of the focus group participants told the Bush team that it had found the issues needed to undermine the Dukakis campaign. It would have been much more difficult to have generated this information through a public opinion survey. As Bush's campaign manager, the late Lee Atwater, commented (Grove 1988b), "Focus groups give you a sense of what makes people tick and a sense of what's going on with people's minds and lives that you simply don't get from reading survey data."

Morin (1992e) has pointed out that focus groups have become very popular among the media; newspapers and television networks frequently commission them. While Morin applauds focus groups as another tool for journalists, he warns that the media often fail to recognize the limitations of this methodology. Certainly one caveat is that focus groups are not mini-public opinion surveys. Focus groups may suffer from problems of external validity; that is, the results of the focus group may not be generalizable to any broader population because the participants in a focus group may not be representative, both because of who they are and how they were selected. Nevertheless, the process of intensive discussion within a focus group may provide insights into what is motivating citizens, insights not readily revealed by a standard public opinion survey. For example, a recent report prepared for the Kettering Foundation relied heavily on focus group methodology (Harwood Group 1993). Entitled "Meaningful Chaos: How People Form Relationships with Public Concerns," the report argued that if political leaders really want to engage citizens in key public policy concerns, they and the media may need to devise new ways of accomplishing this. Among the report's recommendations is a call for more "mediating institutions" where citizens can interact directly and discuss the issues of the day. The Kettering report was sensitive to the limitations of the focus group methodology; in an appendix on methodology, the report stated (p. 49):

> There are, of course, limitations to group discussions. The research is qualitative. Thus, the observations detailed in this report should not be mistaken for findings from a random sample survey. They are, technically speaking, hypotheses, or insights, that would need to be

validated by reliable quantitative methods before being considered definitive. Still, the insights are suggestive of how citizens view public concerns and their relationships to them.

Deliberative Opinion Polls

A deliberative opinion poll combines elements of both the focus group and the standard public opinion poll. That is, a deliberative poll brings together a representative group of citizens, provides them with information and the opportunity for discussion on issues, and then polls them on these issues. The rationale and need for deliberative polls is presented by Fishkin (1992, 1994), who argues that public opinion surveys measure what the public thinks, but not what they would think if they had the opportunity to meet and become immersed in the issues through discussion about and study of the issues. Logistically, a deliberative poll is an expensive and challenging undertaking because it requires bringing together a representative sample and providing fair and balanced materials about the issues at hand.

An example of a deliberative poll is one conducted in Great Britain in 1994 (Fishkin 1994). A sample of 869 randomly selected citizens first responded to a baseline survey about the problem of crime and how it should be handled. Each of the respondents was then invited to Manchester to participate in the actual deliberative process; 302 citizens (largely representative of the original sample) attended. These 302 people then received briefing materials, participated in intensive discussions in small groups, and questioned experts and politicians on the problem of crime. After several days of considering the crime issue, the participants were again polled on their views of how to handle crime and their responses were compared to the baseline survey. Some of the findings attributed to the deliberative process were increased support for alternatives to prison and increased awareness of the rights of defendants. Fishkin concluded that this deliberative exercise was successful and advocated its broader use as a way of empowering citizens.

Although the logistics of deliberative polls make it unlikely that they will become a regular feature of the political landscape, they are suggested as an approach for presidential contests in the United States. Fishkin (1992) has proposed holding a deliberative poll early in 1996 in Austin, Texas. The poll would include 600 randomly selected delegates, the participation of all the presidential contestants before the winnowing process has begun, and intensive study and discussion of issues in small group sessions. Even if the prospects for deliberative polling seem weak, the rationale for the enterprise is clear. Traditional public opinion polls capture what is immediately on the voters' minds and, as noted in chapter 2, they are often plagued by nonattitudes. Moreover, candidates often treat citizens' opinions as something to manipulate through political advertising and campaign rhetoric. A deliberative poll, in contrast, can reveal what citizens think once they are informed about an issue and the results can place some constraints on the strategies of the candidates. Whether deliberative polls could ever have such an influence in the real world of politics and elections remains doubtful.

Exit Polls

Exit polls, as mentioned in chapter 1, are interviews with voters as they leave polling places. These very visible and controversial polls typically ask voters for whom they voted. They also collect some information on the issue positions and demographic characteristics of the respondents. The most prominent exit polls are conducted by the major news organizations to predict and explain presidential election outcomes as well as the results of congressional and major state-level races.

Exit polls have a number of advantages and uses. First, they are polls of actual voters, so they avoid the enduring problem faced by preelection surveys: determining who will actually vote. Second, exit poll samples are collected in many states. This allows state-by-state analysis of the presidential election, an endeavor not feasible with national surveys of 1,500 respondents, which are not amenable to breakdowns by state. (For details on how exit poll samples are selected, see Levy 1983.) Third, exit polls can be quickly tabulated. Almost instantaneous predictions and descriptions of election outcomes are possible. Indeed, this advantage has become a central selling point for exit polls as the networks compete with each other to be the first to call an election. Finally, exit polls generate rich information that enables both journalists and social scientists to understand better the factors that help shape the voters' choices.

Exit polls are generally accurate, although recent developments in the mechanics of how Americans vote might affect the predictive ability of exit polls. For example, numerous states are making it easy to vote by absentee ballot, while some states are experimenting with voting prior to election day. Clearly, these votes will not be captured by election day exit polling. Moreover, there is evidence that exit polls overrepresent the well educated and affluent since they are more willing to fill out the exit poll forms (Morin 1994g).

On rare occasions, exit poll results are inaccurate. For example, an exit poll in the 1989 Virginia gubernatorial race showed the black Democratic candidate Douglas Wilder winning by 10 percent when he actually won by less than one percent of the vote. The explanation for this inaccuracy is that some white respondents in the exit poll indicated that they had voted for Wilder when they had not (Traugott and Price 1992). As another example, the 1992 exit poll in the GOP presidential primary in New Hampshire showed George Bush with only a six-point margin over Pat Buchanan when his lead in the actual vote count was sixteen points. This discrepancy was attributed in part to the greater intensity of Buchanan supporters and their greater willingness to participate in the exit polling (Morin 1992b; Mitofsky 1992). This misleading exit poll actually affected news coverage of the New Hampshire primary by initially reporting Buchanan's showing as stronger than it actually was.

The 1980 Fiasco.   Exit polls created a storm of controversy on election night in 1980. Although the national preelection polls had indicated a close race between Jimmy Carter and Ronald Reagan, as the results came in from the eastern time zone it became evident that a Reagan landslide (especially in the Electoral College) was developing. What troubled many observers was that within minutes after the polls closed in a state, the networks would declare—on the basis of exit polls, and not official election returns—that Reagan had carried that state. By 8:30 p.m. Eastern Standard Time (EST), it was clear from exit poll results that Reagan had won enough states to ensure his election, no matter what happened in those states west of the Mississippi where the polls were still open (strong Reagan states in any event). Hence, the networks declared Reagan the victor while parts of the country were still voting. Moreover, Carter conceded the election before all of the polls had closed. Understandably, many concerns were raised about the effects of media declarations of victory when some voters had not yet cast their ballots. There were numerous anecdotal stories about voters in line at the polling booth leaving when they heard that the presidential race was already decided and about other citizens who decided not to venture to the polls at all. In 1984 Mondale wisely waited until the polls were closed on the West Coast before conceding, as did Dukakis in 1988.

Did the early call of the 1980 presidential election actually deter citizens from voting? The empirical evidence is mixed. Works by Jackson and McGee (1981) and Jackson (1983), based upon a January 1981 reinterview of respondents who had been part of a national election sample months earlier, claimed that a combination of factors, including the early projections based on exit polls and Carter's early concession, reduced overall turnout by 6 percent to 12 percent. Epstein and Strom (1984), using different analysis procedures, challenged these findings, claiming that only four of forty-five respondents in the survey who decided on election day not to vote attributed their decision to their knowledge that Carter had lost. These four respondents represented only 1 percent of the total number of registered nonvoters in the sample ($N = 395$). Had they voted, the overall turnout would have increased by only 0.2 percent. Based upon official election returns from congressional districts, research by Michael X. Delli Carpini (1984) found that the early call of the 1980 election did depress turnout in both the presidential and congressional contests to the detriment of Democratic candidates. He argued that there were between five and fourteen congressional contests in which the Republican margin of victory was less than the advantage provided the GOP by the early reporting of the presidential outcome. Critical of all of the empirical studies of the effects of early reporting in 1980, Sudman (1986) concluded that congressional district turnout was depressed by 1 percent to 5 percent.

The early projections had no significant impact on the outcome of the presidential race in 1980, but in state and local contests turnout effects, no matter how small, could have been much more consequential. In these elections fewer votes are cast, and the margin between victory and defeat is sometimes very small.

Projecting election results for a state before that state's polls are closed raises concerns about the behavior of the media. Although there is some dispute (Busch and Lieske 1985) about how late in the day exit polls must be taken in order to obtain a representative sample and make accurate projections, it is clear that if the polls close in a state at 7:30 p.m., exit polls could in most cases accurately predict the winner by late afternoon. Widespread reporting of such projections by the media could measurably depress turnout within the state. The television networks claim that they are very careful not to make projections in a state until after the polls in that state have closed, but a 1983 study by the League of Women Voters (LWV) and the Committee for the Study of the American Electorate pointed to numerous instances in which 1982 election projections were broadcast while the polls were still open. Sometimes while the polls are open the networks subtly describe the voting trends revealed by the exit polls, but do not declare a winner. "NBC Nightly News" provoked a controversy when it reported two hours before the polls would close that Michael Dukakis "may well be headed for a victory" in the 1988 New York Democratic primary (Boyer 1988).

Public Reaction. The opposition to exit polls has been fierce in many circles. Newspaper columnist Mike Royko once urged readers to lie to exit poll interviewers, thereby undermining the usefulness of the entire enterprise. Some pollsters have been critical of exit polls and early projections. Although Roper (1985) and others believe that exit polls have few if any effects on elections, they argue that their use should still be curtailed since most citizens believe that exit polls can influence election

Reprinted with permission of Tribune Media Services.

outcomes. Exit polls, they claim, cause citizens to lose confidence in the electoral process and become increasingly suspicious of the mass media.

Congress and state governments too have sharply criticized exit polls. The U.S. House Task Force on Elections conducted hearings in 1985 on the news industry's use of exit polls, and called for voluntary restraint on the part of the media (Swift 1985). The state of Washington went further. Recognizing that it would be difficult to prohibit the reporting of election projections and results, Washington State passed a law making it a misdemeanor to conduct any exit interviews within 300 feet of the polls (Abrams 1985). The obvious intention of this law was to make the collection of exit data far more difficult. The law was ultimately invalidated in federal court.

The controversy surrounding exit polls remains and will likely continue to heat up every two years. The networks argue strenuously that governmentally imposed limitations on the reporting of exit polls would be a form of censorship and a violation of First Amendment rights. Also, the news organizations note that if the polls were open simultaneously for twenty-four hours in all fifty states, the problem of early projections would be resolved. State officials reject this option as too expensive and point out that the networks could still make premature projections in the case of states for which they had sufficient information. Broder (1984) has proposed the Canadian solution: the networks could begin their election coverage by time zone from east to west, beginning each regional broadcast just as polls in that region are closing. Thus, the networks might begin election coverage in the East at 8:00 p.m. EST, in the Midwest at 9:00 p.m. EST, in the Mountain States at 10:00 p.m. EST, and on the Pacific Coast at 11:00 p.m. EST.

Consumer Guidelines. Consumers of exit polls should carefully evaluate the news reports throughout election day. Any news about patterns of vote choices among various groups is most likely based upon the exit polls completed to that point. Ask yourself whether such reports might affect your likelihood of voting and your actual choice of candidate. Also note the time of announcement of any election projections; if the projection is made before the polls have closed, then it is based on exit polls and not on official election returns, since the latter are not available until after the polls close. Observe whether the projection is for a state contest or a national race; if the latter, note whether the polls are still open in some states. Finally, try to keep a mental list of the number of early projections that subsequently are contradicted by the actual vote totals.

It is unlikely that exit polls will ever be regulated except by the self-policing of the networks themselves. In their early development, exit polls enabled the television networks to try to scoop their competition by being the first to call an election. The news media invested heavily in the technology of polling and election coverage; the ability to beat the competition and to improve ratings were major payoffs for the networks on their investment. (Consumers of exit polls should keep in mind that the polls play a somewhat different role for newspapers, which are not in a competition to predict election outcomes on election night. Instead, newspapers use exit polls primarily to describe voting patterns and to explain why the election turned out as it did.)

The competition among networks was somewhat mitigated when, beginning with the 1990 midterm elections, ABC, NBC, CBS, and CNN decided to conduct one joint exit poll rather than separate ones as in the past. The major reason for this change was financial; exit polling is very expensive. But as Schneider (1989) has pointed out, with different exit polls conducted on the same election, results have differed; multiple polls enabled investigators to compare the results and make judgments on which were more likely on target. But in the 1990 and 1992 elections, consumers of exit polls did not have the benefit of competition among the exit polls. On the positive side, however, all networks had the same access to the same exit polls, which may have reduced the temptation to try to preempt the competition by prematurely reporting exit poll results. For the 1994 midterm elections, there was competition again between two major exit poll enterprises.

Uses of Polls by Candidates

Candidates use polls to test the political waters in a variety of ways. For example, prospective candidates might commission a private poll and also examine public polls to assess their chances. Their assessments of results can steer their expectations and actions. For example, bad poll news might lead to a decision not to seek office. One reason given for Geraldine Ferraro's decision not to run for the U.S. Senate in 1986 against incumbent Republican senator Alphonse D'Amato was that poll results showed her trailing substantially. On the other hand, California Republican state senator Milton Marks was encouraged to challenge incumbent U.S. representative Phil Burton in 1982 by the National Republican Campaign Committee because a poll showed Marks leading Burton by 7 percent in February (Rothenberg 1982, 2). (Marks ultimately lost.)

A party organization with the financial resources to conduct polls and to provide other election services may use this capability to provide services to recruit candidates. At the national level the Republican party has been much better able than the Democrats to offer such assistance to its candidates and would-be candidates because of its more successful fund-raising operations based upon computerized direct mail.

Sometimes candidates will use positive poll results to generate campaign contributions or to deter contributions to their opponents. For example, in 1985 Idaho Democratic governor John Evans sent results of a poll he conducted to many political action committees (PACs) and potential contributors. The poll showed Evans in a virtual tie with incumbent Republican Steve Symms in a trial heat for the U.S. Senate seat to be voted on in 1986. Evans's action was clearly a signal to contributors that he had a good chance of being the next U.S. senator from Idaho and therefore was worthy of their donations (Rothenberg 1985, 11). Evans ultimately lost by a narrow margin.

Often when published polls show a candidate running poorly, the candidate will try to minimize the potential damage to fund raising and volunteers' morale by attacking the credibility and relevance of the poll. "The only poll that counts is the poll taken on election day," the candidate might argue, and then cite examples of how the polls have been wrong in the past. In a systematic analysis of reactions of the Bush campaign to negative poll results, Bauman and Herbst (1994) found three dominant responses. First was the (often valid) assertion that it was too early to give much credence to poll results. Second was an attack on the pollsters themselves and the journalists that reported the polls. Finally the campaign tried to counter results of published polls with results of its own private polls.

Sometimes the attack on a poll becomes more a matter of methodology. For example, the campaign organization of Jon Kyl, a 1986 candidate for the Republican nomination to the U.S. House in Arizona's Fourth Congressional District, conducted polls showing Kyl gaining strongly on front-runner John Conlan, with a third candidate, Mark Dioguardi, running far behind. Dioguardi challenged the validity of the poll, claiming that before the trial heat question that referred to all three candidates, respondents were asked a series of items that referred only to Kyl and Conlan, thereby giving respondents the misleading impression that the primary was actually a two-candidate race (Rothenberg 1986a, 3).

Likewise, a 1986 newspaper poll in Columbia, Missouri, showed Carrie Franche leading her chief opponent, Ralph Uthlaut, for the Republican nomination in the Ninth Congressional District, 35 percent to 20 percent, with 40 percent undecided. The Uthlaut campaign questioned the validity of the poll because the sample was based on the overall population of the district rather than on past primary turnout (Rothenberg 1986b, 5). In North Dakota a 1986 poll conducted by Decision/Making/Information, Inc. (DMI) for the National Republican Senatorial Campaign Committee showed incumbent Republican senator Mark Andrews far ahead of his Democratic challenger. The Democrats charged that the sample underrepresented Democrats, a criticism rejected by DMI (Rothenberg 1986b, 11). (Andrews's reelection bid was unsuccessful.)

Whatever the merits of these criticisms, it is clear that a candidate "harmed" by polls has a strong incentive to cast doubt on their credibility so that a campaign is taken seriously. If a campaign is not taken seriously, it will have difficulty in raising money and attracting other resources such as free media coverage.

Sometimes candidates deliberately manipulate aspects of their campaign or the polling process to generate results that will advance their candidacies. For example, in the four-way contest for the Republican nomination for governor of Ohio in 1982, one of the candidates, Seth Taft, scheduled his early television advertising to go on the air before the Ohio Republican party conducted a statewide poll assessing the standing of the candidates. The poll showed Taft running first, thereby enhancing his credibility. Undoubtedly, his famous last name and the skillful timing of his commercials gave Taft an early advantage in the polls, but he eventually lost the primary. To demonstrate greater electoral strength than they actually have, candidates often schedule television commercials and mailings in conjunction with party- and media-sponsored polls.

Candidates and campaign managers are also very skillful in selectively leaking information from in-house, private polls to improve their chances of winning. Sometimes these in-house polls are deliberately designed to generate the desired results. For example, before asking a trial heat question about their contenders, pollsters might ask a series of issue questions or candidate qualification items that will predispose the respondent to support one candidate over another. But in leaking the results of the trial heat item to the media, no information will be provided about the questions that preceded it. A candidate can also try to control poll results through sample selection. For example, if a candidate is thought to be more popular among women than men, interviewing might be conducted mainly during the day to obtain a predominantly female sample. But when the results of the poll are leaked, no mention would be made of the gender composition of the sample, thereby inflating the standing of the candidate.

Voters and reporters should be wary of such selective leaking. One tip-off is the refusal of a campaign to reveal additional information about a poll, such as question wording and question order. Although this kind of manipulation is not widespread, many campaigns use whatever tactics they believe will work because the objective of most campaigns is to win. Consumers can only hope that they can exercise good judgment in evaluating election poll results and that reporters and other journalists will not be easily victimized by manipulated campaigns.

Polls in the Presidential Selection Process

Polls are used at all stages of the presidential selection process. During the general election, the major news organizations and the campaigns themselves regularly conduct polls. When a major campaign event occurs, such as a televised debate between the presidential contenders, a slew of polls follows immediately to assess the effect of the event on the campaign. During the primary season, media polls in key states are common, as are national polls measuring the presidential preferences of Democrats and Republicans throughout the nation.

One result of the ubiquity of polls in presidential campaigns is the increasing prominence of the role of pollsters. In the past two decades, individual pollsters such as Pat Caddell, Richard Wirthlin, and Stanley Greenberg achieved celebrity status during the Carter, Reagan, and Clinton campaigns. Such pollsters today are part of the core strategy group that decides themes and tactics, media advertising, public speaking schedules, and other key aspects of the campaign.

Polls do much more than simply reflect the current standing of the candidates in the presidential contest. The polls themselves and the reporting of them shape the very course of the campaign. They have also been instrumental in the raising of campaign funds, although their impact has lessened in this area. Since 1976 presidential campaigns in the general election have been publicly funded. Major party nominees no longer need to worry that poor poll performance will cut off the flow of money to their campaigns. In 1968, however, many Democrats complained that early polls that showed Hubert Humphrey losing the election badly hindered fund raising so that even when it became clear near the end of the campaign that Humphrey had a chance to win, the money available for the final push was inadequate. In contrast to the general election, during the primary season eligible candidates today receive only partial public funding. Public matching funds are contingent on the ability of the candidates to attract private financial support. Thus, bad poll results, as well as poor primary and caucus showings, may deter potential donors from supporting a failing campaign.

The Caucus and Primary Season

The combined effect of polls and media coverage of polls is particularly critical during the caucus and primary season, for at least two reasons. First, many candidates may seek a party's presidential nomination, as happened with both Republicans and Democrats in 1988, with six and seven serious contenders, respectively. Unable to cover all candidates equally, the media give more attention to the most serious and viable candidates, with viability defined by a candidate's standing in the polls.

Second, the caucuses and primaries are a sequence of elections in which media coverage of the outcome in just one state can dramatically affect later polls and primaries. For example, in 1984 John Glenn's campaign conducted a poll in New Hampshire about one week before that state's primary. The actual interviewing was conducted around the time of the Iowa precinct caucuses in which Glenn did much worse than expected. The media coverage of the Iowa results stressed how badly the Glenn campaign was hurt there. Consequently, Glenn's New Hampshire survey showed that interviews completed before the reporting of his poor finish in Iowa had him running much more strongly in New Hampshire than did interviews completed after the reporting of the Iowa results. The combined effect of media coverage and the polls is particularly significant in Iowa and New Hampshire because these states begin the formal process of delegate selection. The "winners" in Iowa and New Hampshire almost invariably enjoy a sizable gain in support in the national polls because of the positive and extensive media coverage they receive.

The presidential primary season can be viewed as a sequential, psychological game in which the perception that a candidate is running strongly, as reflected in good poll results, makes it easier for the campaign to attract money, volunteers, and media coverage; bad poll results have the opposite effect. But strong performance in the polls is itself a function of the amount and content of media coverage that a candidate receives. This is why Iowa and New Hampshire are so critical. Because they are small states in which both a personal and a media campaign can be conducted, they enable a relatively unknown candidate, such as Jimmy Carter in 1976 or Gary Hart in 1984, to do better than expected and thus receive substantial media coverage. This coverage can move a candidate higher in the public opinion polls, which in turn enhances the candidate's media coverage and credibility.

In presidential election years polls become an overt part of campaign strategy during the primary season, when candidates appeal for support on the grounds that they are more electable than their opponents as demonstrated by the polls. Probably the best examples of this phenomenon occurred in 1976 and 1968. In 1976 Gerald Ford and Ronald Reagan were locked in a tight battle for the Republican presidential nomination, the winner most likely having to run against former Georgia governor Jimmy Carter. The Ford campaign conceded the South to Carter no matter who won the GOP nomination, but argued, citing public opinion polls, that Ford was the much stronger candidate to run against Carter nationwide (Phillips 1976). In 1968 Nelson Rockefeller's campaign to win the GOP nomination also depended heavily on the public opinion polls, since he knew that he would have great difficulty winning presidential primaries and caucuses. Rockefeller challenged Richard Nixon, the frontrunner, to cosponsor fifty state polls to see which candidate was the strongest. Rockefeller also commissioned and released polls of key electoral-vote states that showed him running better than Nixon against Democratic candidate Hubert Humphrey (Crossley and Crossley 1969, 7). Rockefeller hoped to sway Republican delegates to his cause by the argument that he was the strongest candidate the party could offer.

Presidential Debates and the General Election

The interaction between poll results and media coverage is well illustrated by the treatment of the presidential and vice-presidential debates before the general election. Often polls taken immediately after a debate produce very different results than do polls taken a few days later. The difference is attributable to the dominant media message in the interim. For example, a CBS News/*New York Times* poll conducted immediately after the first Reagan-Mondale debate in 1984 showed that 43 percent thought Mondale won the debate, 34 percent thought Reagan won, and 16 percent saw it as a tie—a 9 percent Mondale advantage overall. Two days later a CBS News/*New York Times* poll gave Mondale a 49 percent advantage (66 percent thought the winner was Mondale, 17 percent Reagan, and 10 percent saw it as even). The only explanation for this massive shift in sentiment was the intervening news coverage of the debate, which focused heavily on the president's poor performance and for the first time explicitly raised the question of his age.

Another example of influential media coverage is provided by polls conducted after the second Ford-Carter debate in 1976. In that debate

President Ford made a blatant misstatement to the effect that Eastern Europe was not under the domination of the Soviet Union. This was in the pre-Gorbachev era, when Soviet troops were stationed in Poland and the Polish government followed the dictates of Moscow. Telephone polls immediately after the debate showed Carter winning, but only by a narrow margin. Ford received negative media coverage after the debate for his mistake, and his campaign was not very skillful in putting the issue to rest when questioned by reporters as to what the president actually meant. As a result, Carter's narrow margin changed in polls taken a few days later which showed that Americans overwhelmingly viewed him as the winner of the debate.

"Winning" a debate may be less a matter of a candidate's actual performance than a function of the media's coverage and interpretation of that performance. This is why the call-in poll sponsored by the ABC News organization after the Carter-Reagan debate in 1980 was particularly offensive. ABC News invited its viewers to call one of two numbers to indicate whether they thought Reagan or Carter had won; the call cost fifty cents. Despite the self-selection and economic biases inherent in this procedure and the technical difficulty many citizens experienced in trying to complete their calls, ABC News announced that Reagan had won the debate by a two-to-one margin over Carter. Ideally, Americans would have dismissed this instant poll as foolish and unsound. Unfortunately, because it was the first large-scale reaction to the debate to be publicized, the poll and ABC's reporting of it shaped subsequent perceptions of who won the debate.

A final example of the role of polls in presidential debates occurred in 1980 when the League of Women Voters (LWV), the sponsor of the debate, decided to invite candidates whose popular support in public opinion surveys was more than 15 percent. The real issue was whether independent candidate John Anderson would meet the 15 percent test. The Carter strategists wanted Anderson excluded, since they believed that Anderson drew more votes from Carter than from Reagan, an effect that might be heightened if Anderson had the opportunity to share the same platform with Reagan and Carter. Anderson did meet the test and debated Reagan; Carter boycotted the debate. The LWV's use of polls in this fashion sparked much controversy among pollsters. What would the LWV have done had Anderson gotten only 13 percent? Would it have factored in sampling error? How would it have treated the undecided respondents? (See Dionne 1980; Knap 1980.) It was fortunate that Anderson clearly met the standard.

When and Why Election Predictions Are Wrong

In the vast majority of cases polls are on target. Nevertheless, polls can make notorious mistakes, such as those of the *Literary Digest* poll of 1936 (discussed in chapter 4) and the 1948 presidential election polls that indicated that Thomas E. Dewey would beat Harry S. Truman. The bad call in 1948 is widely attributed to the quota method of sampling employed by the polls and, more importantly, to the fact that polling stopped too far in advance of the election and therefore did not reflect the movement of many Democratic defectors back to Truman. In fact, the last polls showed Dewey with only a five-point lead over Truman, and the trend in the polls had been one of a declining Dewey advantage.

National polls have been off target in other important races. In 1980, for example, they failed to predict the magnitude of Reagan's victory. Most polls showed a very tight race even though Reagan beat Carter by ten percentage points. Again the poor predictions were attributed to the fact that many polls did not continue right through to the end of the campaign and thus did not capture the last-minute surge to Reagan by the undecideds and independents. The state-level polls in 1980 were far more accurate in predicting a sizable Reagan victory.

In 1982 the polls projected landslide victories for incumbent Republican governors in Illinois and Pennsylvania but the incumbent governors barely eked out a win. They also incorrectly predicted that Tom Bradley would win in the California gubernatorial contest and Bill Clements in the race for governor of Texas. And in 1988 the polls incorrectly predicted Bob Dole as the victor in the New Hampshire GOP primary, which George Bush won by nine points. Last-minute vote changes, emerging economic problems, and the inability to foresee turnout accurately among various subgroups were all cited as explanations for the polls' faulty projections.

In 1992 the general election presidential polls were quite accurate overall, although critics expressed concerns about the deluge of sometimes conflicting polls and the media reporting of them. One specific set of criticisms focused on the Gallup tracking polls conducted toward the conclusion of the campaign. The polls, which received substantial media attention (Traugott 1992), generated concerns about the actual selection of respondents, the method by which undecided voters were allocated to candidates, and most importantly, a shift in poll analysis from registered voters to likely voters, concerns that created some confusion among the media and the public as to how much the gap between Clinton and Bush had actually narrowed.

The accuracy of predictions depends on several factors. The rest of this section examines four of the factors that affect election predictions: the timing of preelection polls, the treatment of undecided voters, the estimation of voter turnout, and the changing political and economic climate.

The Timing of Polls

The timing of a preelection poll influences its accuracy; the closer to the election the poll is conducted, the more accurate its results are likely to be (Felson and Sudman 1975). The reasons for this are obvious: late polls can capture the effects of last-minute events and campaign activities that may influence outcomes. In contrast, early polls primarily reflect name recognition and perceptions of incumbents' performance. When voters have little information about the candidates, their attitudes about those candidates are highly volatile with the acquisition of some new information about the contenders. This is why the presidential primary polls often have a poorer track record than do the general election polls. In the primaries, especially the early ones with a large field of candidates, information levels are low and voters' commitments to candidates are weak.

In a comprehensive analysis of factors that affected the accuracy of preelection polls, Crespi (1988) found that the most important factor was how close to election day the preelection poll was conducted. The next most important factor was margin of victory and after that, either turnout, or whether the election was a primary or not. These findings suggest that polls would be more accurate if they did a better job identifying likely voters and monitoring trends in voters' preferences in the latter stages of a campaign. This suggestion is directly relevant to the failure of the polls to predict correctly the outcome of the 1988 New Hampshire Republican primary. Most polls failed to predict Bush's comfortable win. Why were most of the polls so wrong? The Gallup Organization offered the explanation that it stopped polling too early (by 4 p.m. on Sunday before the Tuesday election) and therefore did not capture late-breaking developments (Grove 1988a). The one poll that correctly predicted Bush's victory was the CBS survey, which involved a tracking poll on the Sunday and Monday before the election (Morin 1988b), thereby reinforcing Crespi's advice to poll as close to the election as possible. Lau's (1994) analysis of the accuracy of the 1992 presidential polls found that polls that were in the field multiple days were more accurate than overnight polls. He also found that tracking polls were more accurate than standard polls and that polls that interviewed on both weekdays and weekends were more accurate than weekday-only polls.

The Treatment of Undecided Voters

When respondents claim to be undecided they can mean different things. Some genuinely cannot choose among the candidates because they have sufficient, balanced information about them all, which makes it difficult to choose one. This is probably not a very common occurrence. Others may know very little about one or more of the candidates and therefore may be unwilling or unable to make a choice. Finally, "undecided" may be a safe reply for those who do not want to reveal their election choices to the interviewer.

Evidence for this third possibility is provided by the secret ballot technique long used by the Gallup Organization. In this procedure respondents are given a ballot by the interviewer, asked to mark their choices, and then requested to drop the folded ballot into a box. Perry (1979) points out that this approach yields an undecided rate about one-third to one-fourth as large as would be obtained if respondents simply were asked their vote preference by means of a standard survey item. (Note that the secret ballot technique can be used only with personal interviews.)

One way that pollsters may treat undecided respondents is simply to ignore them; results will be tabulated only for those respondents who have already made up their minds — a highly flawed procedure if the undecideds differ in major ways from the decideds. Another way of handling the undecideds is to report their numbers, but then to assume that the undecideds will split in the same way that the decideds already have. Thus, if the decideds vote 60 percent to 40 percent Democratic, the undecideds will be allocated 60 percent to 40 percent Democratic. This is probably a reasonable rule when both candidates are equally well known, and when there is no reason to suspect anything unusual going on among the undecideds.

When one candidate is well known and the other is not, the treatment of the undecideds is more problematical. In a race between a well-known, long-term incumbent and a relatively unknown challenger, an undecided vote can reflect poorly on the incumbent. In 1978 I worked on the campaign of Ohio state representative Charles Kurfess, who was challenging incumbent governor James Rhodes for the GOP gubernatorial nomination. Rhodes had already served three four-year terms as governor and was seeking a fourth. He was certainly the well-known warhorse of the Ohio Republican party. The benchmark survey conducted for the Kurfess campaign showed Rhodes favored over Kurfess, 66 percent to 6 percent, with 28 percent undecided. The final election results were 67 percent to 33 percent in favor of Rhodes. Without panel data one cannot definitively conclude that most of the undecideds moved to support Kurfess. Nevertheless, it seems plausible that the undecided vote in this case was actually a negative comment on the incumbent; in response to another question, the undecideds overwhelmingly preferred a new candidate for governor.

A later contest for the Ohio GOP gubernatorial nomination illustrates the danger in ignoring undecideds. In 1986 the candidates were James Rhodes once again, then seeking his fifth term as governor of Ohio, and state senators Paul Gillmor and Paul Pfeifer, who were not yet household names in the state. Most observers gave the two "Pauls" little chance to win, since they were viewed as splitting the anti-Rhodes vote. At an important stage of the campaign, a major media-sponsored poll that received extensive coverage showed Rhodes with 70 percent of the vote, Gillmor with 19 percent, and Pfeifer with 11 percent. The media coverage focused only on those respondents who had already made up their minds; moreover, the actual wording of the question did not include an undecided category: "Will you support James Rhodes, Paul Pfeifer, or Paul Gillmor for Governor in the Republican primary?" Nowhere in the newspaper reports of the poll (Miller 1986; Kostrzewa 1986b) was there any mention of the proportion of respondents who volunteered that they were undecided.

Ignoring the undecideds yielded a very high and widely publicized estimate of Rhodes's strength. The poll and the reporting of it unwittingly aided the Rhodes campaign by making his lead seem insurmountable and his nomination inevitable. Had undecideds been considered, Rhodes's nomination would not have been a certainty, particularly if one believed that an undecided response in a choice between a sixteen-year former governor and two less well known challengers was a negative reaction to that long-term incumbent. Ultimately, Rhodes, Gillmor, and Pfeifer received 48, 39, and 13 percent of the vote, respectively. The closeness of the outcome surprised many reporters and commentators and led them to wonder what might have happened had the Gillmor campaign been taken more seriously. But because of poll results it was difficult for reporters to view the Gillmor effort as viable; hence, the dominant media focus was the inevitability of Rhodes's nomination. (Rhodes lost badly in the general election.)

The behavior of undecided voters also partially accounts for the failure of the preelection polls to mirror closely the outcome of the two prominent contests in 1989—the New York City mayoralty and the Virginia governorship. Although polls accurately predicted the winners as David Dinkins in New York and Doug Wilder in Virginia, the poll estimates of their margin of victory were much too high. Wilder won in Virginia by less than 1 percent, yet the preelection polls were suggesting a double-digit margin. In New York, Dinkins won by about 2 percent even though the polls showed him between fourteen and twenty-one points ahead (Balz 1989). These contests had high visibility because both Dinkins and Wilder would be the first black Americans to be elected to their respective positions. If, as pollsters increasingly believe, whites who are undecided in a contest between a black and a white candidate vote heavily for the white candidate, then one reason for the polling errors in the Dinkins and Wilder contests was the behavior of the heavily white undecided groups of voters. Other factors also contributed to poll discrepancies in the Dinkins and Wilder victories, including race-of-interviewer effects, turnout effects, last-minute changes in voter preferences, and others. But the fact remains that white undecideds were not revealing their true preferences to the interviewers and in these contests white citizens gave an undecided response to an interviewer querying on a black-versus-white contest, even though they had already decided to support the white candidate.

Estimating Turnout in Elections

Probably the most difficult task pollsters face is estimating which of their respondents will actually vote. If the survey preferences of voters and nonvoters were identical, then this would not be a problem. But often there are marked differences between the two groups.

Pollsters use a variety of means to predict whether a person will vote. The Gallup Organization has used a subsample of likely voters from the overall sample of all possible voters (Perry 1979, 320-321). Among the items in the survey are the respondents' stated intention to vote, registration status, reported frequency of past voting, awareness of where to vote, interest in politics in general, interest in the particular election, and intensity of vote preference. Thus, in Gallup's final survey for the presidential election in 1976, when all respondents were considered, Carter led Ford, 48 percent to 43 percent, with Eugene McCarthy and others receiving 4 percent, and undecideds and those who refused to participate amounting to 5 percent. But when likely voters only were considered, Carter led 48 percent to 46 percent, with 2 percent for other candidates and 4 percent undecided or refusing to respond to the poll.

Other pollsters use similar procedures for determining likely voters. For example, Peter Hart has used respondents' reports of registration status, past voting in other races and current intention to vote, interest in and perceived importance of the election, and awareness of the candidates and where to vote (Goldhaber 1984, 49).

When tracking polls did not correctly predict the outcome of the 1988 New Hampshire primary, ABC News/Washington Post changed the way they determined who the likely voters were (Morin 1988c). In their New Hampshire polling, the ABC News/Washington Post polls had simply asked self-described registered voters the following question: Were they certain to vote, would they probably vote, were the chances 50-50, or would they probably not vote? Anyone who said he or she was certain to vote was considered a likely voter; this resulted in a sample whose projected turnout rate was twice as high as the real percentage because people often say they will vote even when they won't because they want to portray themselves as good citizens. Thus, ABC News/Washington Post decided to make it more difficult to be classified a likely voter by establishing multiple criteria. To be deemed a likely voter, the respondent had to say he or she was certain to vote and also had to have voted in 1986. Other factors were considered, including strength of commitment to a candidate. This more stringent test of likely voters generated more accurate results, but also resulted in more interviews with registered voters being tossed aside when making election predictions.

A somewhat different approach has been used by the *Columbus Dispatch*, which uses mailed questionnaires. As discussed in chapter 4, mailed questionnaires have low response rates and the representativeness of those people who do reply is uncertain. The *Dispatch* partially corrects for these problems by mailing questionnaires to samples selected from lists of registered voters who have voted in the past four primaries (Jordan 1982). This methodology is based on the notion current in the social sciences that voting is a habitual activity and that the best predictor of current voting turnout is past voting participation. The *Dispatch* poll does not rely on respondents' own reports of their past voting behavior, which could suffer from faulty memory and deliberate distortions—some people portray themselves as conscientious citizens who voted even when they did not. Instead it uses highly accurate, official public records of past voter participation in elections. Of course, such records are not very helpful in estimating the likely turnout of newly registered voters. In 1994, the *Dispatch* once again used its mailed questionnaires, but also commissioned telephone surveys conducted by the Gallup Organization. Overall, the *Dispatch* results were much more accurate, most likely because the mail poll did a better job of estimating the likely electorate. Anyone who completes a mailed questionnaire probably has a level of motivation indicative of a likely voter, while the Gallup screen for likely voters simply consisted of registered voters who said they were likely to vote.

The Changing Political and Economic Climate

Pollster Lance Tarrance observes that surveys will predict best when there is a normal voter turnout pattern. This observation applies to the polls in 1982. They performed poorly because they consistently underestimated the Democratic turnout, which was higher that year than expected because of the deepening economic recession and the effective efforts by labor unions and black organizations to mobilize participation among their rank-and-file members. Moreover, although voter turnout is usually low among the unemployed, the 1982 election may have been atypical because many of the newly unemployed had been regular voters and therefore participated at a higher-than-expected rate in 1982 (Rothenberg 1983, 8).

Probably the contest that did the most damage to the polls' reputation in 1982 was the Illinois gubernatorial election. Most polls predicted that incumbent Republican governor James Thompson would score a fifteen- to twenty-point victory over Adlai Stevenson III (Day and Becker 1984; Kohut 1983). But when the votes were tabulated, Thompson narrowly won by less than 0.2 percent.

Day and Becker (1984) and Kohut (1983) tested numerous hypotheses about the inaccuracy of the Illinois polls. They ruled out some, such as last-minute shifts in preference that were missed by the polls; polls were conducted to the very end of the campaign, and they still showed Thompson winning by a large margin. A poor estimate of the likely voters was also ruled out as the cause of the polls' inaccuracies. Instead, the polls' poor performance seemed to be caused mainly by an upsurge in straight-ticket voting among Democrats, including some Democrats who preferred Thompson to Stevenson but still cast a straight Democratic vote. In Chicago the Democratic organization devoted many resources to a "Punch 10" (that is, vote straight Democratic) media campaign, an effort that was particularly effective in black areas where it was part of an overall anti-Reagan theme (Day and Becker 1984, 613; Kohut 1983, 42). Thus, a good part of the Illinois poll debacle was due to political organization and mobilization, developments that are difficult to anticipate and assess by means of a poll.

A more recent example of inaccuracy occurred in the 1994 elections. The Republican victory was more sweeping than had been indicated by the polls weeks before the election. And while part of the discrepancy may have been due to difficulty in estimating the likely Democratic and Republican turnout, many events in the ten days before the elections probably affected the results. The extensive and visible campaigning by President Clinton, for example, may have served to nationalize many of the local contests to the advantage of the GOP. It is the case that the polls conducted right before election day were largely on target in predicting the Republican sweep as many races broke in favor of the GOP over the final weekend of the campaign.

Other ways in which election polls can go wrong include poor question wording, bad samples, and incompetent interviewing. One hopes, of course, that these problems are not prevalent in a survey; if they were, one would have little confidence in the entire enterprise, let alone the specific election predictions. Even if a sample is good, citizens should be aware of the sample size and sampling error. One reason for the relatively poor performance of presidential primary polls is that they often have small samples and large sampling error (Mitofsky and Plissner 1980). Of the fifty-one preprimary polls Mitofsky and Plissner analyzed, only five had a sampling error of three points or less; most had sample sizes of fewer than 500, and some had

© Dennis Renault, The Sacramento Bee.

samples of 200 or fewer. A good preelection survey must successfully address all of the issues discussed in chapters 2 through 5—nonattitudes, question wording, and sampling and interviewing techniques—as well as the unique problems inherent in making election predictions.

How Preelection Polls Affect Voters

Speculation about how polls affect voters has been widespread and contradictory. Some argue that polls that show one candidate ahead of another increase the incentives for supporters of the trailing candidate to change their preference and climb on board the winning candidate's bandwagon. Others emphasize underdog effects: sympathetic voters, they claim, rally around the candidate the polls show to be losing. Little strong evidence supports either of these views. The bandwagon effect would require that leading candidates consistently increase their margin, while the underdog effect predicts that the losing candidate will inexorably gain on the leader. These simple kinds of effects have not shown up consistently in surveys.

An experimental study by de Bock (1976) found some evidence that the reporting of disheartening poll results weakened the support and turnout motivation among a candidate's adherents. However, this finding seems to be more a function of the experimental design itself, in which exposure to the negative polls was much more direct than would be the case in the real-world setting. Other experimental studies have shown that polls can encourage support for the underdog, although the effects are not strong (Marsh 1984).

An ABC News/*Washington Post* poll in 1985 attempted to address the question of the effects of polls on voter choice. The survey asked a sample of Americans whether they were aware of whom the polls favored in 1984 and whether the polls had influenced their voting behavior (Sussman 1985f). Seventy-eight percent correctly knew that the polls had picked Reagan to win, 7 percent said Mondale, and 15 percent did not know or remember what the polls had said. Among the 78 percent who knew the polls had predicted a Reagan victory, 4 percent said it helped them decide for Reagan, 4 percent said it helped them decide for Mondale, and 93 percent said it had no effect. Sussman concluded that the preelection polls could not have had any significant impact on the vote split since the pro-Mondale and pro-Reagan effects almost canceled each other.

Keep in mind three facts about Sussman's study. First, asking people to recall their views seven months after the election may incur many errors of memory. Second, Sussman's procedure requires people to remember explicitly that the polls had influenced them; polls could be influential without voters being consciously aware of it. Third, some people might not be willing to admit that the polls affected their vote lest they appear to be making decisions on inappropriate grounds. Despite these reservations, Sussman's conclusion seems plausible in general and certainly so for the 1984 election.

Bandwagon and underdog effects can and do occur, but their magnitude is small and probably inconsequential. Of course, polls may have an indirect effect on voters through their impact on campaign contributors, campaign workers, and media coverage, as illustrated by the Renault cartoon shown on the preceding page. In addition to affecting voting behavior, polls can influence public opinion itself, a topic addressed in chapter 9. For example, if people become aware of changes in public opinion on an issue, that information may lead them to support the position favored by the trend. Or if they learn that their views are not shared by their fellow citizens, they may become unwilling to express their views. The very act of polling people can sensitize them to politics and campaigns in general and can encourage them to seek out information or become more involved. Given the prominence of polls in elections and in political discourse in general, it is important for citizens to understand both the positive and the manipulative uses made of polls, regardless of original intent.

8 Analyzing and Interpreting Polls

Thus far we have considered how public opinion surveys are conducted, how they are reported in the media, and how they influence elections and campaigns. This chapter focuses on the end products of public opinion surveys—the analysis and interpretation of poll data.

Interpreting a poll is more an art than a science, even though statistical analysis of poll data is central to the enterprise. An investigator examining poll results has tremendous leeway in deciding which items to analyze, which sample subsets or breakdowns to present, and how to interpret the statistical results. Take as an example a poll with three items that measure attitudes toward arms control negotiations. The investigator may construct an index from these three items, as discussed in chapter 3. Or the investigator may emphasize the results from one question, perhaps because of space and time constraints and the desire to keep matters simple, or because those particular results best support the analyst's own policy preferences. The investigator may examine results from the entire sample and ignore subgroups whose responses deviate from the overall pattern. Again time and space limitations or the investigator's own preferences may influence these choices. Finally, two investigators may interpret identical poll results in sharply different ways depending on the perspectives and values they bring to their data analysis; the glass may indeed be half full or half empty.

As the preceding example suggests, analyzing and interpreting data are not automatic objective processes, but instead entail a high degree of subjectivity and judgment. Subjectivity in this context does not mean deliberate bias or distortion, but simply professional judgments about the importance and relevance of information. Certainly, news organizations' interpretations of their polls are generally done in the least subjective and unbiased fashion. But biases can slip in, sometimes unintentionally and sometimes deliberately, as may occur when an organization has sponsored a

Reprinted by permission of NEA, Inc.

poll to promote a particular position. Because this final phase of polling is likely to have the most direct influence on public opinion, this chapter includes several case studies to illustrate the judgmental aspects of analyzing and interpreting poll results.

Choosing Items to Analyze

Many public opinion surveys deal with multifaceted, complex issues. For example, a researcher querying Americans about their attitudes toward tax reform might find initially that they overwhelmingly favor a fairer tax system. But if respondents are asked about specific aspects of tax reform, their answers may reflect high levels of confusion, indifference, or opposition. And depending upon which items the researcher chooses to emphasize, the report might convey support, indifference, or opposition toward tax reform. American foreign policy in the Middle East is another highly complex subject that can elicit divergent reactions from Americans depending on which aspects of the policy they are questioned about.

Some surveys go into great depth on a topic through multiple items constructed to measure its various facets. The problem for an investigator in this case becomes one of deciding which results to report and often, though an extensive analysis is conducted, the media might publicize only an abbreviated version of it. In such a case the consumer of the poll results is at the mercy of the media to portray accurately the overall study. Groups or organizations that sponsor polls to demonstrate support for a particular position or policy option often disseminate results in a selective fashion which enables them to put the organization and its policies in a favorable light.

In contrast with in-depth surveys on a topic, other polls called *omnibus surveys* are more superficial in their treatment of particular topics because of their need to cover many subjects in the same survey. Here the problem for an investigator becomes one of ensuring that the few questions employed to study a specific topic really do justice to the substance and complexity of that topic. It is left to the consumer of both kinds of polls to judge whether they receive the central information on a topic or whether other items might legitimately yield different substantive results.

The issue of prayer in public schools is a good example of how public opinion polling on a topic can be incomplete and potentially misleading. Typically, pollsters ask Americans whether they support a constitutional amendment that would permit voluntary prayer in public schools, and more than three-fourths of Americans respond that they would favor such an amendment. This question misses the mark. Voluntary prayer by individuals is in no way prohibited; the real issue is whether there will be *organized* voluntary prayer. But many pollsters do not include items that tap this aspect of the voluntary prayer issue. Will there be a common prayer? If so, who will compose it? Will someone lead the class in prayer? If so, who? Under what circumstances and when will the prayer be uttered? What about students who do not wish to participate or who prefer a different prayer?

The difficulty with either the in-depth or the omnibus survey is that the full set of items used to study a particular topic is usually not reported and hence the consumer cannot make informed judgments about whether the conclusions of the survey are valid. Recognizing this, individuals should take a skeptical view of claims by a corporate executive or an elected officeholder or even a friend that the polls demonstrate public support for or opposition to a particular position. The first question to ask is, What is the evidence cited to support the claim? From there one might examine the question wording, the response alternatives, the screening for nonattitudes, and the treatment of "don't know" responses. Then one might attempt the more difficult task of assessing whether the questions used to study the topic at hand were really optimal. Might other questions have been used? What aspects of the topic were not addressed? Finally, one might ponder whether different interpretations could be imposed on the data and whether alternative explanations could account for the reported patterns.

In evaluating poll results, there is always the temptation to seize upon those that support one's position and ignore those that do not. The problem is that one or two items cannot capture the full complexity of most issues. For example, a *Newsweek* poll conducted by the Gallup Organization in July 1986 asked a number of questions about sex laws and lifestyles. The poll included the following three items (Alpern 1986, 38):

Do you approve or disapprove of the Supreme Court decision upholding a state law against certain sexual practices engaged in privately by consenting adult homosexuals? [This question was asked of the 73 percent who knew about the Supreme Court decision.]

Disapprove	47%
Approve	41%

In general, do you think that states should have the right to prohibit particular sexual practices conducted in private between consenting adult homosexuals?

No	57%
Yes	34%

Do you think homosexuality has become an accepted alternative lifestyle or not?

Yes	32%
No	61%
Don't know	7%

Note that the first two items tap citizens' attitudes toward the legal treatment of homosexuals, while the third addresses citizens' views of homosexuality as a lifestyle. Although differently focused, all three questions deal with aspects of gay life. It would not be surprising to see gay rights advocates cite the results of the first two questions as indicating support for their position, while opponents of gay rights would emphasize the results of the third question.

An Eyewitness News/*Daily News* poll of New York City residents conducted in February 1986 further illustrates how the selective use and analysis of survey questions can generate very different impressions of popular opinion on an issue. This poll asked a number of gay rights questions:

On another matter, would you say that New York City needs a gay rights law or not?

Yes, need gay rights law	39%
No, do not need gay rights law	54%
Don't know/no opinion	8%

On another matter, do you think it should be against the law for landlords or private employers to deny housing or a job to someone because that person is homosexual or do you think landlords and employers should be allowed to do that if they want to?

Yes, should be against law	49%
No, should not be against law	47%

Volunteered responses

Should be law only for landlord	1%
Should be law only for employers	8%
Don't know/no opinion	3%

Although a definite majority of the respondents oppose a gay rights law in response to the first question, a plurality also believe that it should be illegal for landlords and employers to deny housing and jobs to persons because they are homosexual. Here the two questions both address the legal status of homosexuals, and it is clear which question gay rights activists and gay rights opponents would cite in support of their respective policy positions. It is not clear, however, which question is the better measure of public opinion. The first question is unsatisfactory because one does not know how respondents interpreted the scope of a gay rights law. Did they think it referred only to housing and job discrimination, or did they think it would go substantially beyond that? The second question is inadequate if it is viewed as equivalent to a gay rights law. Lumping housing and jobs together constitutes another flaw, since citizens might have divergent views on these two aspects of gay rights.

Baron (1980, 21-24) compared the results of pairs of questions on various topics to show how question wording—none of it overtly loaded or biased—could generate highly dissimilar portraits of American public opinion. Following are pairs of items on four of the topics studied by Baron:

Détente

Harris Poll (June 1978): Do you favor or oppose détente, that is the United States and Russia seeking out areas of agreement and cooperation?

Favor détente	69%
Oppose détente	19%

CBS News/*New York Times* Poll (June 1978): What do you think the U.S. should do—should the U.S. try harder to relax tensions with the Russians or instead should it get tougher in its dealings with the Russians?

Relax tensions	30%
Get tougher	53%

SALT

Harris Poll (June 1978): Do you favor or oppose the U.S. and Russia coming to a new SALT arms control agreement?

Favor SALT	72%
Oppose SALT	17%

Time/Yankelovich Poll (June 1978): The government is attempting to negotiate a new agreement with Moscow called SALT II, limiting the number of strategic nuclear weapons either country will manufacture. Do you favor our signing this kind of agreement with the Russians or do you think it's too risky?

Favor SALT	32%
Oppose SALT	56%

Abortion rights

CBS News/*New York Times* Poll (October 1977): The right of a woman to have an abortion should be left entirely to the woman and her doctor.

Agree	74%
Disagree	22%

Harris Poll (February 1978): Do you support legalized abortion up to three months of pregnancy?

Yes	42%
No	40%

Pornography

CBS News/*New York Times* Poll (January 1978): Should the government, at some level, restrict the sale of pornography to adults—or should adults be permitted to buy and read whatever they wish?

Restrict	44%
Don't restrict	56%

Time/Yankelovich Poll (November 1977): The government should crack down more on pornography in movies, books and nightclubs.

Agree	74%
Disagree	23%

Note that most of these question pairs were asked at approximately the same time of year, so genuine attitude change probably does not account for the differences between the pairs of items. Instead, the differences can be attributed to question wording, response alternatives, and location of the question in the survey (although no information is provided about location in the Baron article).

Technically, there is no contradiction between the responses to the first pair of questions on détente; one can favor "seeking out areas of agreement and cooperation" with the Soviets on certain issues and getting "tougher with the Russians" on other issues. Nevertheless, it is easy to predict which result foreign policy liberals and conservatives would choose to support their respective policies for dealing with the Soviet Union.

The two items on SALT, the Strategic Arms Limitation Talks, are probably the most flawed, the first because many respondents will simply not know what a SALT agreement entails, and the second because of its highly leading response alternative of "or do you think it's too risky?" Again, two opposing policy stances could be supported, depending on the question cited. The third and fourth pairs on the lifestyle and civil liberties issues of abortion and pornography also demonstrate that ostensibly valid poll results can be found to support potentially conflicting issue positions.

Additional examples of the importance of item selection are based on polls of Americans' attitudes about the Iraqi invasion of Kuwait in 1990. Early in the Persian Gulf crisis, various survey organizations asked Americans different questions concerning how they felt about taking military action against Iraq; not surprisingly, they obtained different results.

Do you favor or oppose direct U.S. military action against Iraq at this time? (Gallup, August 3-4, 1990)

Favor	23%
Oppose	68%
Don't know/refused	9%

Do you agree or disagree that the U.S. should take all actions necessary, including the use of military force, to make sure that Iraq withdraws its forces from Kuwait? (ABC News/*Washington Post*, August 8, 1990)

Agree	66%
Disagree	33%
Don't know	1%

Would you approve or disapprove of using U.S. troops to force the Iraqis to leave Kuwait? (Gallup, August 9-12, 1990, taken from *The Public Perspective*, September/October 1990, 13)

Approve	64%
Disapprove	36%

(I'm going to mention some things that may or may not happen in the Middle East and for each one, please tell me whether the U.S. should or should not take military action in connection with it). . . . If Iraq refuses to withdraw from Kuwait? (NBC News/*Wall Street Journal*, August 18-19, 1990, taken from *The Public Perspective*, September/October, 1990, 13)

No military action	51%
Military action	49%

Note that the responses to these questions indicate varying levels of support for military action even though most of the questions were asked within two weeks of each other. The first question shows the most opposition to military action. This is easily explained, since the question concerns military action *at this time*, an alternative that many Americans may have seen as premature until other means had been tried. The other three questions all indicate majority support for military action, although that support ranges from a bare majority to about two-thirds of all Americans. It is clear which question proponents and opponents of military action would cite to support their arguments.

Throughout the Persian Gulf crisis, public opinion was highly support-ive of President Bush's policies; only in the period between October and December 1990 did support for the president's handling of the situation drop below 60 percent. For example, a November 1990 CBS News/*New York Times* poll showed the following patterns of response:

Do you approve or disapprove of the way George Bush is handling Iraq's invasion of Kuwait?

Approve	50%
Disapprove	41%
Don't know/NA	8%

Likewise, an ABC News/*Washington Post* poll in mid-November reported:

Do you approve or disapprove of the way George Bush is handling the situation caused by Iraq's invasion of Kuwait?

Approve	59%
Disapprove	36%
Don't know/NA	5%

Some opponents of the military buildup tried to use these and similar polls to demonstrate that support for the president's policies was decreasing, since earlier polls had indicated support levels in the 60 percent to 70 percent range. Fortunately, the *Washington Post* poll cited above asked respondents who disapproved of Bush's policy whether the president was moving too slowly or too quickly. It turned out that 44 percent of the disapprovers said "too slowly" and only 37 percent "too quickly." Hence, a plurality of the disapprovers preferred more rapid action against Iraq—a result that provided little support for those critics of the president's policies who were arguing against a military solution.

Shortly before the outbreak of the war, the *Washington Post* con-ducted a survey of American attitudes about going to war with Iraq. To assess the effects of question wording, the *Post* split its sample in half and used two different versions of the same question followed by the identical follow-up question to each item.

Version 1

As you may know, the U.N. Security Council has authorized the use of force against Iraq if it doesn't withdraw from Kuwait by January 15. If Iraq does not withdraw from Kuwait, should the United States go to war against Iraq to force it out of Kuwait at some point after January 15 or not?

Go to war sometime after January 15	62%
No, do not go to war	32%

How long after January 15 should the United States wait for Iraq to withdraw from Kuwait before going to war to force it out?

Do not favor war at any point	32%
Immediately	18%
Less than one month	28%
1-3 months	8%
4 months or longer	2%

Version 2

The United Nations has passed a resolution authorizing the use of military force against Iraq if they do not withdraw their troops from Kuwait by January 15. If Iraq does not withdraw from Kuwait by then, do you think the United States should start military actions against Iraq, or should the United States wait longer to see if the trade embargo and economic sanctions work?

U.S. should start military actions	49%
U.S. should wait longer to see if sanctions work	47%

How long after January 15 should the United States wait for Iraq to withdraw from Kuwait before going to war to force it out?

U.S. should start military actions	49%

For those who would wait:

Less than a month	15%
1-3 months	17%
4 months or longer	9%

Morin (1991) points out how very different portraits of the American public can be painted by examining the two versions with and without the follow-up question. For example, version 1 shows 62 percent of Americans supporting war against Iraq, while version 2 shows only 49 percent;

obviously, these different results are due to the inclusion of the embargo and sanctions option in the second version. Hence it appears that version 2 gives a less militaristic depiction of the American public. But if one considers the follow-up question, one can construct a different picture of the public. For example, the first version shows that 54 percent of Americans (18 + 28 + 8) favor going to war within three months. But the second version shows that 81 percent of Americans (49 + 15 + 17) favor war within three months. The point, of course, is that the availability of different items on a survey can generate differing descriptions of the public's preferences.

The importance of item selection is illustrated in a final example on the Gulf War. It is from an April 3, 1991, ABC News/*Washington Post* poll conducted after the conclusion of the war, and it included the following three questions:

Do you approve or disapprove of the way that George Bush is handling the situation involving Iraqi rebels who are trying to over-throw Saddam Hussein?

Approve	69%
Disapprove	24%
Don't know	7%

Please tell me if you agree or disagree with this statement: The United States should not have ended the war with Iraqi President Saddam Hussein still in power.

Agree	55%
Disagree	40%
Don't know	5%

Do you think the United States should try to help rebels overthrow Hussein or not?

Yes	45%
No	51%
Don't know	4%

Note that the responses to the first item indicate overwhelming approval for the president. But if one analyzed the second question in isolation, one might conclude that a majority of Americans did not support the president and indeed wanted to restart the war against Saddam Hussein. But the third item shows that a majority of Americans oppose helping the rebels. The lesson of this and the previous examples is clear. Constructing an interpretation around any single survey item can generate a very inaccurate description of public opinion. Unfortunately, advocates of particular positions have many opportunities to use survey results selectively and misleadingly to advance their cause.

The health care debate in 1993 and 1994 also provides examples of how the selection of items for analysis can influence one's view of American public opinion. *Washington Post* polls (Morin 1994d) asked Americans whether they thought the Clinton health plan was better or worse than the present system. In one version of the question, the sample was given the response options "better" or "worse," while in the other version respondents could choose among "better," "worse," or "don't know enough about the plan to say." The following responses were obtained.

Version 1		*Version 2*	
better	52%	better	21%
worse	34%	worse	27%
don't know (volunteered)	14%	don't know enough	52%

Clearly, very different portrayals of American public opinion are presented by the two versions of the question. The first version suggests that a majority of Americans believed that the Clinton plan was better than the status quo, while the second version suggests that a plurality of citizens with opinions on the issue felt that the Clinton plan was worse. It is obvious which version of the question supporters and opponents of the Clinton health plan would be more likely to cite.

Another example from the health care reform area deals with Americans' feelings about the seriousness of the health care problem. Certainly, the more seriously the problem was viewed, the greater the impetus for changing the health care system. Different polling organizations asked a variety of questions designed to tap the importance of the health care issue (questions taken from the September/October 1994 issue of *Public Perspective*, pp. 23, 26):

Louis Harris and Associates (April 1994): Which of the following statements comes closest to expressing your overall view of the health care system in this country?. . . There are some good things in our health care system, but fundamental changes are needed to make it better. . . . Our health care system has so much wrong with it that we need to completely rebuild it. . . . On the whole, the health care system works pretty well and only minor changes are necessary to make it work.

Fundamental changes needed	54%
Completely rebuild it	31%
Only minor changes needed	14%

NBC/*Wall Street Journal* (March 1994): Which of the following comes closest to your belief about the American health care system—the system is in crisis; the system has major problems, but is not in crisis; the system has problems, but they are not major; or the system has no problems?

Crisis	22%
Major problems	50%
Minor problems	26%

Gallup (June 1994): Which of these statements do you agree with more: The country has health care problems, but no health care crisis, or, the country has a health care crisis?

Crisis	55%
Problems but no crisis	41%
Don't know	4%

Gallup (June 1994): Which of these statements do you agree with more: The country has a health care crisis, or the country has health care problems, but no health care crisis?

Crisis	35%
Problems but no crisis	61%
Don't know	4%

Certainly if one were trying to make the case that health care reform was an absolute priority, one would cite the first version of the Gallup question in which 55 percent of the respondents labeled health care a crisis. But if one wanted to move more slowly and incrementally on the health care issue, one would likely cite the NBC/*Wall Street Journal* poll in which only 22 percent of Americans said there was a crisis. Health care reform is the kind of controversial public policy issue that invites political leaders to seize upon those poll results to advance their positions. In such situations, citizens should be sensitive to how politicians are selectively using the polls.

Our final example in this section focuses on how the media selects what we learn about a poll even when the complete poll and analyses are available to the citizenry. The example concerns a book entitled *Sex in America: A Definitive Survey* by Robert T. Michael et al., published in 1994, along with a more specialized and comprehensive volume, *The Social Organization of Sexuality: Sexual Practices in the United States* by Edward O. Laumann et al. Both books are based on an extensive questionnaire administered by the National Opinion Research Center to 3,432 scientifically selected respondents. The enterprise was a genuine public opinion survey on sexual behavior unlike the sex pseudo-polls discussed in chapter 1.

Reprinted with special permission of King Features Syndicate.

Because of the importance of the subject matter and because sex sells, media coverage of the survey was widespread. How various media reported the story indicates how much leeway the media have and how influential they are in determining what citizens learn about a given topic. For example, the *New York Times* ran a front-page story on October 7, 1994 entitled "Sex in America: Faithfulness in Marriage Thrives After All." Less prominent stories appeared in subsequent issues including one on October 18, 1994, inaccurately entitled "Gay Survey Raises a New Question."

Two of the three major news magazines featured the sex survey on the covers of their October 17, 1994 issues. The *Time* cover simply read "Sex in America: Surprising News from the Most Important Survey since the Kinsey Report." The *U.S. News & World Report* cover was more risqué, showing a partially clad man and woman in bed; it read "Sex in America: A Massive New Survey, the Most Authoritative Ever, Reveals What We Do Behind the Bedroom Door." In contrast, *Newsweek* simply ran a two-page story with the lead "Not Frenzied, But Fulfilled. Sex: Relax. If you do it — with your mate — around twice a week, according to a major new study, you basically wrote the book of love."

Other magazines and newspapers also reported on the survey in ways geared to their readership. The November issue of *Glamour* featured the survey on its cover with the teaser "Who's doing it? And how? MAJOR U.S. SEX SURVEY." The story that followed was written by the authors of the book. While the cover of the November 15, 1994 *Advocate* read "What That Sex Survey Really Means," the story focused largely on what the survey had to say about the number of gays and lesbians in the population. The lead stated "10%: Reality or Myth? There's little authoritative information about gays and lesbians in the landmark study *Sex in America* — but what there is will cause big trouble." Finally, the *Chronicle of Higher Education*, a weekly newspaper geared to college and university personnel, in its October 17, 1994 issue headlined its story "The Sex Lives of Americans. Survey that had been target of conservative attacks produces few startling results."

Both books about the survey contain a vast amount of information and a large number of results and findings. But most of the media reported on such topics as marital fidelity, how often Americans have sex, how many sex partners people have, how often people experience orgasm, what percentage of the population are gay and lesbian, how long sex takes, the time elapsed between a couple's first meeting and their first sexual involvement, and similar topics. Many of the reports also presented results for married vs. singles, men vs. women, and other analytical groupings. While most of the media coverage cited above was accurate in reporting the actual survey results, it was also selective in focusing on the more titillating parts of the survey, an unsurprising outcome given the need to satisfy their readerships.

Examining Trends with Polling Data

Researchers often use polling data to describe and analyze trends. To isolate trend data, a researcher must ensure that items relating to the topic under investigation are included in multiple surveys conducted at different points in time. Ideally, the items should be identically worded. Even when they are, serious problems of comparability can make trend analysis difficult. Identically worded items may not mean the same thing or provide the same stimulus to respondents over time because social and political changes in society have altered the meaning of the questions. For example, consider this question:

Some say that the civil rights people have been trying to push too fast. Others feel they haven't pushed fast enough. How about you? Do you think that civil rights leaders are trying to push too fast, are going too slowly, or are they moving at about the right speed?

The responses to this item can be greatly influenced by the goals and agenda of the civil rights leadership at the time of the survey. A finding that more Americans think that the civil rights leaders are moving too fast or too slowly may reflect not a change in attitude from past views about civil rights activism but a change in the civil rights agenda itself. In this case, follow-up questions designed to measure specific components of the civil rights agenda are needed to help define the trend.

There are other difficulties in achieving comparability over time. For example, even if the wording of an item were to remain the same, its placement within the questionnaire could change, which in turn could alter the meaning of a question (see chapter 3). Likewise, the definition of the sampling frame and the procedures used to achieve completed interviews could change. In short, comparability entails much more than simply wording questions identically. Unfortunately, consumers of poll results seldom receive the information that enables them to judge whether items are truly comparable over time.

Two studies demonstrate the advantages and disadvantages of using identical items over time. Abramson (1990) complained that the biennial National Election Studies (NES) conducted by the Survey Research Center at the University of Michigan, Ann Arbor, were losing their longitudinal comparability as new questions were added to the surveys and old ones removed. Baumgartner and Walker (1988), in contrast, complained that the use of the same standard question over time to assess the level of group membership in the United States had systematically underestimated the extent of such activity. They argued that new measures of group membership should be employed, which of course would make comparisons between past and present surveys more problematic. One might advocate the inclusion of the old and the new measures in a survey, but this becomes very costly if one also needs to cover many other topics.

Two other studies show how variations in question wording can make the assessment of attitude change over time difficult. Borrelli and colleagues (1987) found that polls measuring Americans' political party loyalties in 1980 and in 1984 varied widely in their results. They attributed the different results in these polls to three factors: whether the poll sampled voters only; whether the poll emphasized "today" or the present in inquiring about citizens' partisanship; and whether the poll was conducted close to election day, which would tend to give the advantage to the party ahead in the presidential contest. The implications of this research for assessing change in party identification over time are evident. That is, to conclude that genuine partisan change occurred in either of the two polls, other possible sources of observed differences, such as modifications in the wording of questions, must be ruled out. In a study of support for aid to the Nicaraguan contras between 1983 and 1986, Lockerbie and Borrelli (1990) argue that much of the observed change in American public opinion was not genuine, but instead was attributable to changes in the wording of the questions used to measure support for the contras. Again, the point is that one must be able to eliminate other potential explanations for observed change before one can conclude that observed change is genuine change.

Smith's (1993) critique of three major national studies of anti-Semitism conducted in 1964, 1981, and 1992 is an informative case study of how longitudinal comparisons may be undermined by methodological differences across surveys. The 1981 and 1992 studies were ostensibly designed to build upon the 1964 effort, thereby facilitating an analysis of trends in anti-Semitism. But, as Smith notes, longitudinal comparisons among the three studies were problematic because of differences in sample definition and interview mode, changes in question order and question wording, and insufficient information to evaluate the quality of the sample and the design execution. In examining an eleven-item anti-Semitism scale, he did find six items that were highly comparable over time that indicated a decline in anti-Semitic attitudes.

Despite the problems of sorting out true opinion change from change that can be attributed to methodological factors, there are times when public opinion changes markedly and suddenly in response to a dramatic occurrence, and one is confident that the observed change is indeed genuine. Two examples from CBS News/New York Times polls in 1991 about the Persian Gulf war illustrate dramatic and extensive attitude change. The first example concerns military action against Iraq. Just before the January 15 deadline imposed by the UN for the withdrawal of Iraq from Kuwait, a poll found that 47 percent of Americans favored beginning military action against Iraq if it did not withdraw, and 46 percent were opposed. Two days after the deadline had passed and after the beginning of the allied air campaign against Iraq, a poll found 79 percent of Americans saying the United States had done the right thing in beginning military action against Iraq. The second example focuses on people's attitudes toward a ground war in the Middle East. Before the allied ground offensive began, only 11 percent of Americans said the United States should begin fighting the ground war soon; 79 percent said bombing from the air should continue. But after the ground war began, the numbers shifted dramatically: 75 percent of Americans said that the United States was right to begin the ground war, and only 19 percent said the nation should have waited longer. Clearly the Persian Gulf crisis was a case when American public opinion moved dramatically in the direction of supporting the president at each new stage.

Examining Subsets of Respondents

Although it is natural to want to know the results from an entire sample, often the most interesting information in a poll comes from examining the response patterns of subsets of respondents defined according to certain theoretically or substantively relevant characteristics. For example, a January 1986 CBS News/New York Times poll showed President Reagan enjoying unprecedented popularity for a six-year incumbent: 65 percent approved of the president's performance, and only 24 percent disapproved. These overall figures mask some analytically interesting variations. For example, among blacks only 37 percent approved of the president's performance, while 49 percent disapproved. The sexes also differed in their views of the president, with men expressing a 72 percent approval rate compared with 58 percent for women. As expected among categories of party loyalists, 89 percent of the Republicans, 66 percent of the independents, and only 47 percent of the Democrats approved of the president's performance. The discovery that blacks and whites or men and women differ in their views of the president prompts one to explore the reasons for these differences.

There is no necessary reason for public opinion on an issue to be uniform across subgroups. Indeed, on many issues there are reasons to expect just the opposite. That is why, in gaining a fuller understanding of American public opinion, it is important to examine the views of relevant subgroups of the sample. In doing so, however, one should note that dividing the sample into subsets places a smaller number of cases in each, thereby increasing the sampling error and lowering the reliability of the sample estimates. For example, a sample of 1,600 Americans might be queried about their attitudes on abortion. After the overall pattern is observed, the researcher might wish to examine abortion attitudes within religious categories to determine whether religious affiliation is associated with specific attitudes toward abortion. Hence, she might break down the sample by religion, yielding 1,150 Protestant, 400 Catholic, and 50 Jewish respondents. The analyst might observe that Catholics on the whole were the most opposed to abortion. To find out which Catholics are most likely to oppose abortion, she might further divide the 400 Catholics into young and old Catholics or regular church attenders and nonregular attenders, or into four categories of young Catholic churchgoers, old Catholic churchgoers, young Catholic nonattenders, and old Catholic nonattenders. The more breakdowns done at the same time, the quicker the sample size in any particular category plummets, perhaps leaving insufficient cases in some categories to make solid conclusions.

Innumerable examples can be cited to demonstrate the advantages of delving more deeply into poll data on subsets of respondents. An ABC News/*Washington Post* poll conducted in February 1986 showed major differences in the attitudes of men and women toward pornography; an examination of only the total sample would have missed these important divergences. For example, in response to the question, "Do you think laws against pornography in this country are too strict, not strict enough, or just about right?" 10 percent of the men said the laws were too strict, 41 percent said not strict enough, and 47 percent said about right. Among women, only 2 percent said the laws were too strict, a sizable 72 percent said they were not strict enough, and 23 percent thought they were about right (Sussman 1986c, 37).

A CBS News/*New York Times* poll of Americans conducted in April 1986 found widespread approval of the American bombing of Libya; 77 percent of the sample approved of the action, and only 14 percent disapproved. Despite the overall approval, differences among various subgroups are noteworthy. For example, 83 percent of the men approved of the bombing compared with 71 percent of the women. Of the white respondents, 80 percent approved in contrast to only 53 percent of the blacks (Clymer 1986c). Even though all of these demographically defined groups gave at least majority support to the bombing, the differences in levels of support are both statistically and substantively significant.

Polls showed dramatic differences by race to the O. J. Simpson case with blacks being more convinced of Simpson's innocence and more likely to believe that he could not get a fair trial. For example, a field poll of Californians (*U.S. News & World Report*, August 1, 1994) showed that only 35 percent of blacks believed that Simpson could get a fair trial compared to 55 percent of whites. Also, 62 percent of whites thought Simpson was "very likely or somewhat likely" to be guilty of murder compared to only 38 percent for blacks. Comparable results were found in a national *Time*/CNN poll (*Time*, August 1, 1994): 66 percent of whites thought Simpson got a fair preliminary hearing compared to only 31 percent of black respondents, while 77 percent of the white respondents thought the case against Simpson was "very strong" or "fairly strong" compared to 45 percent for blacks. A *Newsweek* poll (August 1, 1994) revealed that 60 percent of blacks believed that Simpson was set up (20 percent attributing the setup to the police); only 23 percent of whites believed in a setup conspiracy. When asked whether Simpson had been treated better or worse than the average white murder suspect, whites said better by an overwhelming 52 percent to 5 percent margin, while blacks said worse by a 30 percent to 19 percent margin. These reactions to the Simpson case startled many Americans who could not understand how their compatriots of another race could see the situation so differently.

School busing to achieve racial integration has consistently been opposed by substantial majorities in national public opinion polls. A Harris poll commissioned by *Newsweek* in 1978 found that 85 percent of whites opposed busing (Williams 1979, 48). An ABC News/*Washington Post* poll conducted in February 1986 showed 60 percent of whites against busing (Sussman 1986b). The difference between the two polls might reflect genuine attitude change about busing in that eight-year period, or it might be a function of different question wording or different placement within the questionnaire. Whatever the reason, additional analysis of both these polls shows that whites are not monolithic in their opposition to busing. For example, the 1978 poll showed that 56 percent of white parents whose children had been bused viewed the experience as "very satisfactory." The 1986 poll revealed sharp differences in busing attitudes among younger and older whites. Among whites age thirty and under, 47 percent supported busing and 50 percent opposed it, while among whites over age thirty, 32 percent supported busing and 65 percent opposed it. Moreover, among younger whites whose families had experienced busing firsthand, 54 percent approved of busing and 46 percent opposed it. (Of course, staunch opponents of busing may have moved to escape busing, thereby guaranteeing that the remaining population would be relatively more supportive of busing.)

Another example of the usefulness of examining poll results within age categories is provided by an ABC News/*Washington Post* poll conducted in May 1985 on citizens' views of how the federal budget deficit might be cut. One item read, "Do you think the government should give people a smaller Social Security cost-of-living increase than they are now scheduled to get as a way of reducing the budget deficit, or not?" Among the overall sample, 19 percent favored granting a smaller cost-of-living increase and 78 percent opposed. To test the widespread view that young workers lack confidence in the Social Security system and doubt they will ever get out of the system what they paid in, Sussman (1985d) investigated how different age groups responded to the preceding question. Basically, he found that all age groups strongly opposed a reduction in cost-of-living increases. Unlike the busing issue, this question showed no difference among age groups — an important substantive finding, particularly in light of the expectation that there would be divergent views among the old and young. Too often people mistakenly dismiss null (no difference) results as uninteresting and unexciting; a finding of no difference can be just as substantively significant as a finding of a major difference.

In many instances the categories used for creating subgroups are already established or self-evident. For example, if one is interested in gender or racial differences, the categories of male and female or white and black are straightforward candidates for investigation. Other breakdowns require more thought. For example, what divisions might one use to examine the effects of age? Should they be young, middle-aged, and old? If so, what actual ages correspond to these categories? Is middle age thirty-five to sixty-five, forty to sixty, or what? Or should more than three categories of age be defined? In samples selected to study the effects of religion, the typical breakdown is Protestant, Catholic, and Jewish. But this simple threefold division might overlook some interesting variations; that is, some Protestants are evangelical, some are fundamentalist, and others are considered mainline denomination. Moreover, since most blacks are Protestants, comparisons of Catholics and Protestants that do not also control for race may be misleading.

Establishing categories is much more subjective and judgmental in other situations. For example, religious categories can be defined relatively easily by denominational affiliation, as mentioned earlier, but classifying respondents as evangelicals or fundamentalists is more complicated. Those who actually belong to denominations normally characterized as evangelical or fundamentalist could be so categorized. Or an investigator might identify some evangelical or fundamentalist beliefs, construct some polling questions around them, and then classify respondents according to their responses to the questions. Obviously, this would require some common core of agreement concerning the definition of an evangelical or fundamentalist. Wilcox (1984, 6) argues:

> Fundamentalists and evangelicals have a very similar set of religious beliefs, including the literal interpretation of the Bible, the need for a religious conversion known as being "born-again," and the need to convert sinners to the faith. The evangelicals, however, are less anti-intellectual and more involved in the secular world, while the fundamentalists criticize the evangelicals for failing to keep themselves "pure from the world."

Creating subsets by ideology is another common approach to analyzing public opinion. The most-often-used categories of ideology are liberal, moderate, and conservative, and the typical way of obtaining this information is to ask respondents a question in the following form: "Generally speaking, do you think of yourself as a liberal, moderate, or conservative?" However, one can raise many objections to this procedure, including whether people really assign common meanings to these terms. Indeed, the levels of ideological sophistication and awareness have been an ongoing topic of research in political science.

Journalist Kevin Phillips (1981) has cited the work of political scientists Stuart A. Lilie and William S. Maddox, who argue that the traditional liberal-moderate-conservative breakdown is inadequate for analytical purposes. Instead, they propose a fourfold classification of liberal, conservative, populist, and libertarian, based upon two underlying dimensions: whether one supports or opposes governmental intervention in the economy and whether one supports or opposes expansion of individual behavioral liberties and sexual equality. They define liberals as those who support both governmental intervention in the economy and expansion of personal liberties, conservatives as those who oppose both, libertarians as citizens who favor expanding personal liberties but oppose governmental intervention in the economy, and populists as persons who favor governmental economic intervention but oppose the expansion of personal liberties. According to one poll, populists made up 24 percent of the electorate, conservatives 18 percent, liberals 16 percent, and libertarians 13 percent, with the rest of the electorate not readily classifiable or unfamiliar with ideological terminology.

This more elaborate breakdown of ideology may help us to better understand public opinion, but the traditional categories still dominate political discourse. Thus, when one encounters citizens who oppose government programs that affect the marketplace but support pro-abortion court decisions, proposed gay rights statutes, and the Equal Rights Amendment, one feels uncomfortable calling them liberals or conservatives since they appear to be conservative on economic issues and liberal on lifestyle issues. One might feel more confident in classifying them as libertarians.

A more elaborate classification of the American public was constructed by *Times Mirror* (1987). Three personal orientations (religious faith, alienation, and feelings of financial pressure) and six basic value systems (tolerance/intolerance, beliefs about social justice, militant anticommunism, attitudes toward government, feelings of American exceptionalism, and attitudes toward business corporations) were used to construct the following classification:

Enterprise Republicans. Affluent, educated, 99 percent white, one of two key Republican groups, probusiness and antigovernment.

Moral Republicans. Middle aged, middle income, one of two key Republican groups, mostly white, heavy concentration of southerners, very conservative views on social and foreign policy.

Upbeats. Young, optimistic, strong believers in America, lean solidly toward the Republican party, not critical of government's role in society, mostly white, little or no college, middle income.

Disaffected. Alienated, pessimistic, negative toward big government and big business, lean Republican, feel financial pressure, heavy concentration in Midwest, middle aged, middle income, promilitary.

Bystanders. Young, poorly educated, nonparticipants in American democracy, heavily white, lean Democratic.

Followers. Little interest in politics, little faith in America, lean Democratic but are persuadable, young, poorly educated, blue-collar, little religious commitment, 18 percent Hispanic, 25 percent black.

Seculars. No religious belief, well educated, white, middle aged, strong commitment to personal freedom, heavily concentrated on East and West coasts.

Sixties Democrats. Upper middle class, 60 percent female, well educated, 16 percent black, strong commitment to social justice, support social spending.

New Deal Democrats. Older group, blue-collar, union members, moderate income, religious, intolerant on questions of personal freedom, support many social spending measures.

Passive Poor. Older and poor, solid Democratic, strong faith in America, committed to social justice, less well educated, southern, 31 percent black.

Partisan Poor. Most Democratic group, very low income, high financial pressure, strong concern with social justice, 37 percent black, low income, southern, urban, poorly educated.

Although other analysts have not been quick to use this classification, *Times Mirror* and the Gallup Organization have conducted extensive public opinion polling on issues and presented the results in terms of these categories. For example, polling done in 1988 showed that 60 percent of the Moralists considered acquired immune deficiency syndrome (AIDS) God's punishment for immoral sexual behavior; only 9 percent of the Seculars and 14 percent of the Sixties Democrats shared that view. Fifty-three percent of the Enterprisers said that labor unions were most responsible for the international competitiveness problems of U.S. companies, and only 27 percent blamed the companies; in contrast, 52 percent of the Seculars blamed the companies, and only 21 percent cited the unions.

These examples could be repeated many times over to indicate that these subsets identified by *Times Mirror* have relevance for understanding the shape of public opinion in the United States. Moreover, the identification of these distinct subgroups of citizens gives insight into the difficulties the political parties, especially the Democrats, have in nominating candidates with widespread appeal to the party loyalists. One can see how the Sixties Democrats with their commitment to social justice and high tolerance for alternative lifestyles might clash with New Deal Democrats who are often intolerant on matters of personal freedom.

Additional examples of how an examination of subsets of respondents can provide useful insights into the public's attitudes are provided by two CBS News/*New York Times* surveys conducted in 1991, one dealing with the Persian Gulf crisis and the other with attitudes toward police. Although the rapid and successful conclusion of the ground war against Iraq resulted in widespread approval of the enterprise, before the land assault began, there were differences of opinion among Americans about a ground war. For example, in the February 12-13 CBS News/*New York Times* poll, Americans were asked: "Suppose several thousand American troops would lose their lives in a ground war against Iraq. Do you think a ground war against Iraq would be worth the cost or not?" By examining the percentage saying it would be worth the cost, one finds the following results for different groups of Americans:

All respondents	45%	Independents	46%
Men	56%	Republicans	54%
Women	35%	Eighteen to twenty-nine year-olds	50%
Whites	47%	Thirty to forty-four year-olds	44%
Blacks	30%	Forty-five to sixty-four year-olds	51%
Democrats	36%	Sixty-five years and older	26%

Note that the youngest age group, the one most likely to suffer the casualties, is among the most supportive of a ground war. Note also the sizable differences between men and women, whites and blacks, and Democrats and Republicans.

Substantial racial differences in opinion also expressed in an April 1-3, 1991, CBS News/*New York Times* poll on attitudes toward local police. Overall, 55 percent of the sample said they had substantial confidence in the local police, and 44 percent said little confidence. But among whites the comparable percentages were 59 percent and 39 percent, while for blacks only 30 percent had substantial confidence and fully 70 percent expressed little confidence in the police. Even on issues in which the direction of white and black opinion was the same, there were still substantial racial differences in the responses. For example, 69 percent of whites said that the police in their own community treat blacks and whites the same, and only 16 percent said the police were tougher on blacks than on whites. Although a plurality—45 percent—of blacks agreed that the police treat blacks and whites equally, fully 42 percent of black respondents felt that the police were tougher on blacks. Certainly if one were conducting a study to ascertain citizens' attitudes about police performance, it would be foolish not to examine the opinions of relevant subgroups.

A final example of the importance of examining subsets of respondents is provided by a January 1985 ABC News/*Washington Post* poll that queried Americans about their attitudes on a variety of issues and presented results, not only for the entire sample, but also for subsets of respondents defined by their attentiveness to public affairs (Sussman 1985b). Attentiveness to public affairs was measured by whether the respondents were aware of four news events: the subway shooting in New York City of four alleged assailants by their intended victim; the switch in jobs by two key Reagan administration officials, Donald Regan and James Baker; the Treasury Department's proposal to simplify the tax system; and protests against South African apartheid held in the United States. Respondents then were divided into four levels of awareness, with 27 percent in the highest category, 26 percent in the next highest, 25 percent in the next category, and 22 percent falling in the lowest. The next step in the analysis was to compare the policy preferences of the highest and lowest awareness subsets.

There were some marked differences between these two groups. For example, on the issue of support for the president's military buildup, 59 percent of the lowest awareness respondents opposed any major cuts in military spending to lessen the budget deficit. In contrast, 57 percent of the highest awareness group said that military spending should be limited to help with the budget deficit. On the issue of tax rates, a majority of both groups agreed with the president that taxes were too high, but there was a difference in the size of the majority. Among the lowest awareness respondents, 72 percent said taxes were too high and 24 percent said they were not, while among the highest awareness respondents, 52 percent said taxes were too high and 45 percent said they were not (Sussman 1985b).

These findings raise some interesting normative issues about public opinion polls. As mentioned in chapter 1, the methodology of public opinion polls is very democratic. All citizens have a nearly equal chance to be selected in a sample and have their views counted; all respondents are weighted equally (or nearly so) in the typical data analysis. Yet except at the polls all citizens do not have equal influence in shaping public policy. The distribution of political resources, whether financial or informational, is not uniform across the population. Polls themselves become a means to influence public policy, as various decision makers cite poll results to legitimize their policies. But should the views of all poll respondents be counted equally? An elitist critic would argue that the most informed segments of the population should be given the greatest weight. Therefore, in the preceding example of defense spending, more attention should be given to the views of the highest awareness subset (assuming the validity of the levels of awareness), which was more supportive of reducing military spending. An egalitarian argument would assert that all respondents should be counted equally. We will return to the role of the polls in a democratic political system in the last chapter.

Interpreting Poll Results

An August 1986 Gallup poll on education showed that 67 percent of Americans would allow their children to attend class with a child suffering from AIDS, while 24 percent would not. What reaction might there be to this finding? Some people might be shocked and depressed to discover that almost one-fourth of Americans could be so mean spirited toward AIDS victims when the scientific evidence shows that AIDS is not a disease transmitted by casual contact. Others might be reassured and relieved that two-thirds of Americans are sufficiently enlightened or tolerant to allow their children to attend school with children who have AIDS. Some people might feel dismay: How could 67 percent of Americans foolishly allow their

Reprinted with special permission of King Features Syndicate.

children to go to school with a child who has AIDS when there is no absolute guarantee that AIDS cannot be transmitted casually?

Consider this example from a 1983 poll by the National Opinion Research Center (NORC): "If your party nominated a black for President, would you vote for him if he were qualified for the job?" Eighty-five percent of the white respondents said yes. How might this response be interpreted? One might feel positive about how much racial attitudes have changed in the United States. A different perspective would decry the fact that in this supposedly tolerant and enlightened era, 15 percent of white survey respondents could not bring themselves to say they would vote for a qualified black candidate.

In neither example can we assign a single correct meaning to the data. Instead, the interpretation one chooses will be a function of individual values and beliefs, and purposes in analyzing the survey. This is demonstrated in an analysis of two national surveys on gun control, one sponsored by the National Rifle Association (NRA) and conducted by Decision/Making/ Information, Inc., and the other sponsored by the Center for the Study and Prevention of Handgun Violence and conducted by Cambridge Reports, Inc. (pollster Patrick Caddell's firm). Although the statistical results from both surveys were comparable, the two reports arrived at substantially different conclusions. The NRA's analysis concluded:

> Majorities of American voters believe that we do *not* need more laws governing the possession and use of firearms and that more firearms laws would *not* result in a decrease in the crime rate. (Wright 1981, 25)

In contrast, the center's report stated:

> It is clear that the vast majority of the public (both those who live with handguns and those who do not) want handgun licensing and registration. . . . The American public wants some form of handgun control legislation. (Wright 1981, 25)

Wright carefully analyzed the evidence cited in support of each conclusion and found that

> the major difference between the two reports is not in the findings, but in what is said about or concluded about the findings: what aspects of the evidence are emphasized or de-emphasized, what interpretation is given to a finding, and what implications are drawn from the findings about the need, or lack thereof, for stricter weapons controls. (Wright 1981, 38)

In essence, it was the interpretation of the data that generated the difference in the recommendations.

Two polls on tax reform provide another example of how poll data can be selectively interpreted and reported (Sussman 1985a). The first poll was sponsored by the insurance industry and was conducted by pollster Burns Roper. Its main conclusion, reported in a press conference announcing the poll results, was that 77 percent of the American public "said that workers should not be taxed on employee benefits" and that only 15 percent supported such a tax, a conclusion very reassuring to the insurance industry. However, Roper included other items in the poll that the insurance industry chose not to emphasize. As Sussman points out, the 77 percent opposed to the taxing of fringe benefits were then asked, "Would you still oppose counting the value of employee benefits as taxable income for employees if the additional tax revenues went directly to the reduction of federal budget deficits and not into new spending?" Twenty-six percent were no longer opposed to taxing fringe benefits under this condition, bringing the overall opposition down to 51 percent of the sample.

A second follow-up question asked, "Would you still oppose counting the value of employee benefits as taxable income for employees if the additional tax revenues permitted an overall reduction of tax rates for individuals?" (a feature that was part of the Treasury Department's initial tax proposals). Now only 33 percent of the sample was opposed to taxing fringes, 50 percent supported it, and 17 percent were undecided. Thus, depending upon which results one used, one could show a majority of citizens supportive of or opposed to taxing fringe benefits.

The other poll that Sussman analyzed also tapped people's reactions to the Treasury Department's tax proposal. A number of questions in the survey demonstrated public hostility to the Treasury proposal. One item read:

> The Treasury Department has proposed changing the tax system. Three tax brackets would be created, but most current deductions from income would be eliminated. Non-federal income taxes and property taxes would not be deductible, and many deductions would be limited. Do you favor or oppose this proposal? (Sussman 1985a)

Not surprisingly, 57 percent opposed the Treasury plan, and only 27 percent supported it. But as Sussman points out, the question is highly selective and leading since it focuses on changes in the tax system that hurt the taxpayer. For example, nowhere does it inform the respondent that a key part of the Treasury plan was to reduce existing tax rates so that 80 percent of Americans would be paying either the same amount or less in taxes than they were paying before. Clearly, this survey was designed to obtain a set of results compatible with the sponsor's policy objectives.

Weighting the Sample

As explained in chapter 4, samples are selected to be representative of the population from which they are drawn. Sometimes adjustments must be made to a sample before analyzing and reporting results. These adjustments may be made for substantive reasons or because of biases in the characteristics of the selected sample. An example of the former is pollsters' attempts to determine who the likely voters will be and to base their election predictions not on the entire sample but on a subset of likely voters.

To correct for biases, weights can be used so that the sample's demographic characteristics more accurately reflect the population's overall properties. Because sampling and interviewing involve statistics and probability theory as well as logistical problems of contacting respondents, the sample may contain too few blacks, or too few men, or too few people in the youngest age category. Assuming that one knows the true population proportions for sex, race, and age, one can adjust the sample by the use of weights to bring its numbers into line with the overall population values. For example, if females constitute 60 percent of the sample but 50 percent of the overall population, one might weight each female respondent by five-sixths, thereby reducing the percentage of females in the sample to 50 percent (five-sixths times 60 percent).

A 1986 *Columbus Dispatch* preelection poll on the gubernatorial preferences of Ohioans illustrates the consequences of weighting. In August 1986 the *Dispatch* sent a mail questionnaire to a sample of Ohioans selected from the statewide list of registered voters. The poll showed that incumbent Democratic governor Richard Celeste was leading former GOP governor James Rhodes, 48 percent to 43 percent, with independent candidate and former Democratic mayor of Cleveland Dennis Kucinich receiving 9 percent; an undecided alternative was not provided to respondents (Curtin 1986a). Fortunately, the *Dispatch* report of its poll included the sample size for each category (unlike the practice of the national media). One table presented to the reader showed the following relationship between political party affiliation and gubernatorial vote preference (Curtin 1986b):

Gubernatorial preference	Democrat	Republican	Independent
Celeste	82%	14%	33%
Rhodes	9	81	50
Kucinich	9	5	17
Total %	100	100	100
(*N*)	(253)	(245)	(138)

Given the thrust of the news story that Celeste was ahead, 48 percent to 43 percent, the numbers in the table were surprising, because Rhodes was running almost as well among Republicans as Celeste was among Democrats, and Rhodes had a substantial lead among independents. Because the *N*'s were provided, one could calculate the actual number of Celeste, Rhodes, and Kucinich votes in the sample as follows:

Celeste votes = .82(253) + .14(245) + .33(138) = 287
Rhodes votes = .09(253) + .81(245) + .50(138) = 291
Kucinich votes = .09(253) + .05(245) + .17(138) = 58

Calculating percentages from these totals shows Rhodes slightly *ahead*, 46 percent to 45 percent, rather than trailing. At first I thought there was a mistake in the poll or in the party affiliation and gubernatorial vote preference. In rereading the news story, however, I learned that the sample had been weighted. The reporter wrote, "Results were adjusted, or weighted, slightly to compensate for demographic differences between poll respondents and the Ohio electorate as a whole" (Curtin 1986b). The reporter did inform the reader that the data were weighted, but nowhere did he say that the adjustment affected who was ahead in the poll.

The adjustment probably was statistically valid since the poll respondents did not seem to include sufficient numbers of women and blacks, two groups that were more supportive of the Democratic gubernatorial candidate. However, nowhere in the news story was any specific information provided on how the weighting was done. This example illustrates that weighting can be consequential, and it is probably typical in terms of the scant information provided to citizens about weighting procedures.

When Polls Conflict: A Concluding Example

Because of the variety of factors that can influence poll results and their subsequent interpretation, it is helpful to review them. Useful vehicles for this endeavor are the preelection polls in the 1980, 1984, 1988, and

1992 presidential elections, polls that were often highly inconsistent. For example, in the 1984 election, polls conducted at comparable times yielded highly dissimilar results. A Harris poll had Reagan leading Mondale by nine percentage points, an ABC News/*Washington Post* poll had Reagan ahead by twelve points, a CBS News/*New York Times* survey had Reagan leading by thirteen points, a *Los Angeles Times* poll gave Reagan a seventeen-point lead, and an NBC News poll had the president ahead by twenty-five points (Oreskes 1984). In September 1988, seven different polls on presidential preference were released within a three-day period with results ranging from Bush ahead by eight points to a Dukakis lead of six (Morin 1988d). In 1992, ten national polls conducted in the latter part of August showed Clinton with leads over Bush ranging from 5 to 19 percent (Elving 1992). How can polls on an ostensibly straightforward topic such as presidential vote preference differ so widely? Many reasons can be cited, some obvious and others more subtle in their effects.

Among the more subtle reasons are the method of interviewing and the number of callbacks that a pollster uses to contact respondents who initially were unavailable. According to Lewis and Schneider (1982, 43), Patrick Caddell and George Gallup in their 1980 polls found that President Reagan received less support from respondents interviewed personally than from those queried over the telephone. Their speculation about this finding was that weak Democrats who were going to desert Carter found it easier to admit this in a telephone interview than in a face-to-face situation.

With respect to callbacks, Dolnick (1984) reports that one reason a Harris poll was closer than others in predicting Reagan's sizable victory in 1980 was that it made repeated callbacks, which at each stage "turned up increasing numbers of well-paid, well-educated Republican-leaning voters." A similar situation occurred in 1984. Traugott (1987) found that persistence in callbacks resulted in a more Republican sample, speculating that Republicans were less likely to have been at home or available initially.

Some of the more obvious factors that help account for differences among compared polls are question wording and question placement. Some survey items mention the presidential and vice-presidential candidates, while others mention only the former. Some pollsters ask follow-up questions of undecided voters to ascertain whether they lean toward one candidate or another; others do not. And as noted in chapter 3, question order can influence responses. Normally, incumbents and better known candidates do better when the question on vote intention is asked at the beginning of the survey rather than later. If vote intention is measured after a series of issue and problem questions have been asked, respondents may have been reminded of shortcomings in the incumbent's record and may therefore be less willing to express support for the incumbent.

Summary of Polling Methodology

Designing a "perfect" poll is a bit like creating the "perfect" spaghetti sauce: all cooks start with tomatoes, but each uses his own favorite combination of seasonings—sometimes with widely varied results. Presented below are the ingredients that went into the survey designs of four major national polling organizations this past election year. . . .

CBS/New York Times*

Population sampled from: National adult population telephone survey.
Household selection: Random digit dialing. Up to four attempts to contact household.
Respondent selection: Random selection, appointment made if designated respondent not at home.
Weighting: To correct for household size and to reflect demographics.
Identification of electorate: "Likelihood weight" based on past voting behavior and current intention and reported behavior of similar groups in 1976.
Actual choice: Choice among three major candidates, labeled by party. Leaners included in reported distributions.
Adjustments: None.

Gallup*

Population sampled from: Registered Voters. In-person interviews.
Household selection: Households randomly selected from sample precincts. No callbacks.
Respondent selection: Systematic selection based on age and sex.
Weighting: To correct for "times at home" and to reflect demographics.
Identification of electorate: "Likely voters" identified based on past behavior, interest, and intention to vote, and expected turnout.
Actual choice: "Secret ballot" for tickets, labeled by party. Undecided asked to mark ballot based on leaning.
Adjustments: Undecideds allocated; figures corrected for deviation of sample precincts from national results in 1976.

ABC/Harris*

Population sampled from: Expected electorate (based on 1976). Series of telephone surveys.
Household selection: Random digit dialing. Households not reached retained for one more survey.
Respondent selection: Systematic selection by modified sex quota.
Weighting: To reflect demographics.
Identification of electorate: "Likely voters" identified based on past behavior and intention to vote, and expected turnout.
Actual choice: Choice among three major candidates, labeled by party. Leaners included in reported distributions.*

Adjustments: Survey results from last 12 days combined. (No day-to-day differences noted.) Undecided allocated evenly between Carter and Reagan.

NBC/AP*

Population sampled from: National adult population. Telephone survey.
Household selection: Random digit dialing. No callbacks (except for "busies").
Respondent selection: Systematic selection based on sex quota.
Weighting: None. Sample deemed "self-weighting."
Identification of electorate: "Likely voters" identified based on past behavior, interest, and intention to vote.
Actual choice: Choice among three major candidates, labeled by party (following questions on open-ended preferences and whether respondents had made up minds).
Adjustments: None.

Glossary

National adult population. The sample is designed to reflect the characteristics, including geographic distribution, of the entire adult population.
Registered voters. The same, but the population is registered voters, instead of all adults.
Electorate. The same, but the actual electorate—i.e. taking differential turnout on a geographic basis into account.
Random digit dialing. Procedures giving households (both listed and unlisted numbers) a fair chance to be reached.
Callbacks. Multiple attempts to reach a household.
Random selection. Procedures to give each potential respondent in a household a random chance to come into the sample.
Systematic selection. Selection according to same system, depriving the interviewer of the choice of respondent.
Likelihood weight. An estimate of how likely someone is to vote. Someone who is 80 percent likely will count twice as much in the final figures as someone only 40 percent.
Likely voters. An attempt to separate respondents into two groups: "likely voters" and "non-likely voters." Only the former enter into the reported distributions.
Allocation. Division of the undecided based on other information, such as their partisan preference, issue positions, or data from other surveys.*

Note: This overview cannot capture the full details of procedures used—for example what precise "demographics" were used.

* AP conducted a survey on its own following the last joint survey.

Source: Everett C. Ladd and G. Donald Ferree, "Were the Pollsters Really Wrong?" *Public Opinion,* vol. 3, no. 6 (December/January 1981): 18. Reprinted with permission of American Enterprise Institute for Public Policy Research.

There can be differences among comparable polls in how the sample is selected and how it is treated for analytical purposes. Some polls sample registered voters; others query adult Americans. There are also differences in the methods used to identify likely voters, as discussed in chapter 7. As Lipset (1980) points out, the greater the number of respondents who are screened out of the sample because they do not seem to be likely voters, the more likely it is that the remaining respondents will be relatively more Republican in their vote preferences. Some samples are weighted to guarantee demographic representativeness; others are not.

It is also possible that discrepancies among polls are not due to any of these above factors, but may simply reflect statistical fluctuations. For example, if one poll with a 4 percent sampling error shows Reagan ahead of Mondale, 52 percent to 43 percent, this result is statistically congruent with other polls that might have a very narrow Reagan lead of 48 percent to 47 percent or other polls that show a landslide Reagan lead of 56 percent to 39 percent.

The box on pages 160 and 161 summarizes some of the major features of the 1980 election polls. The summary makes clear that many factors affect the data reported by the media, even when the readers or viewers are not given information about them. In considering the array of influences listed in the box one must also factor in the values and goals of the public opinion analyst. As we have shown in this chapter, the interpretation of poll data can be a highly subjective enterprise that is affected not only by a poll's design, but by the perspective and the intentions of the investigator.

9 Advice to Poll Consumers

It's very clear
The polls are here to stay;
Not for a year,
But ever and a day.

The interviews and the questionnaires
And the pollsters that we know
Aren't just passing fancies—
Oh, my goodness, no!

The media
Love polls in every way.
It matters not
If polls have scant to say.

In time statistics may numb you,
Results may stun you.
Wait for another day,
For—the polls are here to stay.
—with apologies to George Gershwin

To death and taxes should be added public opinion polls, an integral and unavoidable part of American society today. Public opinion polling is a contemporary manifestation of classical democratic theory; it attests to the ability of the rational and wise citizen to make informed judgments on the major issues of the day. Polling makes it possible for political organizations to demonstrate that public opinion is on their side as they promote their ends. Polling is also enamored by news organizations, in part because polls seem to elevate the citizen (and thus the media audience) into a more prominent political role; in effect, the polls transform the amorphous citizenry into a unified actor in the political process. Poll results that are not supportive of government actions provide the media with stories of conflict between the government and the people, just as points of contention between the president and the Congress or between the House and the Senate become a media focus.

As the technology of polling has been continually refined, upgraded, and made more available, many institutions, organizations, and private groups have gained the ability to sponsor and conduct polls. These organizations can readily hire pollsters for surveys that will promote their aims, or, if they want to be absolutely sure that the poll results will be favorable, they can conduct their own surveys. Such self-serving polls are replete with loaded questions, skewed samples, and faulty interpretations similar to the surveys done by the Tobacco Institute and by the Michigan Tobacco and Candy Distributors and Vendors Association to try to head off higher cigarette taxes and antismoking legislation (Morin 1989a; Perlstadt and Holmes 1987).

Adding to the proliferation of surveys, the major news organizations have heavily invested in their own in-house polling operations. The resulting increase in the number of polls they conduct justifies their investment and enables them to keep up with the competition. That is, for certain news stories, such as presidential debates, a news organization that fails to conduct and report a poll on who wins is open to the criticism of incomplete news coverage. The unseemly contest among the media to be the first to "call" the outcome of particular elections illustrates how the pressures of competition and ratings promote the widespread use of polls. The media operate under the assumption that the public reactions to major news events are meaningful and that public opinion polls enhance the news value of a story.

How to Evaluate Polls: A Summary

Polls are a significant way for citizens to participate in society and to become informed about the relationship between the decisions of government and the opinions of the citizenry. As more organizations conduct polls and disseminate their results, whether to inform or to sway public opinion, citizens should become wary consumers, sensitive to the factors that can affect poll results. Gaining this sensitivity does not require familiarity with statistics or survey research experience. Consumers need only treat polls with a healthy skepticism and keep in mind the following questions as tools to evaluate poll results.

One basic question poll consumers should ask is whether a public opinion survey is measuring genuine opinions or nonattitudes. Are respondents likely to be informed and have genuine opinions about the topic? Or is

Doonesbury

BY GARRY TRUDEAU

DOONESBURY copyright 1989 by G. B. Trudeau.
Reprinted with permission of Universal Press Syndicate. All rights reserved.

the focus so esoteric that their responses reflect the social pressures of the interview situation, pressures that cause respondents to provide answers even when they have no real views on the subject at hand? The answers to questions about nonattitudes are not easy to find, for as W. Russell Neuman (1986) argues, there is often not a clear demarcation between attitudes and nonattitudes. Indeed, Neuman coined the term *quasi-attitude* to designate something between an attitude and a nonattitude, and he points out that citizens' responses to survey questions are "a mixture of carefully thought-out, stable opinions, half-hearted opinions, misunderstandings, and purely random responses" (Neuman 1986, 184).

Another question to consider when evaluating polls concerns screening. Have the researchers made any effort to screen out respondents who lack genuine attitudes on the topic? Unfortunately, reports frequently omit information about prior screening questions and their effects. Often one cannot tell what proportion of the total sample has answered a particular item and what proportion has been screened out. To do a better job of reporting this information, news organizations should, at minimum, provide the number of respondents who answered a particular question. When this number is substantially smaller than the total sample size, they should explain the discrepancy.

When screening information is not presented, citizens are forced to form impressionistic judgments about whether the measurement of nonattitudes has been a problem in the survey. Of course, some issues of public policy that have been hotly debated and contested by political elites, even issues such as tax reform, may not be of much interest to many Americans and thus may be highly susceptible to the measurement of nonattitudes.

Citizens are in a better position to evaluate the potential effects of question wording than the presence of nonattitudes. Because the media usually provide the actual wording of questions, citizens can judge whether any words or phrases in the questions are blatantly loaded, whether the alternatives are presented in a fair and balanced fashion, and whether a question accurately reflects the topic under study. If a report of a survey omits question wording, particularly on items dealing with controversial issues, the consumer should be wary and ask why.

Question wording is just one reason a complete questionnaire should be made available with a survey report. A complete questionnaire is also helpful when a survey contains many questions on a topic but reports the results for only one or two items. Without the complete questionnaire, a poll consumer is unable to assess whether the selective release of results has created any misleading impressions.

Another reason to examine the entire questionnaire is to assess the potential effects of question order. This is seldom possible, since press releases (other than those issued by news organizations) and news stories rarely include the complete survey form. However, it is important for citizens to be aware that the way earlier questions are asked can affect responses to subsequent queries. This is a subtle phenomenon for which most citizens have little intuitive feel, yet the strategic placement of questions is one of the most effective ways to "doctor" a survey. While each individual question may be balanced and fair, the overall order of the questions may stimulate specific responses preferred by the sponsor of the survey. One clue that this problem exists is the refusal of an organization, such as a political campaign team, to release the entire poll results.

The next question consumers should address is sampling. Although it is the most mysterious part of polling for most poll consumers, sampling is probably the least important for them to understand in detail. Sampling error is *not* where polls typically go astray. Reputable pollsters pick good samples and typically report sampling error and confidence level so that citizens can form independent judgments about the significance of results. To make sure that a sample properly reflects the aims of a poll, a poll consumer should pay close attention to how a sample is defined. And certainly the consumer should confirm that a sample is a scientifically selected probability sample rather than a purposive sample that an investigator selected for reasons of convenience.

One aspect of sampling that citizens should not overlook is the proportion of the total sample to which a particular finding applies. For a variety of reasons, such as the use of screening questions or the need to study analytically interesting subsets of the original sample, the proportion of respondents on which a result is based may be substantially smaller than the overall sample. Thus, one should know not only the sampling error of the total sample, but also the sampling error of the subsets.

As consumers evaluate polls, they also need to be aware that interviewers and interviewing are aspects of polling that can influence outcomes, but they are aspects that are not easily questioned. It is almost impossible for citizens to evaluate the effects of interviewing on poll results because reports usually provide too little information about the interviewing process beyond the method of interviewing (for example, telephone or personal) and the dates of the interviews. The poll consumer must normally assume that an interview was performed competently, undoubtedly a safe assumption with reputable polling firms. But consumers should note that an interviewer with the intention of generating biased responses has many opportunities to achieve that end while asking questions. The best way for the poll consumer to gain some sense of potential interviewer effects is to be a poll respondent who carefully observes the performance of the inter-viewer — an opportunity that may or may not come one's way.

The final questions to ask when evaluating a poll relate to the end products, analyses and interpretation. Most citizens do not have access to raw poll data; instead they must rely upon the analyses and interpreta-tions provided by the media and other sources. Therefore, poll consumers need to ask whether a source is likely to have a vested interest in a particular poll outcome. If so, they should scrutinize poll results even more carefully. For example, a poll sponsored by the insurance industry purporting to demonstrate that the liability insurance crisis is due to the rapacious behavior of trial lawyers should be viewed with greater skepticism than a similar poll sponsored by an organization with a less direct interest in the outcome. Likewise, election poll results released by a candidate should be viewed more cautiously than those released by a respected news organization.

After evaluating the source of a poll, the consumer then faces the more difficult task of ascertaining whether the pollster's conclusions follow from the data. This task is problematical because often, as noted previously, only a portion of the relevant evidence is presented in a news story or press release. Or a poll may have included many items on a particular topic, yet the report may present only a subset of those items. Without knowledge of the total questionnaire, one can only hope that the analyst has reported a representative set of results, or speculate on how different items on the same topic might have yielded different results. Likewise, reports might include results from the entire sample, but not important variations in the responses of subsets of the sample. Lacking direct access to the data, the citizen is left to ponder how the overall results might differ within subsets of respondents.

The interpretation of a poll is not an automatic, objective enterprise; different analysts examining the same polling data may come to different conclusions. Although this may occur for a variety of reasons, an obvious one is that analysts bring different values and perspectives to the interpretation of polls. Often there are no objective standards on what constitutes a high or low level of support on an issue; it may indeed be partly cloudy or partly sunny depending upon one's perspective. Hence, poll consumers should ask themselves a fundamental question — whether they would necessarily come to the same conclusions on the basis of the data that have been presented. Just because the poll is sponsored by a prestigious organization and conducted by a reputable firm does not mean that one has to defer automatically to the substantive conclusions of the sponsors. And if a poll is conducted by an organization with an obvious vested interest in the results, then the poll consumer is certainly warranted in making an independent judgment.

Polls and Their Effect on the Political System

Do polls promote or hinder citizens' influence in their society? Is the overall effect of the polls on the political system positive or negative? These questions continue to be vigorously debated. Writing in 1940, Cherington argued that polls enhanced the public's influence since they provided a way for the voices of a representative cross-section of Americans to be heard; no longer would the views of a tiny segment of the population be the only ones to gain prominence. Meyer (1940) further argued that the polls provided political decision makers with accurate information about the preferences of the citizenry, thereby enabling political leaders to resist the pressures of narrow groups pushing their own special agenda in the name of the broader public.

The preceding arguments are still true today, yet the limitations inherent in polls as a mode of citizen influence must be recognized. First of all, as discussed in chapter 1, the United States is a representative democracy that includes, in addition to elected representatives, a wide variety of organized groups trying to promote their own interests. Any assumption that the results of public opinion polls can be translated directly into public policy is naive. Moreover, it might not be desirable if public opinion polls were routinely translated into public policy. After all, polls at times may tap only the most ephemeral and transitory of opinions. Little deliberation and thought may have gone into the responses offered by the public. And certainly the rich complexities of issues can never be captured in a public opinion poll as well as they can be in a legislative debate or a committee hearing.

Second, even if the public's views as reflected in the polls were well formed, the implementation of those views might be objectionable. Polling

ROB ROGERS reprinted by permission of UFS, Inc.

often demonstrates that there is no majority view on an issue; opinion may be split in many different ways. The problem then becomes one of determining which subset of public opinion merits adoption. But automatically opting for the majority or plurality position would call into question such cherished values as the protection of minority rights. One can envisage situations in which the unqualified use of public opinion polls might threaten rather than enhance representative democracy and related values.

Third, a focus on poll results ignores the processes by which the public's opinions are formed and modified. For example, one factor that shapes popular opinion is the behavior of political elites. Thus, when the White House orchestrates a massive public relations campaign laden with a nationally televised presidential address, subsequent highly publicized presidential travels, and the submission of a legislative package to Congress, it is not surprising to see public opinion shift in the direction intended by the White House. Public opinion is not always an independent expression of the public's views; it can be an opinion that has been formed, at least in part, from manipulation by elites.

Sometimes the behavior of political elites initiates a shift in opinion, and sometimes the behavior is the result of a shift. For example, the president may take the lead on an unpopular issue, as typically occurs during an international crisis. After the president delivers a major address to the nation, public opinion polls usually indicate an upsurge of support for the president's actions emerging from feelings of patriotism and a desire for national unity in times of crisis. Such was the case with the Persian Gulf crisis that arose in 1990.

In reverse, the president may scramble to catch up with and then shape public opinion. This happened in the summer and fall of 1986 in response to Americans' heightened concern about the drug abuse problem. With the tragic deaths of famous athletes and increased media coverage of the drug crisis, a CBS News/*New York Times* poll conducted in August 1986 showed that a plurality of Americans cited drugs as the nation's most important problem (Clymer 1986d). Congress, particularly House Democrats, trying to get out in front on this issue, proposed a major antidrug offensive. The White House responded by taking the initiative from Congress: President Reagan offered his own proposals, and he and the first lady gave an unprecedented joint address on national television. Major new legislation was passed to address the drug problem. Then, in 1989 President Bush declared a war on drugs and named a drug czar to coordinate federal initiatives. The president announced many antidrug proposals, which, according to the polls, were supported overwhelmingly by Americans even though they felt strongly that Bush's plan did not go far enough.

What do the preceding examples have to say about citizen influence? Certainly, the drug example suggests the potency of popular opinion on issues that arouse the public. But even here the salience of the issue was very much a function of the behavior of media and political elites who brought it to the fore; the public responded to the issue, but did not create it. The adoption of antidrug measures into law suggests that public opinion, once aroused, spurs government policy initiatives. But when the media and political leaders stop talking about drugs, the issue becomes less salient and recedes from popular consciousness, and citizens may have a misguided feeling that somehow the problem has been resolved. Certainly the prominence of the crime issue in the 1994 elections was due in part to the skillful exploitation of the issue by the candidates and the heavy media emphasis on the topic.

The Persian Gulf example raises a different problem — namely, elites' misinterpretation (deliberate or unintentional) of what the polls are actually saying. Unfortunately, political leaders sometimes fail to recognize the limitations and circumstances of poll responses and automatically construe supportive poll results as ringing endorsements of a broad policy agenda. The tendency of Americans to rally around the leadership of the president during an international crisis should not be blindly interpreted as a popular mandate for particular policies, even though in the case of the Persian Gulf crisis, citizen support for the president's policies at each stage of the crisis was genuine.

Ginsberg (1986) has argued that polling weakens the influence of public opinion in a democratic society. He asserts that there are many ways besides participating in a poll for citizens to express their opinions, such as demonstrations and protests, letter-writing campaigns, and interest group activities. But because polling is deemed to be scientific and representative of the broad public, it has dominated these other types of expression.

Ginsberg identifies four basic changes in the nature of public opinion that are attributable to the increased frequency of polling. First, responding to a public opinion survey is an easier form of expression than writing a letter or participating in a protest—activities usually performed by citizens who are intensely committed to their positions. Anyone can respond to a poll question, whether or not the feelings about an issue are strong. Hence, in a public opinion poll the intense opinions of a small minority can be submerged by the indifferent views of the sizable majority. Indeed, government leaders may try to dismiss the views of dissidents by citing polls that indicate that most Americans do not support their position.

Second, polling changes public opinion from a *behavior*, such as letter writing or demonstrating, to an *attitude*, as revealed in a verbal response to a poll question. Ginsberg argues that public opinion expressed through polls is less threatening to political elites than are opinions expressed through behavioral mechanisms. Moreover, polls can inform leaders about dissidents' attitudes before they become behaviors. The information on attitudes gives government a form of early warning as well as an opportunity to change attitudes either by seeking remedies to problems or by relying on public relations techniques to manipulate opinions.

Third, polls convert public opinion from a characteristic of groups to an attribute of individuals. This enables public officials to ignore group leaders and instead to attend directly to the opinions of citizens. Unfortunately, this attention may effectively weaken individuals' political power because organized activity, not individual activity, is the key to citizen influence in the United States. If government leaders are able to use the polls as an excuse to ignore group preferences, then citizen influence will be lessened.

Finally, polling reduces citizens' opportunities to set the political agenda. The topics of public opinion polls are those selected by the polls' sponsors rather than by the citizenry. Therefore, citizens lose control over the agenda of issues, and the agenda as revealed through the polls may differ in major ways from the issues that really matter to people.

Ginsberg's fundamental conclusion is that polling makes public opinion safer and less threatening for government. Opinions expressed through the polls place fewer demands and constraints on decision makers and provide political leaders with an enhanced ability "to anticipate, regulate, and manipulate popular attitudes" (Ginsberg 1986, 85). In short, Ginsberg's thesis is that the advent and growth of public opinion polling have been detrimental to citizen influence.

Ginsberg has raised some important issues about potential dangers inherent in the increased amount of public opinion polling, even if one does not agree with all of his conclusions. Clearly, we must be on guard against allowing public opinion to become synonymous with the results of public opinion polls. Public opinion manifests itself in many ways, including those Ginsberg mentioned — protests, letter-writing campaigns, direct personal contact with decision makers, and many others. Political elites recognize the potential costs of ignoring these alternative forms of political expression, but it is critical that the media also recognize that polls are not the only legitimate expression of public opinion. We too must avoid allowing a passive activity such as responding to a poll to replace more active modes of political participation.

Although there is evidence that direct electoral participation has declined in the United States, other group-based activities are on the rise. And if groups have the resources, they can use polls to promote their agenda when it differs from that of the political elites. And, contrary to Ginsberg's assertion, polls need not make public opinion a property of individuals rather than groups. Polls can identify clusters of citizens (often defined by demographic characteristics) who do not share the prevailing views of the citizenry at large. Whether Ginsberg's concerns are overstated or not, the polls are playing an increasing role in American political life, in campaigns, in governance, and in popular discourse.

Observers have been concerned about the effect of polls not only on citizens' political clout but also on the performance of elected officeholders. More than forty years ago Bernays (1945) warned that the polls would dominate the political leadership, and that decision makers would slavishly follow the polls in order to please the people and maintain their popularity. The polls might even paralyze political leaders, preventing them from taking unpopular positions and from trying to educate the public on controversial issues. Political observers like Bernays still contemptuously deride politicians who run around with polls in their pockets, lacking the courage to act on their own convictions no matter what the polls say.

Some officeholders do blindly follow the polls, but today the greater concern is over those who use, abuse, manipulate, and misinterpret them. In particular, presidents have increasingly tried to manage and manipulate public opinion. For example, Altschuler (1986) describes how President Johnson tried to take the offensive when his poll ratings began to decline.

To convince key elites that he was still strong, Johnson attacked the public polls, selectively leaked private polls, and tried to influence poll results and poll reporting by cultivating the acquaintance of the pollsters.

The Reagan presidency developed one of the most skillful public relations efforts; in-house polling was a central part of the enterprise (Blumenthal 1981). Writing about the Reagan administration, Beal and Hinckley (1984) argued that polls became more important after the presidential election than before it, that polls were a much more important tool of governing than was commonly recognized. Likewise, polling is central to the operation of the Clinton White House. Certainly, no one would deny the president and other elected officials their pollsters. But the measure of an incumbent's performance should not simply be the degree of success achieved in shaping public opinion in particular ways.

One final effect of polls on the political system merits consideration — namely, the contribution of polls to political discourse. Whether as topics of conversation or more structured exchange, the polls contribute to political debate. And because they often are cited as evidence in support of particular positions, they become a central part of political discussion. But polls have more subtle effects; in particular, Americans' awareness of the attitudes of their fellow citizens as learned through the polls may alter their opinions and subsequent behaviors. This phenomenon has been explained in terms of the theories of the spiral of silence and pluralistic ignorance.

The spiral of silence thesis, developed by Noelle-Neuman (1974, 1977), argues that individuals desire to be respected and popular. To accomplish this, they become sensitive to prevailing opinions and how they are changing. If individuals observe that their opinions seem to be in the minority and are losing support, they are less likely to express them publicly. Consequently, such opinions will seem to the individuals to be weaker than they actually are. On the other hand, if people perceive that their views are popular and on the ascendance, they are more likely to discuss them openly. Such opinions then gain more adherents and seem stronger than they actually are. Thus, one opinion becomes established as dominant, while the other recedes to the background. Pluralistic ignorance (O'Gorman 1975; O'Gorman and Garry 1976-1977) refers to people's misperception of what other individuals and groups believe. This, in turn, affects their own views and their willingness to express them. Lang and Lang (1984) link the notions of pluralistic ignorance and the spiral of silence in a discussion of American racial attitudes:

> Typical of pluralistic ignorance has been the unwillingness of many whites to acknowledge their own antiblack prejudice, which they

Reprinted by permission of UFS, Inc.

believe to contradict an accepted cultural ideal. As a way of justifying their own behavior, these whites often attribute such prejudice to other whites by saying "I wouldn't mind having a black neighbor except that my neighbors wouldn't stand for it."

But what if such fears about their neighbors' reactions proved unjustified? What if polls showed an expressed readiness for a range of desegregation measures that these whites do not believe others are prepared to accept? Such a finding contrary to prevailing belief would be controversial. Where the real opinion lies may be less important than the change in perception of the climate of opinion. A definitive poll finding can destroy the premise that underlies the justification for behavior clearly at variance with professed ideals. In these circumstances a spiral of silence about the real opinion fosters a climate inhospitable to segregationist sentiment and drives it underground. (Lang and Lang 1984, 141)

As this example illustrates, public opinion polls provide us with a mechanism for knowing what our fellow citizens think and believe. If the polls can accurately measure the underlying beliefs and values of the citizenry, then we no longer have to be at the mercy of unrepresentative views that mistakenly are thought of as the majority voice. The polls can tell us a lot about ourselves as part of American society, and this self-knowledge may foster a healthier and more open political debate.

Conclusion

As the "Peanuts" cartoon above makes clear, Americans have ambivalent feelings about the polls. We resent the polls when they become too intrusive and seem to be telling us what we will be doing even before we do it. Yet we are also fascinated by what the polls tell us about ourselves. We are suspicious because we seldom are respondents in a poll, yet we readily cite the surveys conducted by reputable and even disreputable pollsters. We complain about the pervasiveness of polls, yet are apt to raise questions that can be answered only by polls.

Perhaps this ambivalence arises out of our uncertainty about just what goes into a poll. Polls are called scientific, yet we know that they are sometimes wrong. Politicians on one day swear by the polls, while on the next day they swear at them. Clearly we are in a better position to evaluate polls if we understand the factors that can affect poll results. Thus, the aim of this book has been to remove the mystery of public opinion research and to help the consumer come to terms with polls. Only then can citizens master the polls rather than be mastered by them.

References

Abrams, Floyd. 1985. "Press Practices, Polling Restrictions, Public Opinion and First Amendment Guarantees." *Public Opinion Quarterly* 49 (spring): 15-18.

Abramson, Paul R., Brian D. Silver, and Barbara Anderson. 1987. "The Effects of Question Order in Attitude Surveys: The Case of the SRC/CPS Citizen Duty Items." *American Journal of Political Science* 31 (November): 900-908.

————. 1990. "The Decline of Overtime Comparability in the National Election Studies." *Public Opinion Quarterly* 54 (summer): 177-190.

Akron Beacon Journal. 1994. "Foreign Poll-icy." Editorial, 8 May, A14.

Aldrich, John H., Richard Niemi, George Rabinowitz, and David Rohde. 1982. "The Measurement of Public Opinion About Public Policy: A Report on Some New Issue Question Formats." *American Journal of Political Science* 26 (May): 391-414.

Alpern, David M. 1986. "A *Newsweek* Poll: Sex Laws." *Newsweek,* 14 July, 38.

Altschuler, Bruce E. 1986. "Lyndon Johnson and the Public Polls." *Public Opinion Quarterly* 50 (fall): 285-299.

Anderson, Barbara A., Brian D. Silver, and Paul R. Abramson. 1988a. "The Effects of Race of the Interviewer on Measures of Electoral Participation by Blacks in SRC National Election Studies." *Public Opinion Quarterly* 52 (spring): 53-83.

————. 1988b. "The Effects of the Race of the Interviewer on Race-Related Attitudes of Black Respondents in SRC/CPS National Election Studies." *Public Opinion Quarterly* 52 (fall): 289-324.

Apple, R. W. Jr. 1986. "President Highly Popular in Poll; No Ideological Shift Is Discerned." *New York Times,* 28 January, A-1, A-14.

Aquilino, William S. 1994. "Interview Mode Effects in Surveys of Drug and Alcohol Use." *Public Opinion Quarterly* 58 (summer): 210-240.

Aquilino, William S., and Leonard A. Losciuto. 1990. "Effects of Interview Mode on Self-Reported Drug Use." *Public Opinion Quarterly* 54 (fall): 362-395.

Asher, Herbert B. 1974a. "The Reliability of the Political Efficacy Items." *Political Methodology* 1 (May): 45-72.

_____. 1974b. "Some Consequences of Measurement Error in Survey Data." *American Journal of Political Science* 18 (May): 469-485.

_____. 1974c. "Some Problems in the Use of Multiple Indicators." Paper presented at the Conference on Design and Measurement Standards for Research in Political Science, Delevan, Wis., 13-15 May.

_____. 1992. *Presidential Elections and American Politics.* 5th ed. Pacific Grove, California: Brooks/Cole.

Baker, Russell. 1988. "Nearing Rope's End." *New York Times,* 9 November, 31.

_____. 1990. "Paralyzing Polls." *New York Times,* 4 April, A-15.

Balz, Dan. 1989. "About Those Predictions We Made Last Tuesday. . ." *Washington Post* National Weekly Edition, 13-19 November, 38.

Banaszak, Lee Ann, and Eric Plutzer. 1993. "The Social Bases of Feminism in the European Community." *Public Opinion Quarterly* 57 (spring): 348-357.

Barnes, James A. 1993. "Polls Apart." *National Journal* 25 (10 July): 1750-1754.

Baron, Alan. 1980. "The Slippery Art of Polls." *Politics Today* 7 (January/February): 21-24.

Bauman, Sandra, and Susan Herbst. 1994. "Managing Perceptions of Public Opinion: Candidates' and Journalists' Reactions to the 1992 Polls." *Political Communication* 11:133-144.

Baumgartner, Frank R., and Jack L. Walker. 1988. "Survey Research and Membership in Voluntary Associations." *American Journal of Political Science* 32 (November): 908-928.

Beal, Richard S., and Ronald H. Hinckley. 1984. "Presidential Decision Making and Opinion Polls." *Annals of the American Academy of Political and Social Science* 472 (March): 72-84.

Bernays, Edward L. 1945. "Attitude Polls—Servants or Masters?" *Public Opinion Quarterly* 9 (fall): 264-268b.

Bernick, E. Lee, and David J. Pratto. 1994. "Improving the Quality of Information in Mail Surveys: Use of Special Mailings." *Social Science Quarterly* 75 (March): 212-219.

Bisconti, Ann Stouffer. 1991. "Energy: Is There a Problem? Nuclear: Is It the Answer?" *The Public Perspective* 2 (January/February): 1-8.

Bishop, George F. 1987. "Experiments with the Middle Response Alternative in Survey Questions." *Public Opinion Quarterly* 51 (summer): 220-232.

_____. 1990. "Issue Involvement and Response Effects in Public Opinion Surveys." *Public Opinion Quarterly* 54 (summer): 209-218.

Bishop, George F., Robert W. Oldendick, and Alfred J. Tuchfarber. 1980. "Pseudo-Opinions on Public Affairs." *Public Opinion Quarterly* 44 (summer): 198-209.

_____. 1982. "Political Information Processing: Question Order and Context Effects." *Political Behavior* 4:177-200.

_____. 1984. "What Must My Interest in Politics Be If I Just Told You 'I Don't Know'?" *Public Opinion Quarterly* 48 (summer): 510-519.

Black, Joan S. 1991. "Presidential Address: Trashing the Polls." *Public Opinion Quarterly* 55 (fall): 474-481.

Blumenthal, Sidney. 1981. "Marketing the President." *New York Times Magazine*, 13 September, 110-118.

Boyer, Peter J. 1988. "Vow Aside, NBC Calls Winner Early." *New York Times*, 20 April, 16.

Broder, David S. 1982. "Daily Polls Helped GOP Keep Senate Edge." *Washington Post*, 7 November, 1.

———. 1984. "The Needless Exit-Polls Battle." *Washington Post* National Weekly Edition, 2 January, 4.

Broh, C. Anthony. 1980. "Horse-Race Journalism: Reporting the Polls in the 1976 Presidential Election." *Public Opinion Quarterly* 44 (winter): 514-529.

Buchwald, Art. 1987. "The Poll Watcher's Compendium." *Washington Post*, 20 August, C-1.

Busch, Ronald J., and Joel A. Lieske. 1985. "Does Time of Voting Affect Exit Poll Results?" *Public Opinion Quarterly* 49 (spring): 94-104.

Campbell, Bruce A. 1981. "Race-of-Interviewer Effects Among Southern Adolescents." *Public Opinion Quarterly* 45 (summer): 231-244.

Cherington, Paul T. 1940. "Opinion Polls as the Voice of Democracy." *Public Opinion Quarterly* 4 (June): 236-238.

Church, Allan H. 1993. "Estimating the Effect of Incentives on Mail Survey Response Rates: A Meta-Analysis." *Public Opinion Quarterly* 57 (spring): 62-79.

Clymer, Adam. 1985. "Pollsters Cite Surveys Indicating Confidence in Their Work." *New York Times*, 20 May, B-7.

———. 1986a. "Most Blacks Back Reagan, Poll Finds." *New York Times*, 5 January, 20.

———. 1986b. "One Issue That Seems To Defy a Yes or No." *New York Times*, 23 February, 22-E.

———. 1986c. "A Poll Finds 77% in U.S. Approve Raid on Libya." *New York Times*, 17 April, A-23.

———. 1986d. "Public Found Ready to Sacrifice in Drug Fight." *New York Times*, 2 September, D-16.

Columbus Dispatch. 1994a. "This Is How Dispatch Poll Was Conducted." 11 September, 5B.

———. 1994b. "Random Sampling of Voters Used to Create Gallup Survey." 25 September, 2C.

Converse, Jean M. 1976-1977. "Predicting No Opinion in the Polls." *Public Opinion Quarterly* 40 (winter): 515-530.

Converse, Philip E. 1970. "Attitudes and Nonattitudes: Continuation of a Dialogue." In *The Quantitative Analysis of Social Problems*, edited by Edward Tufte. Reading, Mass.: Addison-Wesley, 168-189.

Coombs, Clyde H., and Lolagene C. Coombs. 1976-1977. " 'Don't Know': Item Ambiguity or Respondent Uncertainty?" *Public Opinion Quarterly* 40 (winter): 497-514.

Cotter, Patrick R., Jeffrey Cohen, and Philip B. Coulter. 1982. "Race-of-Interviewer Effects on Telephone Interviews." *Public Opinion Quarterly* 46 (summer): 278-284.

Crespi, Irving. 1980. "Polls as Journalism." *Public Opinion Quarterly* 44 (winter): 462-476.

————. 1988. *Pre-Election Polling: Sources of Accuracy and Error.* New York: Russell Sage Foundation.

Crossley, Archibald M., and Helen M. Crossley. 1969. "Polling in 1968." *Public Opinion Quarterly* 33 (spring): 1-16.

Curtin, Michael. 1986a. "Celeste Leading Rhodes 48% to 43%, with Kucinich Trailing." *Columbus Dispatch*, 10 August, 1-A.

————. 1986b. "Here Is How Poll Was Taken." *Columbus Dispatch*, 10 August, 8-E.

Day, Richard, and Kurt M. Becker. 1984. "Preelection Polling in the 1982 Illinois Gubernatorial Contest." *Public Opinion Quarterly* 48 (fall): 606-614.

de Bock, Harold. 1976. "Influence of In-State Election Poll Reports on Candidate Preference in 1972." *Journalism Quarterly* 53 (autumn): 457-462.

Delli Carpini, Michael X. 1984. "Scooping the Voters? The Consequences of the Networks' Early Call of the 1980 Presidential Race." *The Journal of Politics* 46 (August): 866-885.

Delli Carpini, Michael X., and Scott Keeter. 1991. "Stability and Change in the U.S. Public's Knowledge of Politics." *Public Opinion Quarterly* 55 (winter): 583-612.

Dionne, E. J. Jr. 1980. "The Debate Decision Put Polls and Pollsters on the Firing Line." *New York Times*, 14 September, E-3.

Dolnick, Edward. 1984. "Pollsters Are Asking: What's Wrong." *Columbus Dispatch*, 19 August, C-1.

Dutka, Solomon. 1982. "Bringing Polls to Justice." *Public Opinion* 5 (October/November): 47-49.

Elving, Ronald D. 1989. "Proliferation of Opinion Data Sparks Debate over Use." *Congressional Quarterly Weekly Report*, 19 August, 2187-2192.

————. 1992. "Polls Confound and Confuse in This Topsy-Turvy Year." *Congressional Quarterly Weekly Report*, 12 September, 2725-2727.

Epstein, Laurily, and Gerald Strom. 1984. "Survey Research and Election Night Projections." *Public Opinion* 7 (February/March): 48-50.

Erikson, Robert S. 1976. "The Relationship Between Public Opinion and State Policy: A New Look Based on Some Forgotten Data." *American Journal of Political Science* 20 (February): 25-36.

————. 1993. "Counting Likely Voters in Gallup's Tracking Poll." *The Public Perspective* 4 (March/April): 22-23.

Eubank, Robert B., and David John Gow. 1983. "The Pro-Incumbent Bias in the 1978 and 1980 National Election Studies." *American Journal of Political Science* 27 (February): 122-139.

Faulkenberry, G. David, and Robert Mason. 1978. "Characteristics of Nonopinion and No Opinion Response Groups." *Public Opinion Quarterly* 42 (winter): 533-543.

Felson, Marcus, and Seymour Sudman. 1975. "The Accuracy of Presidential Preference Primary Polls." *Public Opinion Quarterly* 39 (summer): 232-236.

Finkel, Steven E., Thomas M. Guterbock, and Marian J. Borg. 1991. "Race-of-Interviewer Effects in a Preelection Poll: Virginia 1989." *Public Opinion Quarterly* 55 (fall): 313-330.

Fishkin, James. 1992. "A Response to Traugott." *The Public Perspective* 3 (May/June): 29-30.

———. 1994. "Britain Experiments with the Deliberative Poll." *The Public Perspective* 5 (July/August): 27-29.

Fletcher, Joseph F. 1989. "Mass and Elite Attitudes About Wiretapping in Canada: Implications for Democratic Theory and Politics." *Public Opinion Quarterly* 53 (summer): 225-245.

Fowler, Floyd Jackson Jr. 1992. "How Unclear Terms Affect Survey Data." *Public Opinion Quarterly* 56 (summer): 218-231.

Fox, Richard J., Melvin R. Crask, and Jonghoon Kim. 1988. "Mail Survey Response Rate: A Metaanalysis of Selected Techniques for Inducing Response." *Public Opinion Quarterly* 52 (winter): 467-491.

Frey, James H. 1983. *Survey Research by Telephone.* Beverly Hills, Calif.: Sage Publications.

Gallup, George. 1947. "The Quintamensional Plan of Question Design." *Public Opinion Quarterly* 11 (fall): 385-393.

———. 1965-1966. "Polls and the Political Process—Past, Present, and Future." *Public Opinion Quarterly* 29 (winter): 544-549.

Galtung, Johan. 1969. *Theory and Methods of Social Research.* New York: Columbia University Press.

Gawiser, Sheldon R., and G. Evans Witt. Undated. *Twenty Questions a Journalist Should Ask About Poll Results.* National Council on Public Polls.

Gilljam, Mikael, and Donald Granberg. 1993. "Should We Take Don't Know for an Answer?" *Public Opinion Quarterly* 57 (fall): 348-357.

Ginsberg, Benjamin. 1986. *The Captive Public: How Mass Opinion Promotes State Power.* New York: Basic Books.

Goldhaber, Gerald M. 1984. "A Pollster's Sampler." *Public Opinion* 7 (June/July): 47-50, 53.

Goldman, Ari L. 1991. "Portrait of Religion in U.S. Holds Dozens of Surprises." *New York Times*, 10 April, A-1.

Gow, David John, and Robert B. Eubank. 1984. "The Pro-Incumbent Bias in the 1982 National Election Study." *American Journal of Political Science* 27 (February): 224-230.

Goyder, John. 1985. "Face-to-Face Interviews and Mailed Questionnaires: The Net Difference in Response Rate." *Public Opinion Quarterly* 49 (summer): 234-252.

Greenberg, Daniel S. 1980. "The Plague of Polling." *Washington Post*, 16 September, A-17.

Grove, Lloyd. 1988a. "New Hampshire Confounded Most Pollsters." *Washington Post*, 18 February, A-1.

———. 1988b. "Focus Groups: Politicians' Version of Taste-Testing." *Washington Post*, 6 July, A-5.

Harwood, Richard. 1992. "The 'Bumps' and the Reality Are Polls Apart." *Cleveland Plain Dealer*, 29 August, 4-C.

Harwood Group. 1993. *Meaningful Chaos: How People Form Relationships with Public Concerns*. A Report Prepared for the Kettering Foundation, Dayton, Ohio.

Hatchett, S., and H. Schuman. 1975-1976. "White Respondents and Race-of-Interviewer Effects." *Public Opinion Quarterly* 39 (winter): 523-528.

Herbers, John. 1982. "Polls Find Conflict in Views on Aid and Public Welfare." *New York Times*, 14 February, 19.

Huddy, Leonie, and John Bracciodieta. 1992. "The Effects of Interviewer Gender on the Survey Response." Paper presented at the annual meeting of the American Political Science Association, Chicago.

Hull, Jon D. 1994. "Anger from the Grass Roots." *Time*, 29 August, 38-39.

Hyman, Herbert H., and Paul B. Sheatsley. 1950. "The Current Status of American Public Opinion." In *The Teaching of Contemporary Affairs*, edited by J. C. Payne. Twenty-First Yearbook of the National Council of Social Studies. Washington, D.C.: Council for Social Studies, National Education Association, 11-34.

Jackson, John. 1983. "Election Night Reporting and Voter Turnout." *American Journal of Political Science* 27 (November): 615-635.

Jackson, John, and William McGee. 1981. "Election Reporting and Voter Turnout." Report of the Center for Political Studies, University of Michigan, Ann Arbor.

James, Jeannine M., and Richard Bolstein. 1990. "The Effect of Monetary Incentives and Follow-Up Mailings on the Response Rate Quality in Mail Surveys." *Public Opinion Quarterly* 54 (fall): 346-361.

Johnson, Timothy P. 1989. "Obtaining Reports of Sensitive Behavior: A Comparison of Substance Use Reports from Telephone and Face-to-Face Interviews." *Social Science Quarterly* 70 (March): 174-183.

Jordan, Gene. 1982. "Polls Reflect Participants' Mood at Time Taken." *Columbus Dispatch*, 16 May, C-1.

Kagay, Michael R. with Janet Elder. 1992. "Numbers Are No Problem For Pollsters. Words Are." *New York Times*, 9 August.

Kane, Emily W., and Laura J. Macaulay. 1993. "Interview Gender and Gender Attitudes." *Public Opinion Quarterly* 57 (spring): 1-28.

Keene, Karlyn H., and Victoria A. Sackett. 1981. "An Editors' Report on the Yankelovich, Skelly and White 'Mushiness Index.'" *Public Opinion* 4 (April/May): 50-51.

Kifner, John. 1994. "Pollster Finds Error on Holocaust Doubts." *New York Times*, 20 May, A-6.

Kinder, Donald R., and Lynn M. Sanders. 1986. "Survey Questions and Political Culture: The Case of Whites' Response to Affirmative Action for Blacks." Paper presented at the Annual Meeting of the American Political Science Association, Washington, D.C., 28-31 August.

Knap, Ted. 1980. "League Weighs Anderson's Standing for Debates." *Columbus Citizen-Journal*, 9 September, 7.

Koch, Nadine S. 1985. "Perceptions of Public Opinion Polls." Ph.D. diss., Ohio State University.

Kohut, Andrew. 1983. "Illinois Politics Confound the Polls." *Public Opinion* 5 (December/January): 42-43.

———. 1993. "The Vocal Minority in American Politics." *Times Mirror* Center for the People and the Press, Washington, D.C., 16 July.

Kostrzewa, John. 1986a. "Celeste Holds Early Lead in Race." *Akron Beacon Journal*, 23 March, A-1.

———. 1986b. "Rhodes Has Solid Edge over Primary Rivals." *Akron Beacon Journal*, 23 March, A-5.

Krosnick, Jon A. 1989. "Question Wording and Reports of Survey Results: The Case of Louis Harris and Associates and Aetna Life and Casualty." *Public Opinion Quarterly* 53 (spring): 107-113.

Krosnick, Jon A., and Duane F. Alwin. 1987. "An Evaluation of a Cognitive Theory of Response-Order Effects in Survey Measurement." *Public Opinion Quarterly* 51 (summer): 201-219.

Krosnick, Jon A., and Matthew K. Berent. 1993. "Comparisons of Party Identification and Policy Preferences: The Impact of Survey Question Format." *American Journal of Political Science* 37 (August): 941-964.

Ladd, Everett Carll. 1980. "Polling and the Press: The Clash of Institutional Imperatives." *Public Opinion Quarterly* 44 (winter): 574-584.

———. 1994. "The Holocaust Poll Error: A Modern Cautionary Tale." *The Public Perspective* 5 (July/August): 3-5.

Lang, Kurt, and Gladys Engel Lang. 1984. "The Impact of Polls on Public Opinion." *Annals of the American Academy of Political and Social Science* 472 (March): 130-142.

Lardner, George Jr. 1985. "A Majority of the People Are Against the 'Star Wars' Defense Plan." *Washington Post* National Weekly Edition, 9 September, 37.

Lau, Richard R. 1994. "An Analysis of the Accuracy of 'Trial Heat' Polls During the 1992 Presidential Election." *Public Opinion Quarterly* 58 (spring): 2-20.

Laumann, Edward O. et al. 1994. *The Social Organization of Sexuality.* Chicago: University of Chicago Press.

Lavrakas, Paul J. 1986. "Surveying the Survey Differences." *Chicago Tribune*, 17 June, 12.

———. 1987. *Telephone Survey Methods: Sampling, Selection, and Supervision.* Newberry Park, Calif.: Sage Publications.

Levy, Mark R. 1983. "The Methodology and Performance of Election Day Polls." *Public Opinion Quarterly* 47 (spring): 54-67.

Lever, Janet. 1994. "Sexual Revelations." *The Advocate* (23 August): 15-24.

Lewis, I. A., and William Schneider. 1982. "Is the Public Lying to the Pollsters?" *Public Opinion* 5 (April/May): 42-47.

Lipset, Seymour Martin. 1980. "Different Polls, Different Results in 1980 Politics." *Public Opinion* 3 (August/September): 19-20, 60.

Lockerbie, Brad, and Stephen A. Borrelli. 1990. "Question Wording and Public Support for Contra Aid, 1983-1986." *Public Opinion Quarterly* 54 (summer): 195-208.

Margolis, Michael. 1984. "Public Opinion, Polling, and Political Behavior." *Annals of the American Academy of Political and Social Science* 472 (March): 61-71.

Marsh, Catherine. 1984. "Do Polls Affect What People Think?" In *Surveying Subjective Phenomena*, edited by Charles F. Turner and Elizabeth Martin. New York: Russell Sage Foundation, 565-591.

Meislin, Richard J. 1987. "Racial Divisions Seen in Poll on Howard Beach Attack." *New York Times*, 8 January, 16.

Meyer, Eugene. 1940. "A Newspaper Publisher Looks at the Polls." *Public Opinion Quarterly* 4 (June): 238-240.

Michael, Robert T., John H. Gagnon, Edward O. Laumann, and Gina Kolata. 1994. *Sex in America: A Definitive Survey*. Boston: Little, Brown & Company.

Miller, M. Mark, and Robert Hurd. 1982. "Conformity to AAPOR Standards in Newspaper Reporting of Public Opinion Polls." *Public Opinion Quarterly* 46 (summer): 243-249.

Miller, Tim. 1986. "Statewide Poll Has Rhodes Far Ahead in GOP." *Dayton Daily News*, 23 March, 1.

Mills, Kim I. 1993. "Cheers' Fans Wanted To See Sam Malone Single." *Akron Beacon Journal*, 2 May, A-13.

Mitofsky, Warren J. 1992. "What Went Wrong with Exit Polling in New Hampshire." *The Public Perspective* 3 (March/April): 17.

Mitofsky, Warren J., and Martin Plissner. 1980. "A Reporter's Guide to Published Polls." *Public Opinion* 3 (June/July): 16-19.

Moore, David W., and Frank Newport. 1994. "Misreading the Public: The Case of the Holocaust Poll." *The Public Perspective* 5 (March/April): 28-29.

Morganthau, Tom. 1986. "Four More Years?" *Newsweek*, 8 September, 16-17.

Morin, Richard. 1987. "Pay Your Taxes and You, Too, Can Give a Useless Opinion." *Washington Post* National Weekly Edition, 7 December, 38.

————. 1988a. "A-Tracking We Will Go." *Washington Post* National Weekly Edition, 15-21 February, 38.

————. 1988b. "What Went Wrong?" *Washington Post* National Weekly Edition, 22-28 February, 37.

————. 1988c. "Tracking a Formula for Success." *Washington Post* National Weekly Edition, 25 April-1 May, 37.

————. 1988d. "Behind the Numbers: Confessions of a Pollster." *Washington Post*, 16 October, C-1, C-4.

————. 1989a. "Where There's a Smoking Poll, There's Smoke." *Washington Post* National Weekly Edition, 30 January-5 February, 37.

————. 1989b. "A Half a Million Choices for American Voters." *Washington Post* National Weekly Edition, 6-12 February, 38.

————. 1989c. "The Answer May Depend on Who Asked the Question." *Washington Post* National Weekly Edition, 6-21 November, 38.

————. 1990. "Women Asking Women About Men Asking Women About Men." *Washington Post* National Weekly Edition, 15-21 January, 37.

————. 1991. "2 Ways of Reading the Public's Lips on Gulf Policy." *Washington Post*, 14 January, A-9.

————. 1992a. "Another Contribution to SLOPpy Journalism." *Washington Post* National Weekly Edition, 10-16 February, 37.

————. 1992b. "This Time in New Hampshire, A Somewhat More Graceful Exit." *Washington Post* National Weekly Edition, 24 February-1 March, 37.

————. 1992c. "Surveying the Surveyors." *Washington Post* National Weekly Edition, 2-8 March, 37.

————. 1992d. "Polling '92: Who's on First." *Washington Post*, 6 June, A-1.

————. 1992e. "Putting the Focus on Presidents and Peanut Butter." *Washington Post* National Weekly Edition, 19-25 October, 37.

————. 1993a. "Getting a Handle on the Religious Right." *Washington Post* National Weekly Edition, 5-11 April, 37.

————. 1993b. "If Only the Birds and Bees Could Count." *Washington Post* National Weekly Edition, 26 April-2 May, 37.

————. 1993c. "Economics: A Puzzle to Many." *Washington Post* National Weekly Edition, 31 May-6 June, 37.

————. 1993d. "Racism Knows No Party Lines." *Washington Post* National Weekly Edition, 20-26 September, 37.

————. 1993e. "Wrong About the Religious Right." *Washington Post* National Weekly Edition, 1-7 November, 37.

————. 1993f. "Ask and You Might Deceive." *Washington Post* National Weekly Edition, 6-12 December, 37.

————. 1994a. "Public Enemy No. 1: Crime." *Washington Post* National Weekly Edition, 24-30 January, 37.

————. 1994b. "A Few Questions About the Questions." *Washington Post* National Weekly Edition, 28 February-6 March, 37.

————. 1994c. "Those Who Live in a House Divided Against Itself." *Washington Post* National Weekly Edition, 7-13 March, 37.

————. 1994d. "Don't Know Much About Health Care Reform." *Washington Post* National Weekly Edition, 14-20 March, 37.

————. 1994e. "The Answer Depends on the Question." *Washington Post* National Weekly Edition, 21-27 March, 37.

————. 1994f. "From Confusing Questions, Confusing Answers." *Washington Post* National Weekly Edition, 18-24 July, 37.

————. 1994g. "When the Data Tell Shockingly Different Stories." *Washington Post* National Weekly Edition, 8-14 August, 37.

Munro, Ralph, and Curtis B. Gans. 1988. "Let's Say No to Exit Polls." *New York Times*, 4 November, 27.

Neuman, W. Russell. 1986. *The Paradox of Mass Politics: Knowledge and Opinion in the American Electorate*. Cambridge, Mass.: Harvard University Press.

Newman, Jody. 1983. "Taking on an Incumbent: The Remarkable Woods-Danforth 1982 U.S. Senate Race." *Campaigns and Elections* 4 (spring): 29-39.

Nietzel, Michael T., and Ronald C. Dillehay. 1983. "Psychologists as Consultants for Changes of Venue: The Use of Public Opinion Surveys." *Law and Human Behavior* 7 (December): 309-335.

Noelle-Neumann, Elisabeth. 1974. "The Spiral of Silence: A Theory of Public Opinion." *Journal of Communication* 24 (spring): 43-51.

———. 1977. "Turbulence in the Climate of Opinion: Methodological Applications of the Spiral of Silence Theory." *Public Opinion Quarterly* 41 (summer): 143-158.

Norpoth, Helmut, and Milton Lodge. 1985. "The Difference Between Attitudes and Nonattitudes in the Mass Public: Just Measurement?" *American Journal of Political Science* 29 (May): 291-307.

O'Gorman, Hubert J. 1975. "Pluralistic Ignorance and White Estimates of White Support for Racial Segregation." *Public Opinion Quarterly* 39 (fall): 313-330.

O'Gorman, Hubert J., and Stephen L. Garry. 1976-1977. "Pluralistic Ignorance—A Replication and Extension." *Public Opinion Quarterly* 40 (winter): 449-458.

Oldendick, Robert W., and Michael W. Link. 1994. "The Answering Machine Generation: Who are They and What Problem Do They Pose for Survey Research." *Public Opinion Quarterly* 58 (summer): 264-273.

Oreskes, Michael. 1984. "Pollsters Offer Reasons for Disparity in Results." *New York Times*, 20 October, A-8.

———. 1990. "Drug War Underlines Fickleness of Public." *New York Times*, 6 September, A-22.

Orton, Barry. 1982. "Phony Polls: The Pollster's Nemesis." *Public Opinion* 5 (June/July): 56-60.

Page, Benjamin I., and Robert Y. Shapiro. 1983. "Effects of Public Opinion on Policy." *American Political Science Review* 77 (March): 175-190.

———. 1992. *The Rational Public: Fifty Years of Trends in Americans' Policy Preferences*. Chicago: University of Chicago Press.

Paletz, David L., Jonathan Y. Short, Helen Baker, Barbara Cookman Campbell, Richard J. Cooper, and Rochelle M. Oeslander. 1980. "Polls in the Media: Content, Credibility, and Consequences." *Public Opinion Quarterly* 44 (winter): 495-513.

Payne, Stanley L. 1951. *The Art of Asking Questions*. Princeton, N.J.: Princeton University Press.

Perlstadt, Harry, and Russell E. Holmes. 1987. "The Role of Public Opinion Polling in Health Legislation." *American Journal of Public Health* 77 (May): 612-614.

Perry, Paul. 1979. "Certain Problems in Election Survey Methodology." *Public Opinion Quarterly* 43 (fall): 312-325.

Peterson, Robert A. 1984. "Asking the Age Question: A Research Note." *Public Opinion Quarterly* 48 (spring): 379-383.

Phillips, Kevin P. 1976. "Polls Used to Reflect Electability." *Columbus Dispatch*, 19 July, B-2.

———. 1981. "Polls Are Too Broad in Analysis Divisions." *Columbus Dispatch*, 8 September, B-3.

Piazza, Thomas. 1993. "Meeting the Challenge of Answering Machines." *Public Opinion Quarterly* 57 (summer): 219-231.

Piekarski, Linda B. 1989. "Choosing Between Directory Listed and Random Digit Dialing in Light of New Demographic Findings." Paper presented at the AAPOR Conference, St. Petersburg, Fla.

Pierce, John C., Maryann E. Steger, Nicholas P. Lovrich Jr., and Brent S. Steel. 1988. "Public Information on Acid Rain in Canada and the United States." *Social Science Quarterly* 69 (March): 193-202.

Presser, Stanley, and Howard Schuman. 1980. "The Measurement of a Middle Position in Attitude Surveys." *Public Opinion Quarterly* 44 (spring): 70-85.

Public Opinion Quarterly. 1987. Fiftieth Anniversary Issue. 51, supplement (winter): S1-S191.

Public Perspective. 1994. September/October: 23, 26.

Rasinski, Kenneth A. 1989. "The Effect of Question Wording on Public Support for Government Spending." *Public Opinion Quarterly* 53 (fall): 388-394.

Reese, Stephen D., Wayne A. Danielson, Pamela J. Shoemaker, Tsan-Kuo Chang, and Huei-Ling Hsu. 1986. "Ethnicity-of-Interviewer Effects Among Mexican-Americans and Anglos." *Public Opinion Quarterly* 50 (winter): 563-572.

Robbins, William. 1986. "Surge in Sympathy for Farmer Found." *New York Times,* 25 February, A-1.

Robinson, Michael J., and Margaret A. Sheehan. 1983. *Over the Wire and on TV: CBS and UPI in Campaign '80.* New York: Russell Sage Foundation.

Roper, Burns W. 1985. "Early Election Calls: The Larger Dangers." *Public Opinion Quarterly* 49 (spring): 5-9.

Rothenberg, Stuart, ed. 1982. *The Political Report* 5 (27 October).

————. 1983. *The Political Report* 6 (5 August).

————. 1985. *The Political Report* 8 (25 October).

————. 1986a. *The Political Report* 9 (11 July).

————. 1986b. *The Political Report* 9 (25 July).

————. 1986c. *The Political Report* 9 (12 September).

Salwen, Michael B. 1985a. "Does Poll Coverage Improve as Presidential Vote Nears?" *Journalism Quarterly* 62 (winter): 887-891.

————. 1985b. "The Reporting of Public Opinion Polls During Presidential Years, 1968-1984." *Journalism Quarterly* 62 (summer): 272-277.

Saar, Andrus, and Liivi Joe. 1992. "Polling, Under the Gun: Political Attitudes in Estonia, Surveyed at the Height of the Soviet Coup Attempt, August 1991." *Public Opinion Quarterly* 56 (winter): 519-523.

Schneider, William. 1989. "One Poll May Be Worse than None." *National Journal* 2 (December): 2970.

Schuman, Howard, and Jean M. Converse. 1971. "The Effects of Black and White Interviewers on Black Responses in 1968." *Public Opinion Quarterly* 35 (spring): 44-68.

Schuman, Howard, Graham Kalton, and Jacob Ludwig. 1983. "Context and Contiguity in Survey Questionnaires." *Public Opinion Quarterly* 47 (spring): 112-115.

Schuman, Howard, and Stanley Presser. 1977. "Question Wording as an Independent Variable in Survey Analysis." *Sociological Methods and Research* 6 (November): 151-170.

_____. 1980. "Public Opinion and Public Ignorance: The Fine Line Between Attitudes and Nonattitudes." *American Journal of Sociology* 85 (March): 1214-1225.

_____. 1981. *Questions and Answers in Attitude Surveys: Experiments on Question Form, Wording, and Context.* New York: Academic Press.

Schuman, Howard, Stanley Presser, and Jacob Ludwig. 1981. "Context Effects on Survey Responses to Questions About Abortion." *Public Opinion Quarterly* 45 (summer): 216-223.

Shipler, David K. 1986. "Public Is Confused on Contra Aid Issue, Poll Indicates." *New York Times*, 15 April, 4.

Sigelman, Lee. 1981. "Question-Order Effects on Presidential Popularity." *Public Opinion Quarterly* 45 (summer): 199-207.

_____. "Disarming the Opposition: The President, the Public and INF Treaty." *Public Opinion Quarterly* 54 (spring): 37-47.

Smith, Eric R. A. N., and Peverill Squire. 1990. "The Effects of Prestige Names in Question Wording." *Public Opinion Quarterly* 54 (spring): 97-116.

Smith, Ted. J. III, and J. Michael Hogan. 1987. "Public Opinion and the Panama Canal Treaties of 1977." *Public Opinion Quarterly* 51 (spring): 5-30.

Smith, Ted J. III, and Derek O. Verrall. 1985. "A Critical Analysis of Australian Television Coverage of Election Opinion Polls." *Public Opinion Quarterly* 49 (spring): 58-79.

Smith, Tom W. 1984. "Nonattitudes: A Review and Evaluation." In *Surveying Subjective Phenomena*, vol. 2. Edited by Charles F. Turner and Elizabeth Martin. New York: Russell Sage Foundation, 215-255.

_____. 1987a. "That Which We Call Welfare by Any Other Name Would Smell Sweeter: An Analysis of the Impact of Question Wording on Response Patterns." *Public Opinion Quarterly* 51 (spring): 75-83.

_____. 1987b. "The Use of Public Opinion Data by the Attorney General's Commission on Pornography." *Public Opinion Quarterly* 57 (summer): 249-267.

_____. 1987c. "How Comics and Cartoons View Public Opinion Surveys." *Journalism Quarterly* 64:208-211.

_____. 1988. "Speaking Out: Hite vs. Abby in Methodological Messes." *AAPOR News* (spring): 3-4.

_____. 1993. "Actual Trends or Measurement Artifacts? A Review of Three Studies of Anti-Semitism." *Public Opinion Quarterly* 57 (fall): 380-393.

Sniderman, Paul, Edward Carmines, Philip Tetlock, and Anthony Tyler. 1993. In Richard Morin, "Racism Knows No Party Lines." *Washington Post* National Weekly Edition, 20-26 September, 37.

Squire, Peverill. 1988. "Why the 1936 *Literary Digest* Poll Failed." *Public Opinion Quarterly* 52 (spring): 125-133.

Squires, Sally, and Richard Morin. 1987. "What Is This Thing Called Love?" *Washington Post* National Weekly Edition, 16 November, 37.

Steeh, Charlotte G. 1981. "Trends in Nonresponse Rates, 1952-1979." *Public Opinion Quarterly* 45 (spring): 40-57.

Stinchcombe, Arthur L., Calvin Jones, and Paul Sheatsley. 1981. "Nonresponse Bias for Attitude Questions." *Public Opinion Quarterly* 45 (fall): 359-375.

Sudman, Seymour. 1986. "Do Exit Polls Influence Voting Behavior?" *Public Opinion Quarterly* 50 (fall): 331-339.

Sussman, Barry. 1984a. "Why Both Parties Are Courting 50 Million Opinion-Switchers." *Washington Post* National Weekly Edition, 16 January, 37.

————. 1984b. "Already the Polls Are Getting Difficult to Follow." *Washington Post*, 26 January, A-2.

————. 1984c. "Do-It-Yourself Tax Reform: Many Think Cheating Is Okay." *Washington Post* National Weekly Edition, 28 May, 36.

————. 1984d. "Some Answers to the Polls' Critics." *Washington Post* National Weekly Edition, 12 November, 37.

————. 1985a. "To Understand These Polls, You Have to Read the Fine Print." *Washington Post* National Weekly Edition, 4 March, 37.

————. 1985b. "Reagan's Support on Issues Relies Heavily on the Uninformed." *Washington Post* National Weekly Edition, 1 April, 37.

————. 1985c. "Americans Prefer Tax Cheating to Being Paid to Inform the IRS." *Washington Post* National Weekly Edition, 13 May, 37.

————. 1985d. "Social Security and the Young." *Washington Post* National Weekly Edition, 27 May, 37.

————. 1985e. "Pollsters Cheer Up About Public's Opinions of Polls." *Washington Post* National Weekly Edition, 3 June, 37.

————. 1985f. "Do Pre-Election Polls Influence People to Switch Their Votes?" *Washington Post* National Weekly Edition, 10 June, 37.

————. 1985g. "Loaded Questions, Faulty Data." *Washington Post* National Weekly Edition, 14 October, 37.

————. 1985h. "These Polls Are Part Public Opinion, Part Public Relations." *Washington Post* National Weekly Edition, 4 November, 37.

————. 1985i. "On 'Star Wars,' It All Depends on How You Ask the Question." *Washington Post* National Weekly Edition, 25 November, 37.

————. 1986a. "Do Blacks Approve of Reagan? It Depends on Who's Asking." *Washington Post* National Weekly Edition, 10 February, 37.

————. 1986b. "It's Wrong to Assume that School Busing Is Wildly Unpopular." *Washington Post* National Weekly Edition, 10 March, 37.

————. 1986c. "With Pornography, It All Depends on Who's Doing the Looking." *Washington Post* National Weekly Edition, 24 March, 37.

————. 1986d. "Right Now Hart Would Beat Bush." *Washington Post* National Weekly Edition, 9 June, 14.

Survey Sampling, Inc. 1994. "Sacramento Most Unlisted Market for 1993." *The Frame* (March): 1.

Swift, Al. 1985. "The Congressional Concern About Early Calls." *Public Opinion Quarterly* 49 (spring): 2-5.

Swim, Janet, and Eugene Borgida. 1987. "Public Opinion on the Psychological and Legal Aspects of Televising Rape Trials." *Journal of Applied Social Psychology* 17:507-518.

Tanur, Judith M. 1994. "The Trustworthiness of Survey Research." *The Chronicle of Higher Education* 25 May, B1-B3.

Taylor, Marylee C. 1983. "The Black-and-White Model of Attitude Stability: A Latent Class Examination of Opinion and Nonopinion in the American Public." *American Journal of Sociology* 89 (September): 373-401.

Times Mirror. 1987. "The People, Press, and Politics." A *Times Mirror* Study of the American Electorate Conducted by the Gallup Organization, September.

Townley, Rod. 1980. "TV's Campaign Polls: How Much Can We Believe?" *TV Guide*, 6 September, 23-26.

Traugott, Michael W. 1987. "The Importance of Persistence in Respondent Selection for Preelection Surveys." *Public Opinion Quarterly* 51 (spring): 48-57.

————. 1992. "A General Good Showing, But Much Work Remains to be Done." *The Public Perspective* 4 (November/December): 14-16.

Traugott, Michael W., and Vincent Price. 1992. "Exit Polls in the 1989 Virginia Gubernatorial Race: Where Did They Go Wrong?" *Public Opinion Quarterly* 56 (summer): 245-253.

Tuckel, Peter S., and Barry M. Feinberg. 1991. "The Answering Machine Poses Many Questions for Telephone Survey Researchers." *Public Opinion Quarterly* 55 (summer): 232-237.

Washington Post. 1985. "A Grain of Salt Please" (editorial). 17 June.

Weeks, Michael F., and R. Paul Moore. 1981. "Ethnicity-of-Interviewer Effects on Ethnic Respondents." *Public Opinion Quarterly* 45 (summer): 245-249.

Wilcox, William Clyde. 1984. "The New Christian Right and the White Fundamentalists: An Analysis of a Potential Political Movement." Ph.D. diss., Ohio State University.

Williams, Dennis A. 1979. "A New Racial Poll." *Newsweek*, 26 February, 48, 53.

Williams, Juan. 1985. "Poll Irks Black Leaders." *Washington Post*, 30 September, A-11.

Wright, James D. 1981. "Public Opinion and Gun Control: A Comparison of Results from Two Recent National Surveys." *Annals of the American Academy of Political and Social Science* 455 (May): 24-39.

Xu, Minghua, Benjamin J. Bates, and John C. Schweitzer. 1993. "The Impact of Messages on Survey Participation in Answering Machine Households." *Public Opinion Quarterly* 57 (summer): 232-237.

Yammarino, Francis J., Steven J. Skinner, and Terry L. Childers. 1991. "Understanding Mail Survey Response Behavior: A Meta-Analysis." *Public Opinion Quarterly* 55 (winter): 613-639.

Index

ABC/Harris polls, 1980 election methodology, 160-161
ABC News
  exit polls, 115
  pseudo-polls, 11
ABC News/Station WLS surveys, 68
ABC News/*Washington Post* polls, 3
  on black support for Reagan, 66-67
  on busing, 148
  after Carter-Reagan debate in 1980, 121
  conflicts, 159
  determining likely voters, 126-127
  on effects of polls on voter choice, 129-130
  on federal budget deficit, 149
  on health care debate, 141
  news releases on, 67
  on Persian Gulf crisis, 137, 138-139, 140
  on pornography, 147
  question order in, 52, 53
  race-of-interviewer effects in, 80
  on Reagan's surgery, 3-4
  on Star Wars, 45-46, 69-70
  subsets of respondents, 153-154
  on U.S.-Soviet military strength, 34
  versions of questions in, 45-46
Abortion polls, 78-79, 91-92, 136
Acquired immune deficiency syndrome (AIDS) polls, 4, 152, 154

Advisory Commission on Intergovernmental Relations surveys, 46
Advocate, 13, 143
Aetna Life and Casualty, 95
Age, ways of measuring, 45
Age groups, 149
AIDS polls, 4, 152, 154
Akron Beacon Journal, 22
"America on the Line" (CBS), telephone call-in surveys, 12
American Association for Public Opinion Research (AAPOR), standards for reporting results, 83, 84-86
American College of Surgeons, 6
American Enterprise, poll result summaries, 5
American Farmland Trust, 7, 10
American Foundation for AIDS Research, 44
American Jewish Committee polls, 6, 47
American National Election Studies (ANES), 53, 78
  1984 screening questions, 28, 29-31
  1992 screening questions, 31-33
Anderson, John, 47, 121
Andrews, Mark, 117
Answering machines, 71
Anti-Semitism, national studies of, 145-146
AP polls. *See* NBC/AP polls

ADJ 6542
2497588

College Library

COLLEGE LIBRARY